IMAGES
of America

HILLSBORO

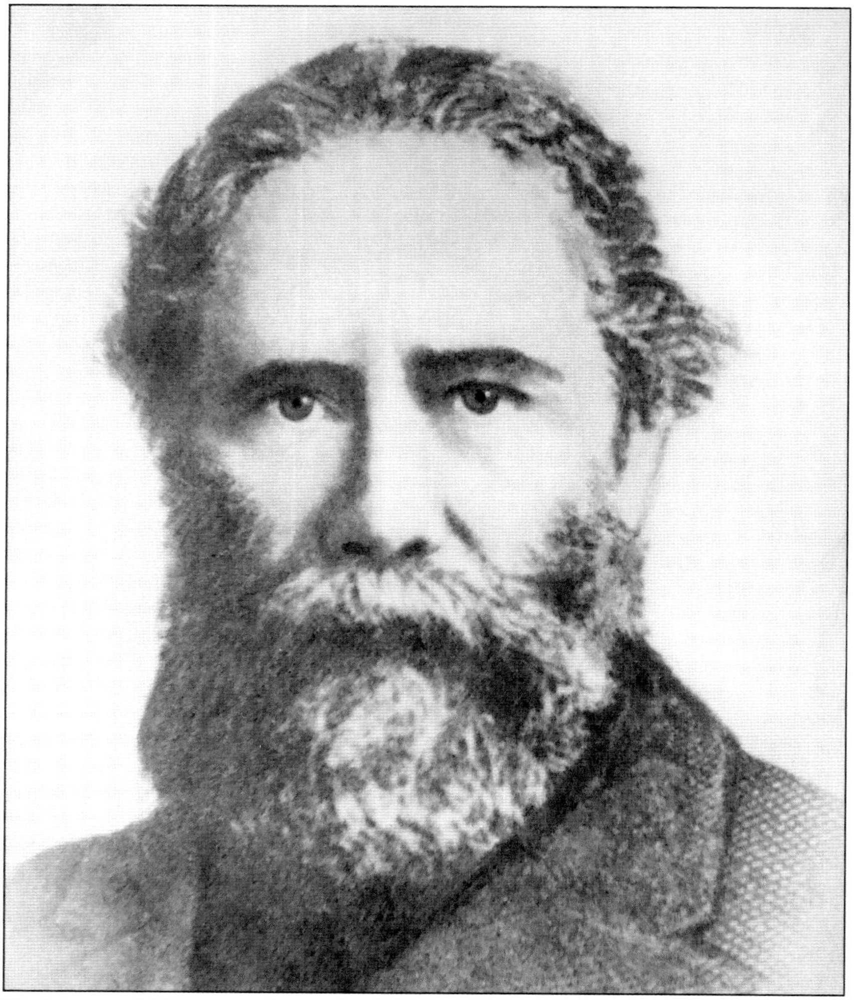

George Washington Hill received a medical degree from Transylvania University in Lexington, Kentucky, and began his medical practice in Franklin, Texas, at the age of 23. After being appointed an Indian agent by Republic of Texas president Sam Houston in 1837, he established a trading post in what is now Spring Hill in Navarro County. Dr. Hill served in the Congress of the Republic of Texas from 1839 to 1842 and then as the secretary of state for the Republic from 1843 to 1845. He served a term as a senator representing Henderson, Limestone, and Navarro Counties in the regular session of the Fourth Legislature of the State of Texas (1851–1852) and in a special session from January 10 to February 7, 1853. (Cell Block Museum.)

On The Cover: Since 1853, Hillsboro has been a close-knit community that has taken pride in providing quality service to its citizens. Fire protection and public safety have been key elements of Hillsboro's character over the years. Hillsboro Hook & Ladder Co. No. 1 was formed in June 1883, and the first fire station was located at 118 South Waco Street. Here, proud local citizens, firemen, and canine friends board a new Hillsboro fire truck with enthusiasm. (Cell Block Museum.)

IMAGES
of America

HILLSBORO

The Hillsboro Heritage League

ARCADIA
PUBLISHING

ISBN 978-0-7385-9958-8

Published by Arcadia Publishing
Charleston, South Carolina

Printed in the United States of America

Library of Congress Control Number: 2013941712

For all general information, please contact Arcadia Publishing:
Telephone 843-853-2070
Fax 843-853-0044
E-mail sales@arcadiapublishing.com
For customer service and orders:
Toll-Free 1-888-313-2665

Visit us on the Internet at www.arcadiapublishing.com

For all who have called Hillsboro home and who treasure the lives shared and memories made throughout the years.

Contents

ACKNOWLEDGMENTS

This book is a photographic glimpse into Hillsboro's past. The Hillsboro Heritage League Editorial Board thanks members of the Hillsboro Heritage League and the community at large who assisted in locating photographs for the book. Our appreciation extends to those committed to preserving Hillsboro's past who trusted us with photographs. Thanks to Will Lowrance, editor, and Anita Tufts, project director, who coordinated work on the project, and to the members of the George and Alva Hudson Smith Foundation for their generous financial support.

Photographs are from the collections of Catherine Andrews, Linda Bacon, Larry Cole, Tom Curtis, Bill Galiga, Lynn Gray, Jack Loftis, Will and Betty Lowrance, Rose Mary Magrill, Art Mann, Sandra McCown, Robert and Carole Moore, Erin Russell Ripple, C.H. Stubblefield, Linda Teague, Anita Tufts, Usa Lee Tufts, John and Denise Tuggle, Apex Grain, Christ Lutheran Church, First United Methodist Church, the Hillsboro Independent School District, the Monday Review Club, the Sesame Club, Marshall and Marshall Funeral Directors, Johnson Studios, the Bob Bullock Collection in the Poage Legislative Library at Baylor University, the Tarlton Law Library in the Jamail Center for Legal Research at the University of Texas School of Law, and the Lyndon B. Johnson Presidential Library. All unattributed photographs are courtesy of private donors.

A special acknowledgment goes to former Hillsboro municipal judge Florence Logan, who kindly made her library available. Other research sources included the Hill County Historical Commission, the Hill County Cell Block Museum, the Historical Research Center in the Texas Heritage Museum at Hill College, the Hillsboro City Library, the Hill County Genealogical Society, The *Heritage of Hill County* Volumes I and II, *Humble Farm Family* magazine, *Fine Families of Hill County*, *Hill College: An Illustrated History*, "Phoenix Rising: Destroyed Hill County Courthouse Emerges from the Ashes" by Mary Alice Robbins, *100% Cotton* by Jack and Jane Pruitt, and *Bond's Alley* by Jane Pruitt.

We also want to express our thanks for unfailing guidance throughout this endeavor to Laura Bruns, our editor at Arcadia Publishing, through whose support and expert advice this photographic record of Hillsboro's history was made possible.

INTRODUCTION

Hillsboro was surveyed as the county seat of Hill County in September 1853, just three months after the county was organized at Lexington Village, on Jack's Branch. A log courthouse was constructed in the center of town, and, from that humble beginning, Hillsboro has become a community of pride and respect across Texas and the nation.

The early years in Hillsboro were dusty and dangerous. Settlers were pushing the limits of the frontier as they moved westward toward the Brazos River, Hill County's western boundary. Early pioneers were adventurous farmers and ranchers eager to begin a new life and put their personal stamp on this new area open to settlement. The presence of Fort Graham on the Brazos made settlement possible, but the threat from native Indians soon vanished, and the county seat town of Hillsboro attracted new settlers.

In 1881, the railroad came to Hillsboro, and a new chapter in the city's history was opened. Rail access meant that farmers could produce and ship cotton to markets much more easily than before. The railroads began a serious marketing campaign in the older southern states to attract new settlers to Hillsboro and Hill County. From 1881 until 1900, families were moving to this area at a rapid rate, and the culture of Hillsboro took on a more family-friendly atmosphere. Churches, schools, and fraternal organizations flourished in this period, and cotton gins, a compress, a cottonseed oil mill, and a cotton textile mill were established to promote the cotton industry.

The period from 1900 to 1930 saw a maturing of culture in Hillsboro that was highlighted by the opening of Hillsboro Junior College in 1923. The college was an integral part of the public school system, and educators from all parts of Texas came to study the system. Impressive business, educational, and religious structures were constructed that reflected the strong cotton-based economy. Downtown businesses and homes were remodeled frequently to move away from the Victorian gingerbread style to the massive Greek Revival architectural style. In 1912, the interurban commuter rail line opened for business; it was a strong feature of life in Hillsboro until 1948. The line provided easy rider access to Dallas, Waco, and other points.

Hillsboro then saw a decline, beginning in the Depression years and continuing after World War II. Returning veterans frequently moved to urban areas to follow employment opportunities that were not available in the agricultural economy of Hillsboro and Hill County. With the rise of synthetic fibers and mechanized farming, there was a drastic decline in emphasis on cotton, and the cotton gins, compress, cottonseed oil mill, and textile mill closed. It was not until the 1980s that an economic revival began to move Hillsboro forward, and the Main Street program was an effective means of developing pride in historic Hillsboro. The outlet mall on Interstate 35 has proven to be a major point of identity for Hillsboro and has brought thousands to rediscover Hillsboro.

The community has long been known for political leadership and as the home of individuals who have made major contributions in state and national affairs. These include Lt. Gov. Bob Bullock, Attorney General Crawford Martin, Speakers of the House Thomas S. Smith and Robert Lee Bobbitt, who also served as justice of the 4th Court of Appeals. Others include Texas Supreme Court chief justices Nelson Phillips and Robert W. Calvert, as well as Supreme Court Associate Justice Sam D. Johnson, who later served on the US Fifth Circuit Court of Appeals. Wright C. Morrow served as presiding judge of the Texas Court of Criminal Appeals. Frank G. McDonald served as chief justice of the 10th Court of Appeals.

One

The Courthouse

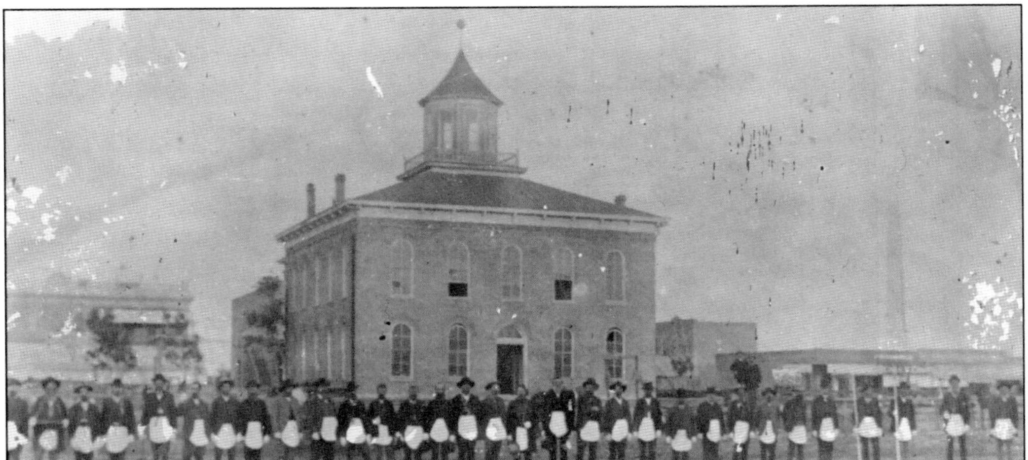

Hillsboro, the county seat of Hill County, was surveyed and laid out in streets after a Commissioners Court order on September 24, 1853. Building a courthouse then became a priority. C.N. Brooks was hired to build the modest structure, which was constructed of elm poles, boards, and a clapboard door. Later, a more substantial courthouse was built. That two-story brick structure burned in September 1872. Its replacement, a similar structure, cost $15,000 and served until a more formidable building was constructed in 1890. This 1874 scene shows the dedication of the cornerstone by Hillsboro Lodge No. 196 of Ancient Free and Accepted Masons.

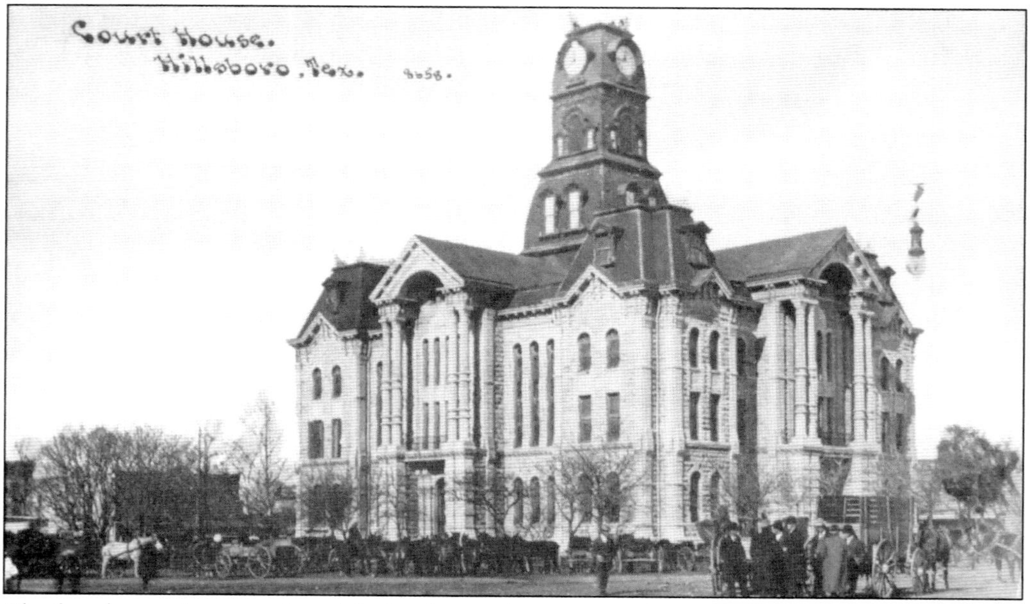

The fourth courthouse replaced the brick courthouse erected in 1874. Contractors Lovell, Miller & Hood built the rusticated limestone structure in 1890 for a cost of $83,000. Waco architect W.C. Dodson designed the modified French Second Empire styling. The three-story courthouse is topped by a 70-foot clock tower. The courthouse is a Recorded Texas Historic Landmark and a State Archaeological Landmark, as recorded by the Hill County Historical Commission.

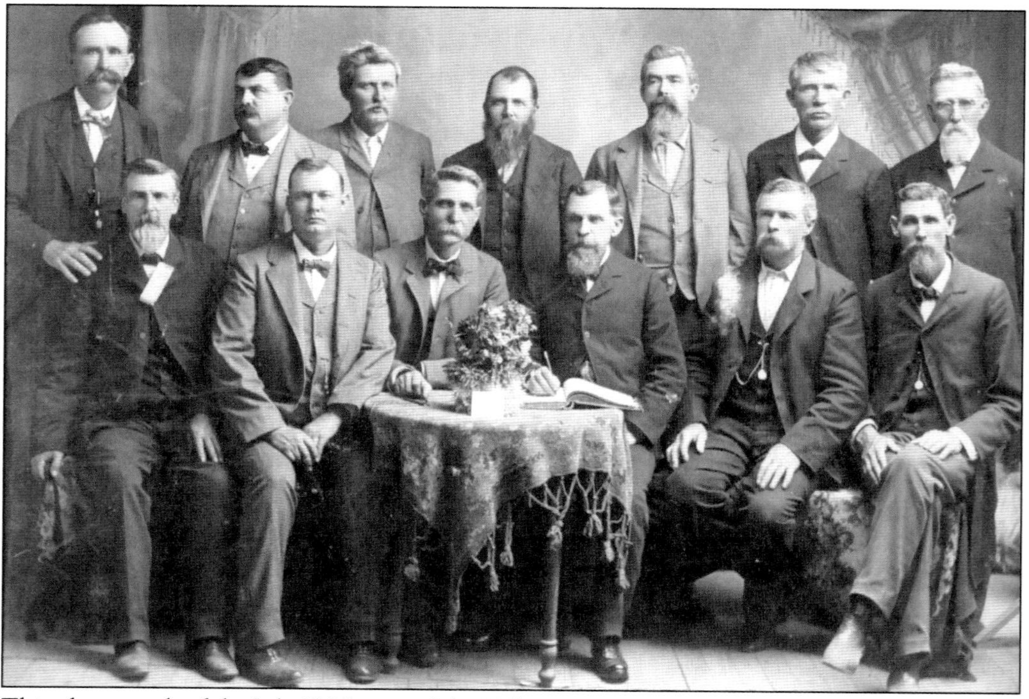

This photograph of the July 1906 term of the Hill County grand jury, 66th District Court of Hill County, was taken in Blanchard Studio. The members of the jury were, in no particular order, district attorney A.M. Frazier, foreman James T. Frazier, J.O. Files, Johnson Thompson, L.P. Miracle, Galbreath R. Priddy, John Rose, William Gamblin, Eli Luske, P.W. Frazier, Jim Tinsley, and Pat Evers.

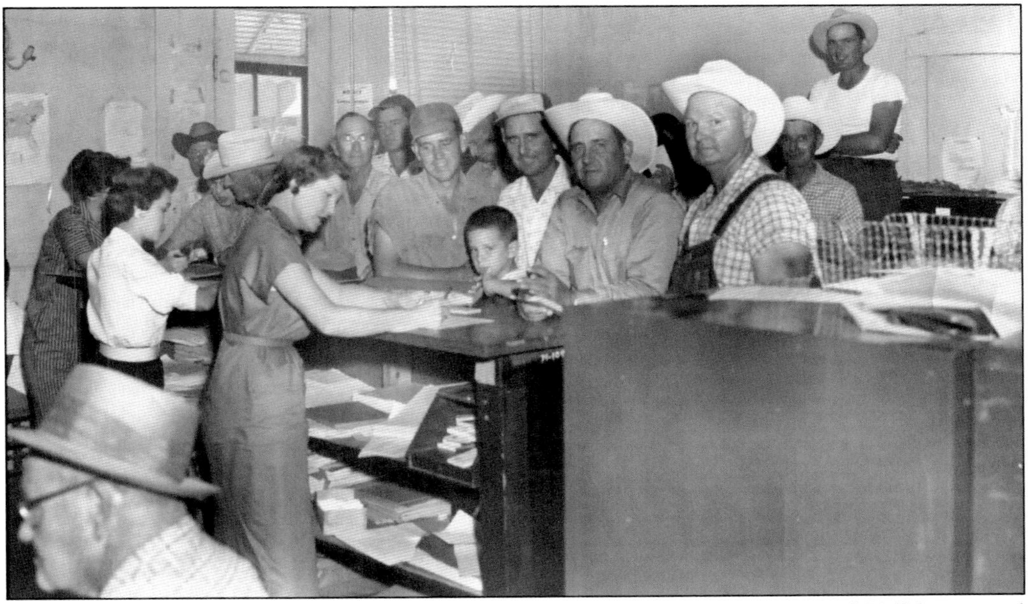

Cotton farming and other agricultural pursuits flourished on the farms around Hillsboro until the 1920s. After a period of surplus cotton and grain brought low prices, farmers were assisted by the Agricultural Adjustment Agency, a precursor to the Farm Service Agency that operated in the Hill County Courthouse from 1933 to 1936.

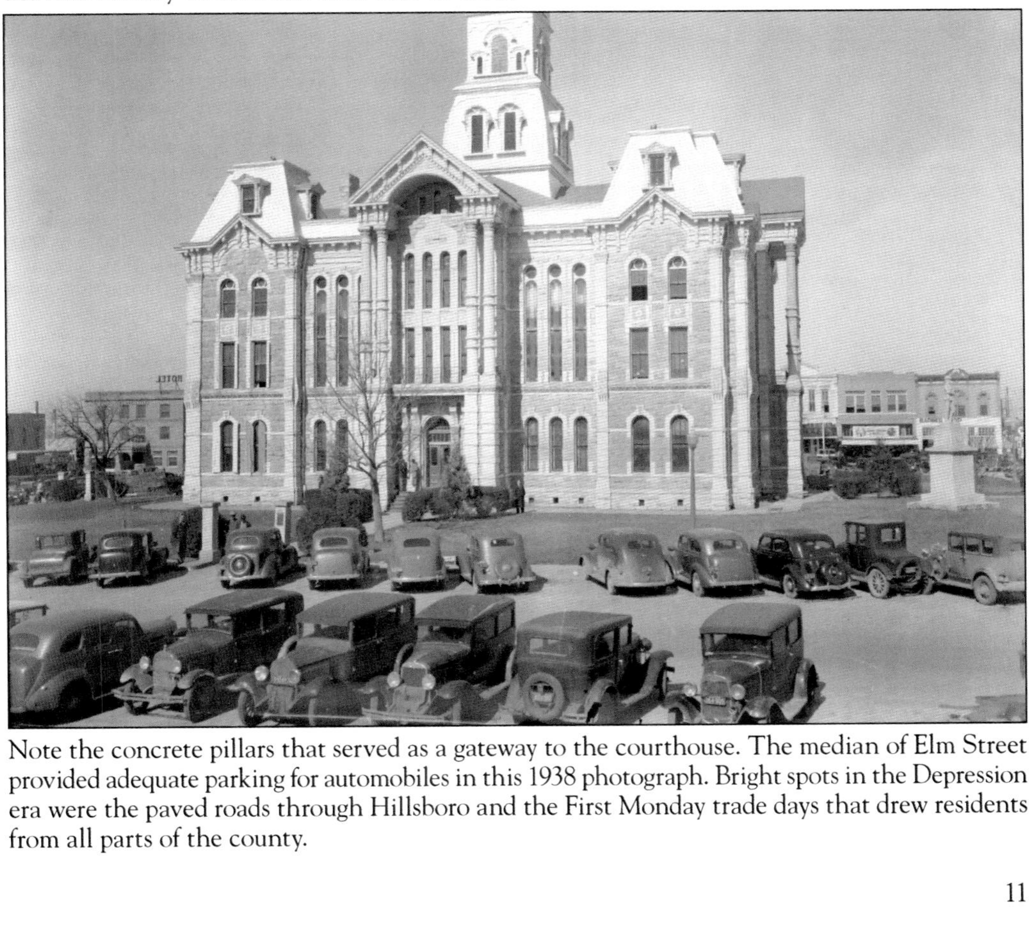

Note the concrete pillars that served as a gateway to the courthouse. The median of Elm Street provided adequate parking for automobiles in this 1938 photograph. Bright spots in the Depression era were the paved roads through Hillsboro and the First Monday trade days that drew residents from all parts of the county.

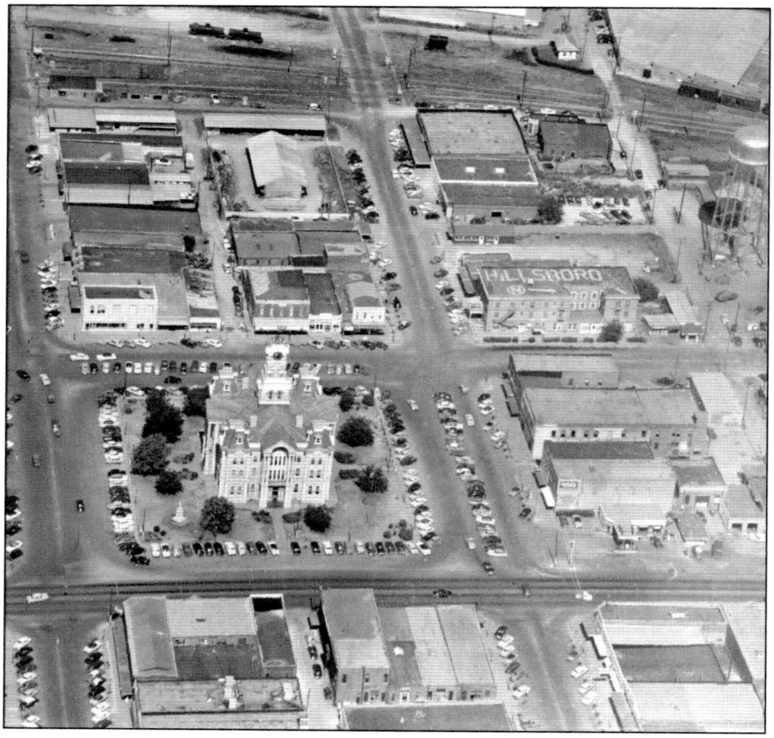

This aerial view to the west shows the courthouse around 1950, surrounded by post–World War II buildings. The Cooper Wholesale Grocery and Texas Power & Light Distribution Center are between West Franklin and Fancher Streets east of the railroad tracks. O.L. Wilkirson Lumber Yard occupied the northeast corner of West Elm and Bois d'Arc Streets and the southeast corner of West Franklin and Bois d'Arc Streets. Note "Hillsboro" spelled out on the roof of the Wear Hotel.

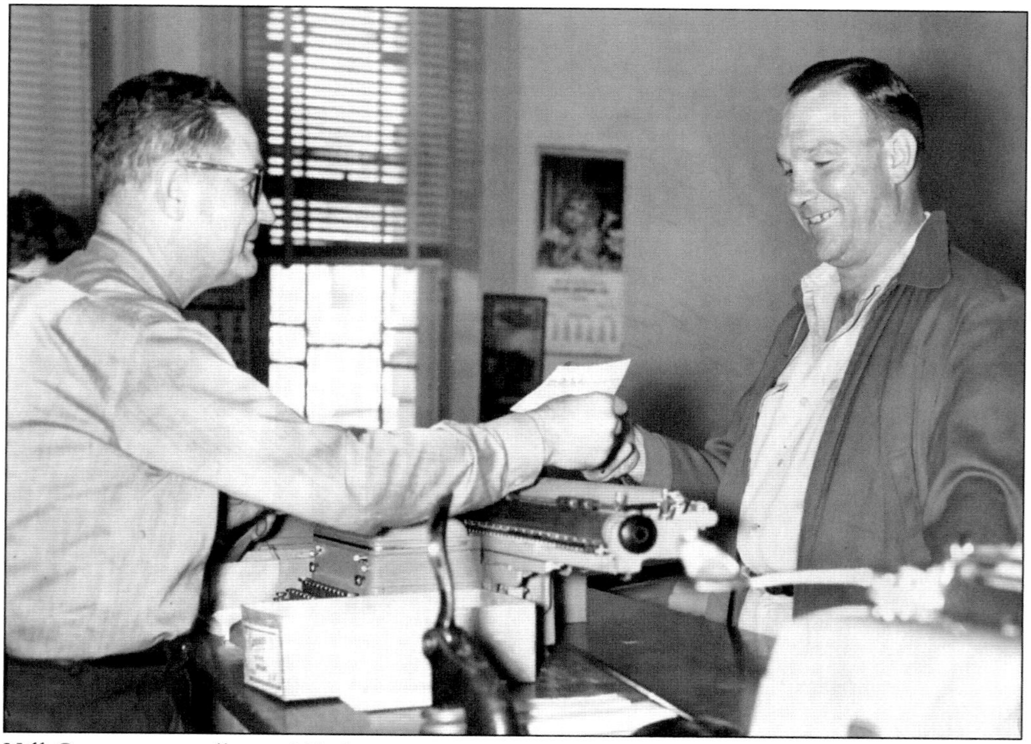

Hill County tax collector J.E. Scott assists a taxpayer in a first-floor office of the courthouse around 1959. The interior of the courthouse features stained-glass windows, high ceilings, and a basement with unadorned limestone walls.

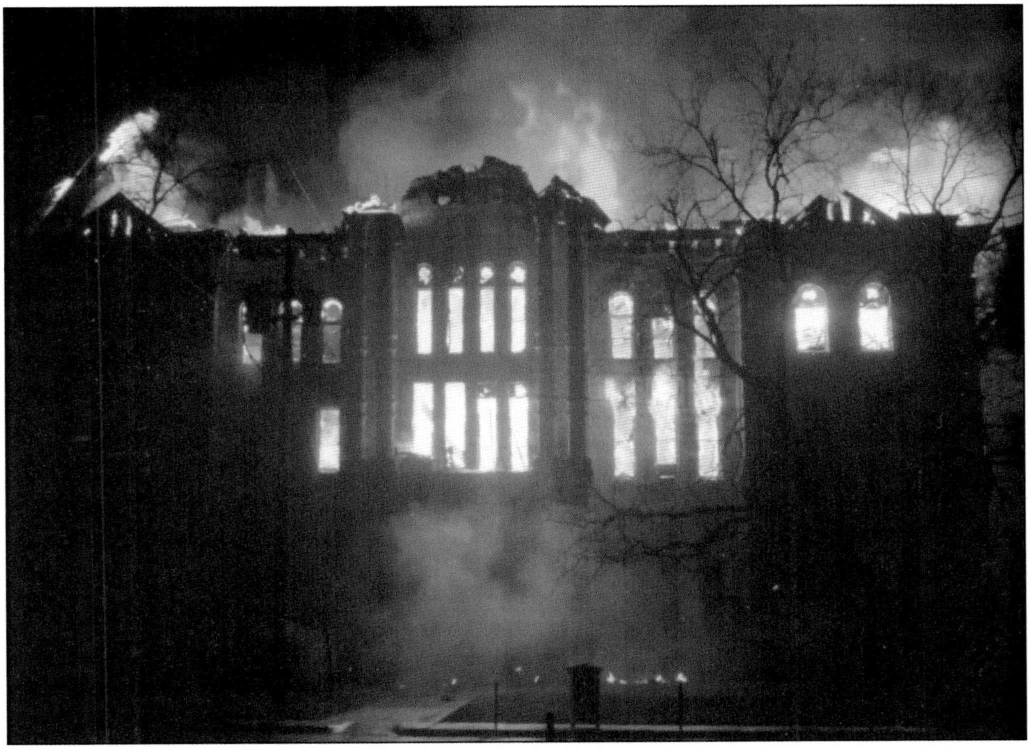

On New Year's Day 1993, the courthouse suffered the same fiery fate as the county's second courthouse. Fortunately, it was not completely destroyed, and the Texas Historical Commission (THC) certified that it could be restored. The only caveat was that it had to meet THC's standards. The insurance on the structure was insufficient to accomplish this goal, and the Hill County Historical Commission headed the effort to restore the important landmark. The restoration project grew into a statewide and even national project. All 254 counties in Texas contributed funds, as did many émigrés from the county. Hill County native and country singer Willie Nelson (right) gave benefit concerts for the restoration project in 1993 and 1999.

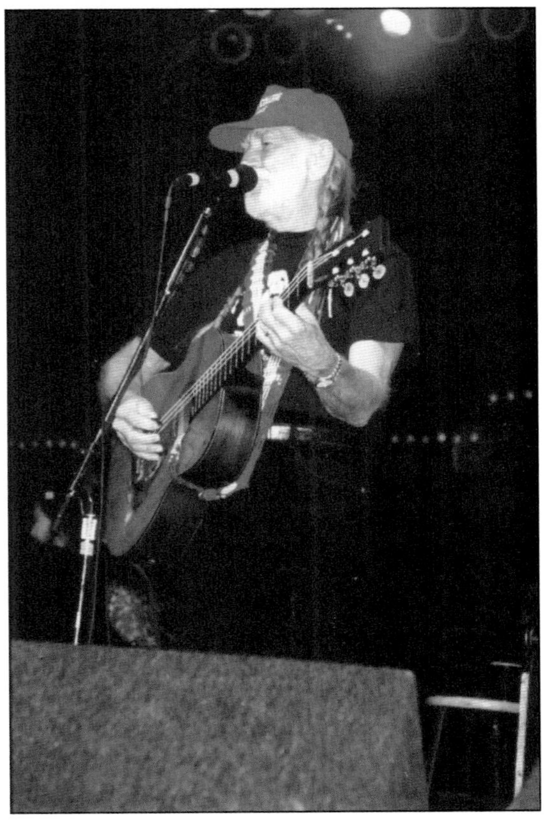

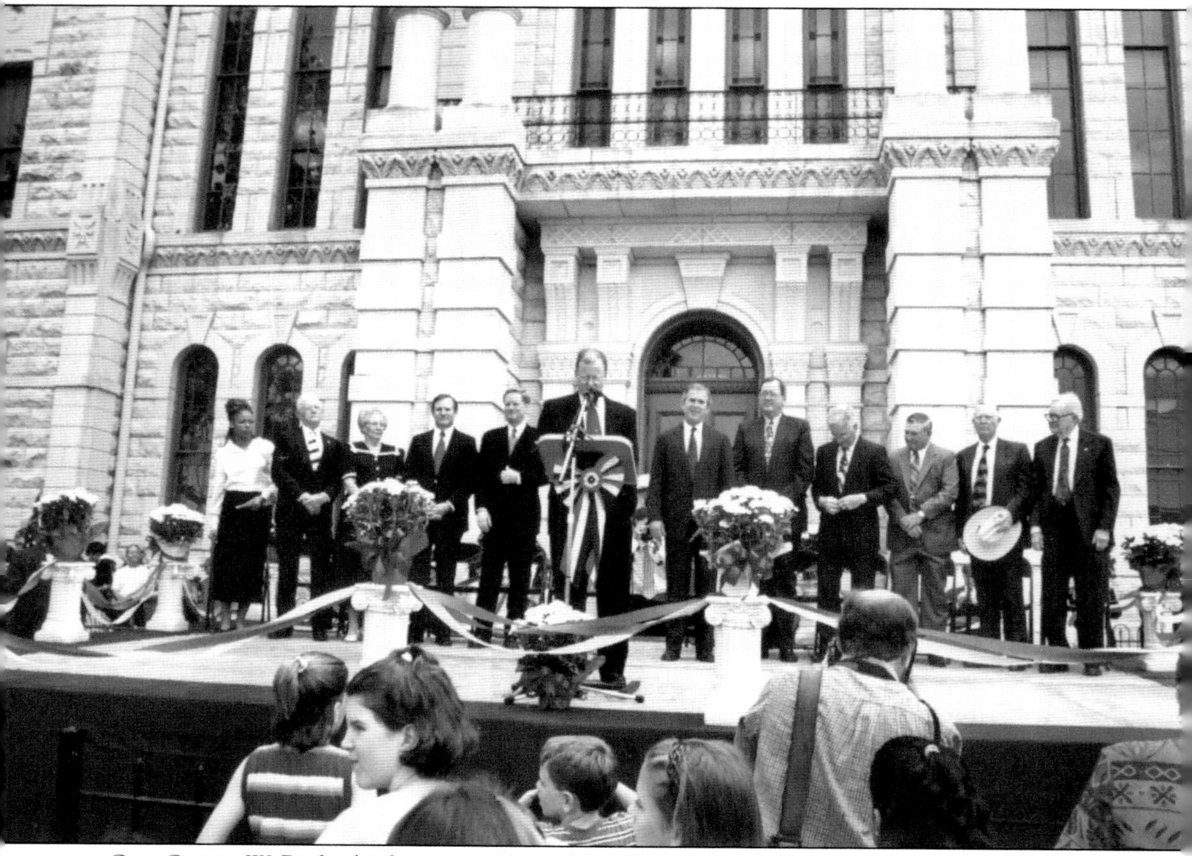

Gov. George W. Bush, the future president of the United States, dedicated the restored courthouse to the people of Hill County on May 10, 1999. Seen here on stage are, from left to right, Tiffaney Gipson, the singer of the national anthem; commissioners John Erwin and Mildred Brustrom; US congressman Chet Edwards; state representative Jim Pitts; master of ceremonies Arthur Mann; Governor Bush; state senator David Sibley; county judge Kenneth Davis; commissioners Kenneth Reid and J.K. Lane; and 10th Court of Appeals justice Frank G. McDonald. Courthouse restoration efforts were headed by Dallas architect Craig Melde, principal with ArchiTexas.

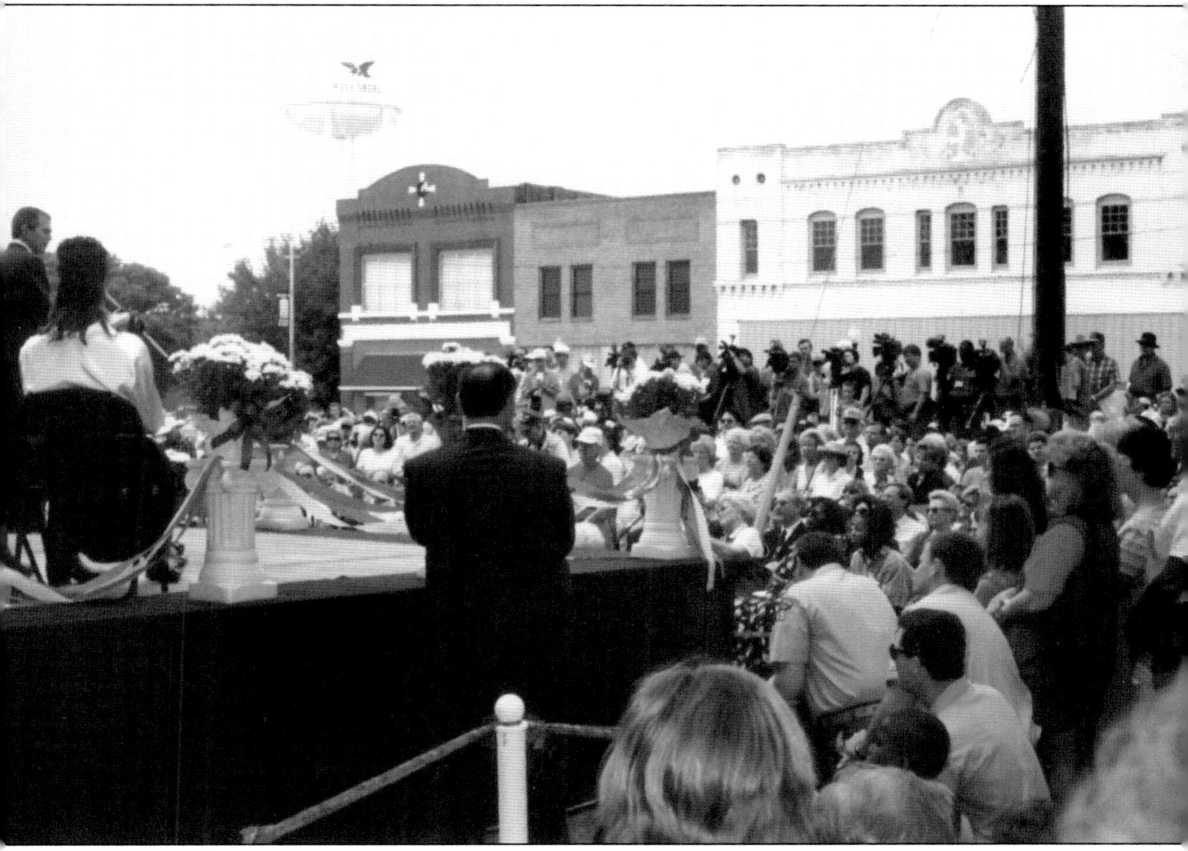

Governor Bush (on stage, left) addresses the crowd at the 1999 courthouse dedication. The city water tower, featuring the Hillsboro Independent School District's Eagle emblem, looms in the distance. The buildings in the background, on the 100 block of West Franklin Street, are the Wear office building (Eastland Title), Terry Cunningham Construction (formerly Aderhold & Marshall Funeral Home), and the former Montgomery Ward store, which was originally the home of the Colonial Trust Company.

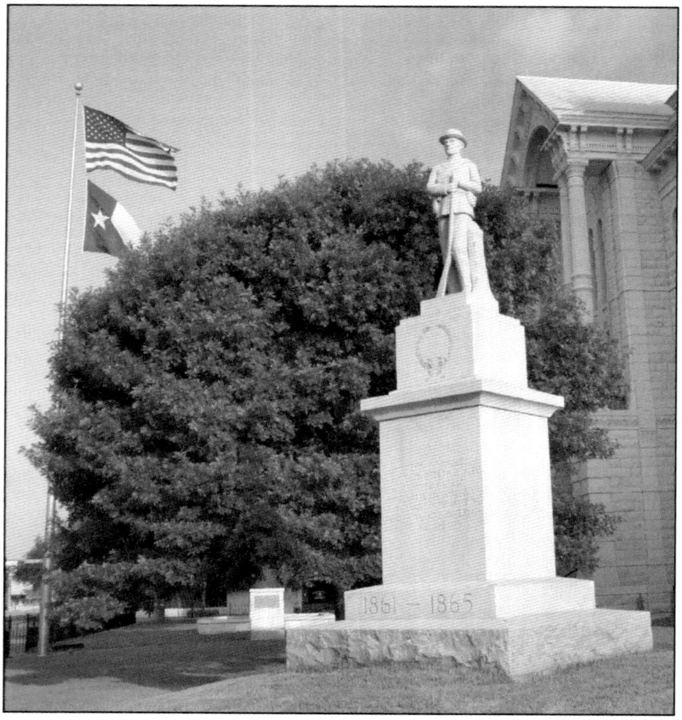

The courthouse is seen here in 2013. Note the 1925 Confederate soldier monument in the foreground. The gray granite statue, which stands sentinel on the southeast corner of the courthouse square, was erected by the Sons of Confederate Veterans Camp No. 966 under the leadership of former sheriff Fred Long and Capt. Joseph T. Bobbitt. The design and construction contract was awarded to Alex Park of Hillsboro Monument Company. (Art Mann.)

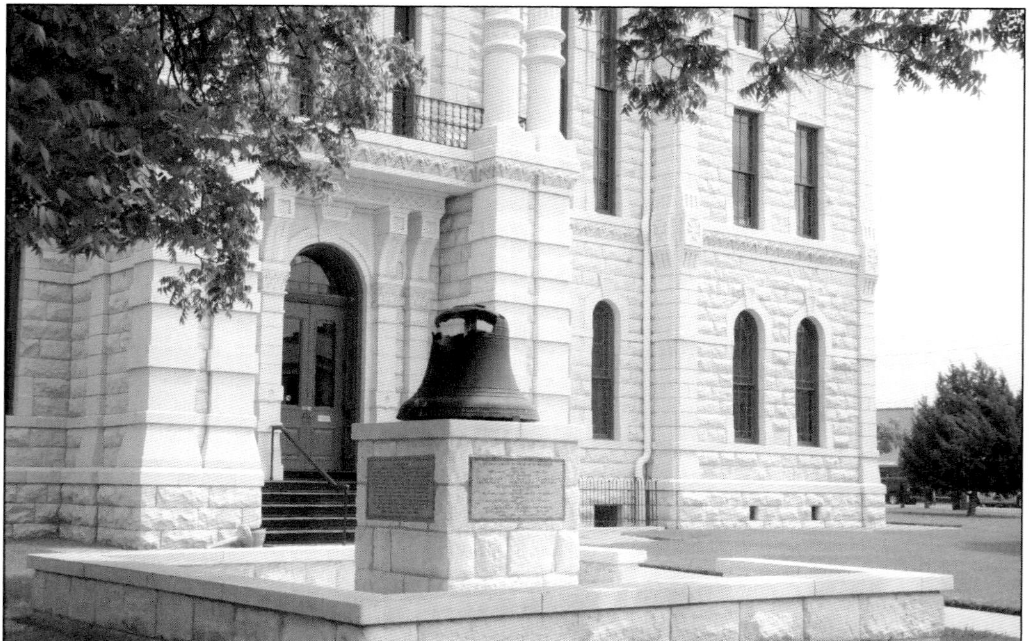

The Hill County Courthouse Bell Plaza is on the south lawn of the courthouse. The plaza is constructed from limestone blocks salvaged from the oldest building in neighboring Abbott. A pedestal holding the bell in the center of the plaza features four plaques, with information on the history of the courthouse, the 1993 fire, the restoration effort, and a list of officials involved in the restoration. Partial funding for a new courthouse bell came from the Taco Bell corporation, according to the Hill County Historical Commission. (Anita Tufts.)

Two

Cotton Culture and Industry

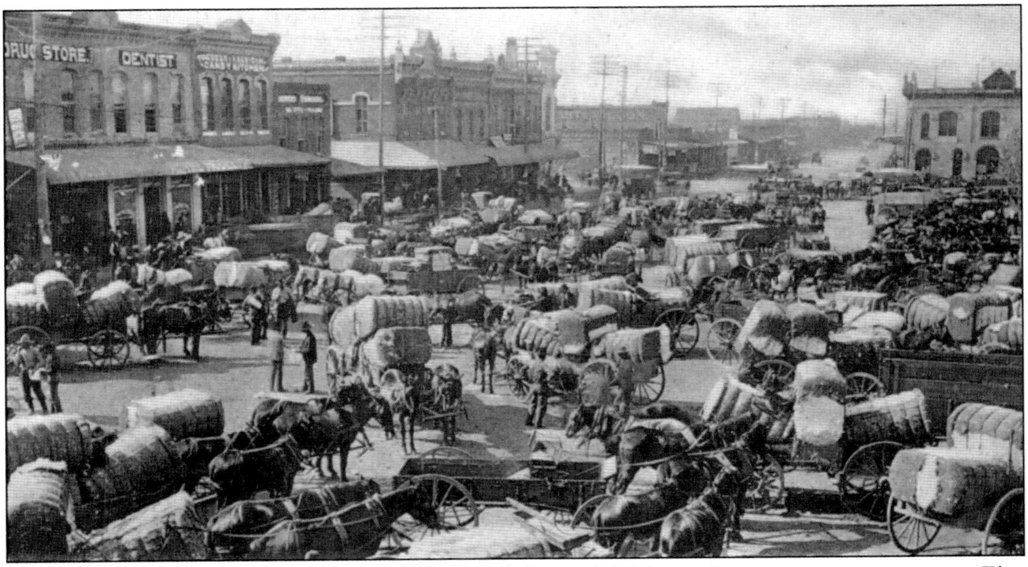

This 1890s scene of farmers bringing cotton bales to Hillsboro shows cotton wagons on Elm Street, on the south side of the courthouse, looking west. The population of Hillsboro at that time was 2,541. Hill County was one of the top cotton-producing counties in the South, and the entire county lived on the results of the year's cotton crop, according to *100% Cotton*, by Jack and Jane Pruitt.

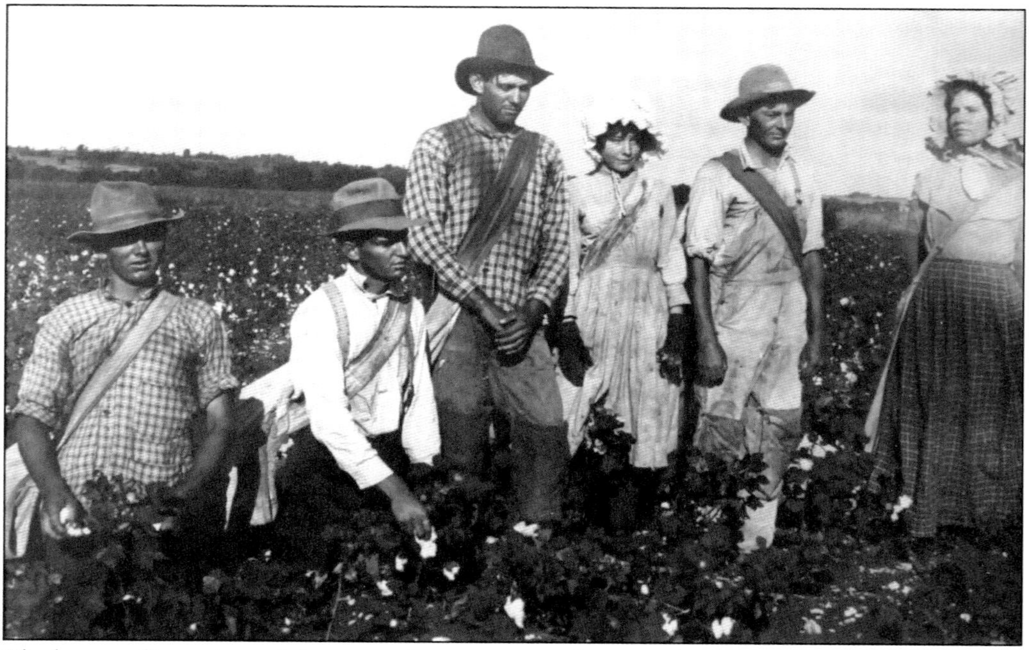

The human dimensions of the years when cotton was king can be seen in the faces of the Flores family, who farmed in the Lakenon area in Hill County in the 1920s. (Cell Block Museum.)

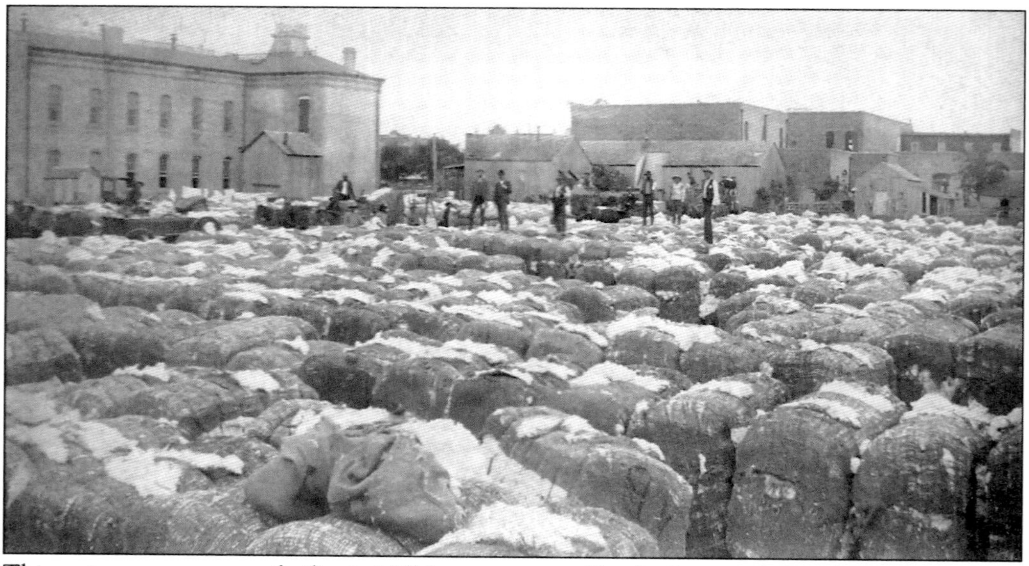

This major cotton storage facility in Hillsboro was owned by the Farmers & Merchants Warehouse, organized in 1914. The warehouse had a capacity of 2,400 bales, was fireproof, and had a capital of $20,000. The original board of directors included A.L. Smith, president, and E.S. Davis, secretary. Both retained offices until their deaths. Later officials and directors of the company included Marion Clyette, R.C. West, David N. Glass, F.J. Cloyed, H.M. "Mack" Lowrance, and Willis Thompson, according to *100% Cotton*.

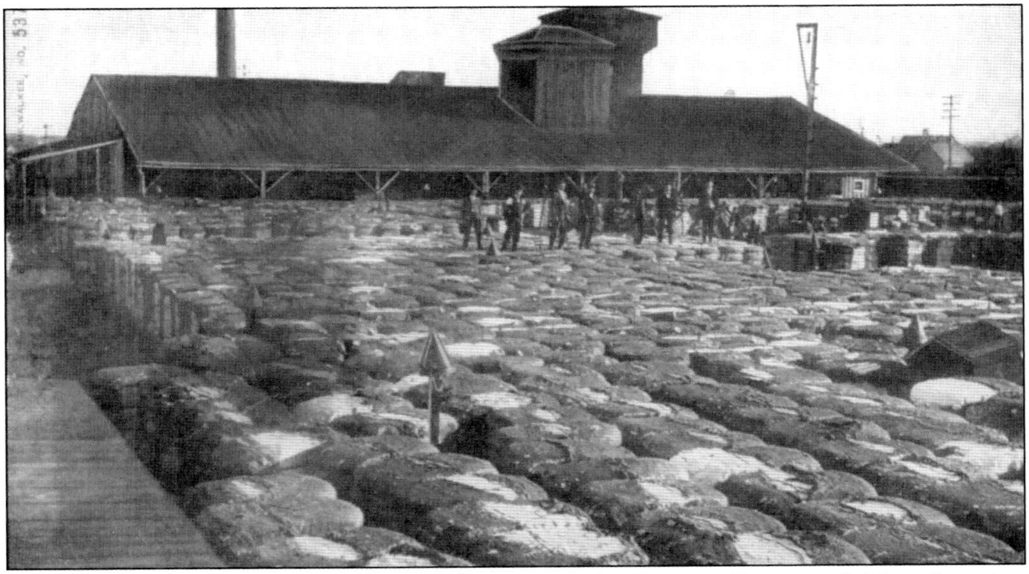

Jack and Jane Pruitt state in *100% Cotton* that in 1890, the Shippers Compress & Manufacturing Company began business in Hillsboro, with G.R. Bennett, president; H.C. Denney, vice president; J.L. Watson, secretary and manager; and J.J. Warren, treasurer. The plant was located on Franklin Street between the Missouri, Kansas & Texas (MKT) and Cotton Belt railroads. Other cotton yards were the Farmers Union and Farmers & Merchants.

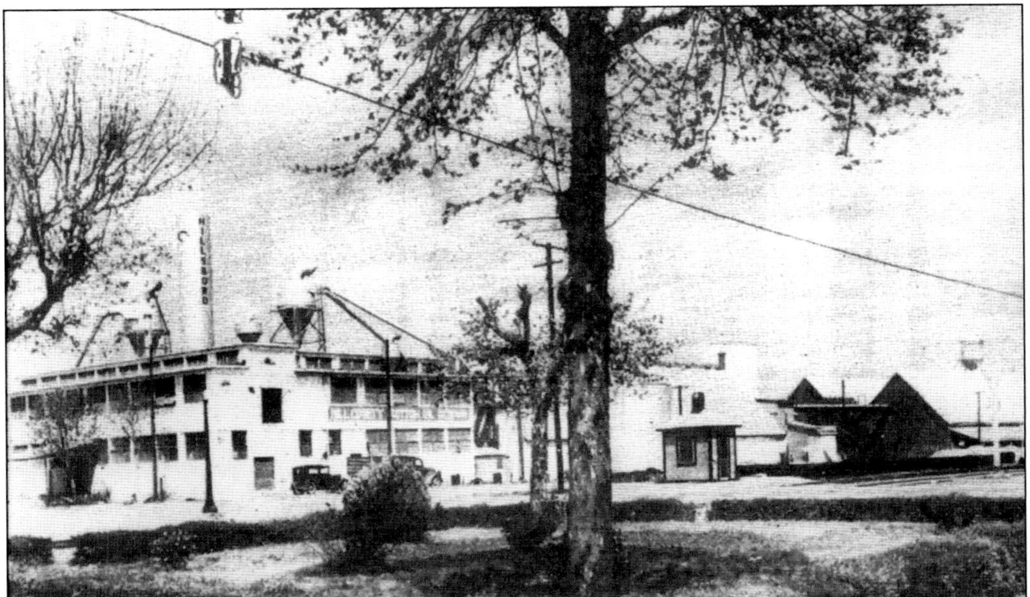

Located on West Franklin Street, the Hill County Cotton Oil Company was established in 1902. Ed Woodall was one of the principal factors and it had a capacity of 100 tons per day. The executive board included G. Luther White, president; John R. Griffin, vice president; and Edward Woodall, secretary-treasurer and manager, according to *100% Cotton*. Another oil-producing company was the Hillsboro Oil Company, which was organized in 1891 with a total capacity of 70 tons of cottonseed a day.

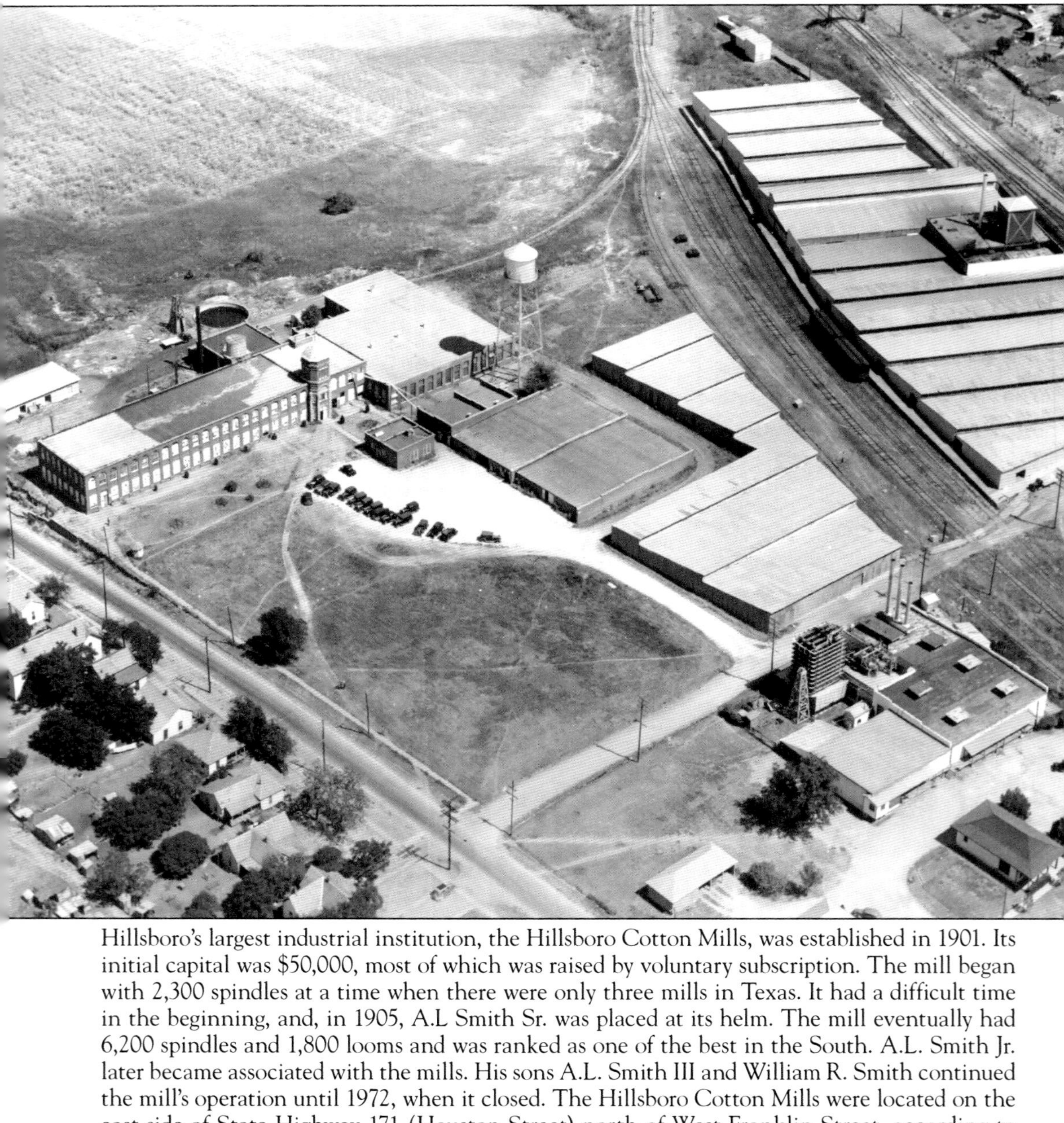

Hillsboro's largest industrial institution, the Hillsboro Cotton Mills, was established in 1901. Its initial capital was $50,000, most of which was raised by voluntary subscription. The mill began with 2,300 spindles at a time when there were only three mills in Texas. It had a difficult time in the beginning, and, in 1905, A.L Smith Sr. was placed at its helm. The mill eventually had 6,200 spindles and 1,800 looms and was ranked as one of the best in the South. A.L. Smith Jr. later became associated with the mills. His sons A.L. Smith III and William R. Smith continued the mill's operation until 1972, when it closed. The Hillsboro Cotton Mills were located on the east side of State Highway 171 (Houston Street) north of West Franklin Street, according to *100% Cotton*.

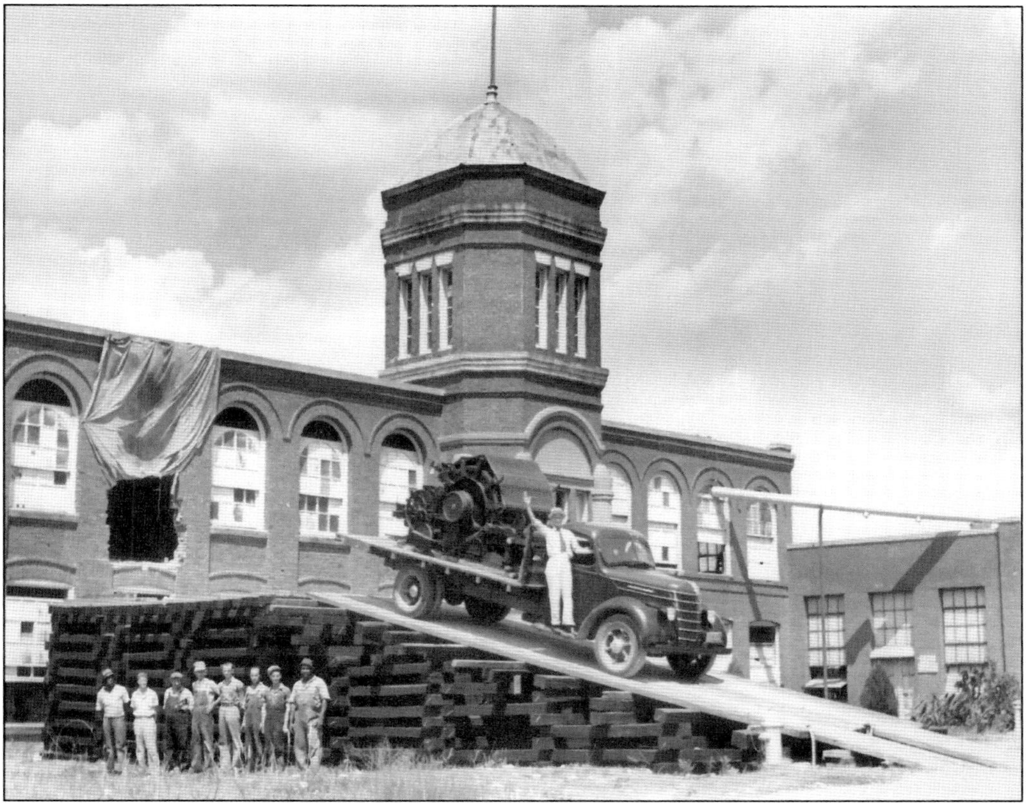

Employees of Hillsboro Cotton Mills are seen here in the process of installing new looms. Note the ramp and the large opening required to allow installation of the equipment.

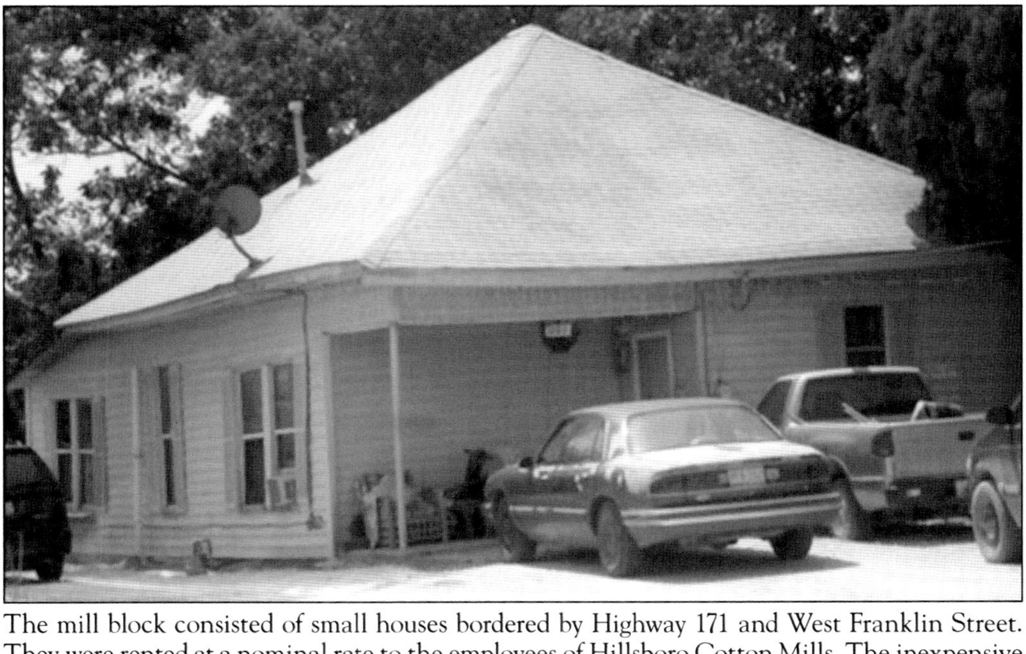

The mill block consisted of small houses bordered by Highway 171 and West Franklin Street. They were rented at a nominal rate to the employees of Hillsboro Cotton Mills. The inexpensive housing assisted those struggling to recover from the Great Depression.

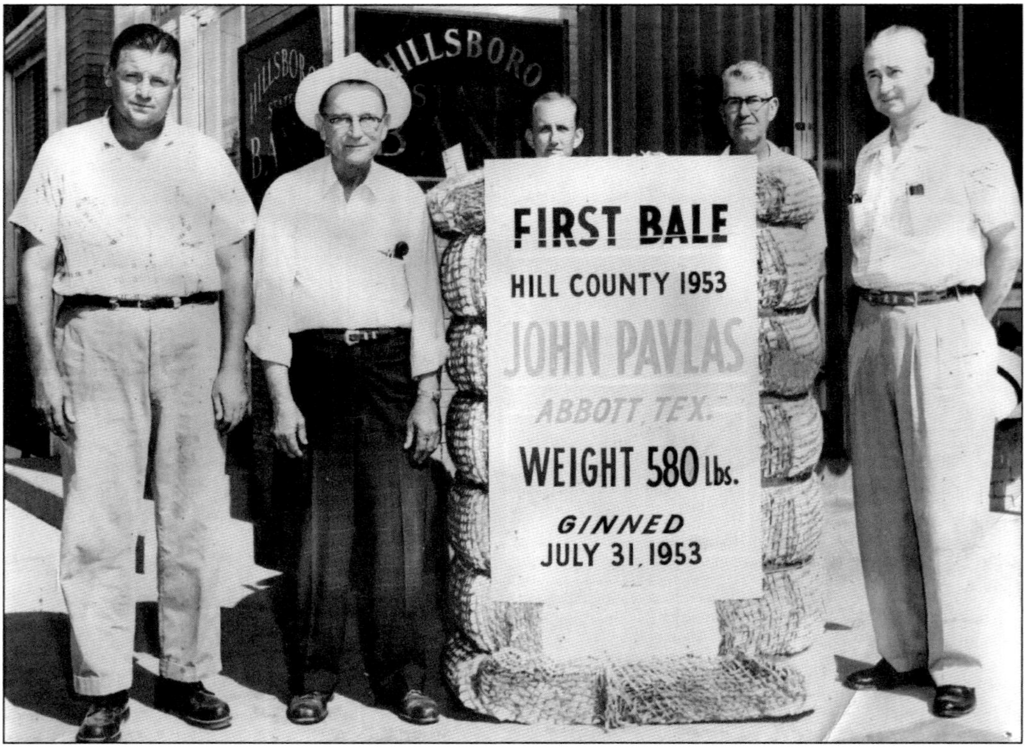

The first bale of cotton ginned in the county has always been a celebrated event in Hillsboro and Hill County. On July 31, 1953, John Pavlas produced and ginned the first bale of cotton in the county. It weighed in at 580 pounds. Seen here in front of the Hillsboro State Bank are, from left to right, Jean Kirkland, John Pavlas, S.J. Vaughan III, Chester Morgan, and Aubrey Moore.

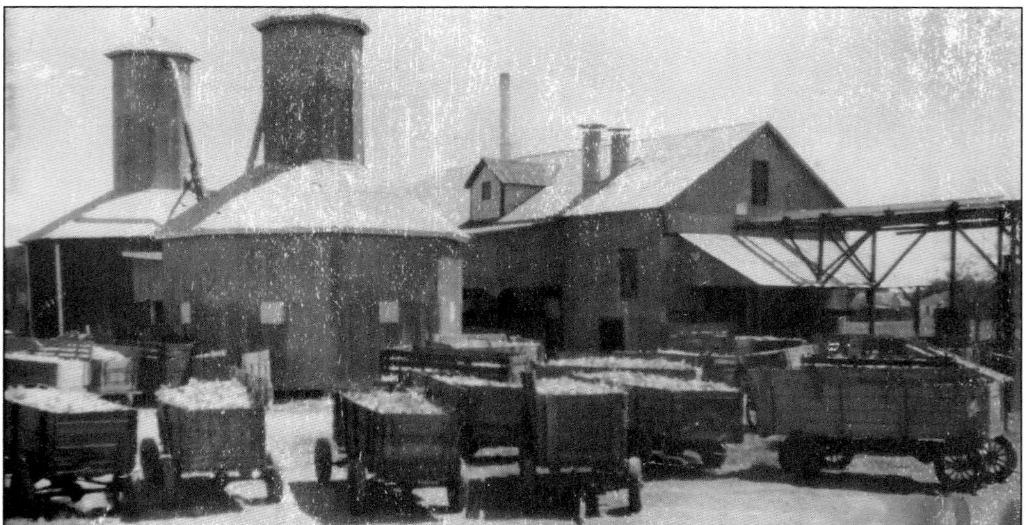

W.C. Robertson Gin & Grain served area farmers beginning in 1903. This 1930s photograph shows the cotton gin, at 430 South Waco Street, in the background with two cotton houses in front. Wagons of corn ready for the corn sheller sit in the yard. A.N. Robertson managed the gin on South Waco Street while W.C. Robertson Jr. managed the Farmer's Co-operative Gin, at 301 Chestnut Street. (Apex Grain, John and Denise Tuggle.)

Cecil Stubblefield, the owner and cotton buyer for C. Stubblefield & Co., grades a sample of cotton. The firm exported cotton throughout the world and, in 1955, bought the first 200 bales of cotton produced in the United States. The office was located at 103 ½ West Elm Street in 1940 before relocating to 105 West Elm Street. Another buyer was the Cotton Exchange, located in one of the oldest structures on the courthouse square on the northwest corner of Elm and Covington Streets. (C.H. Stubblefield)

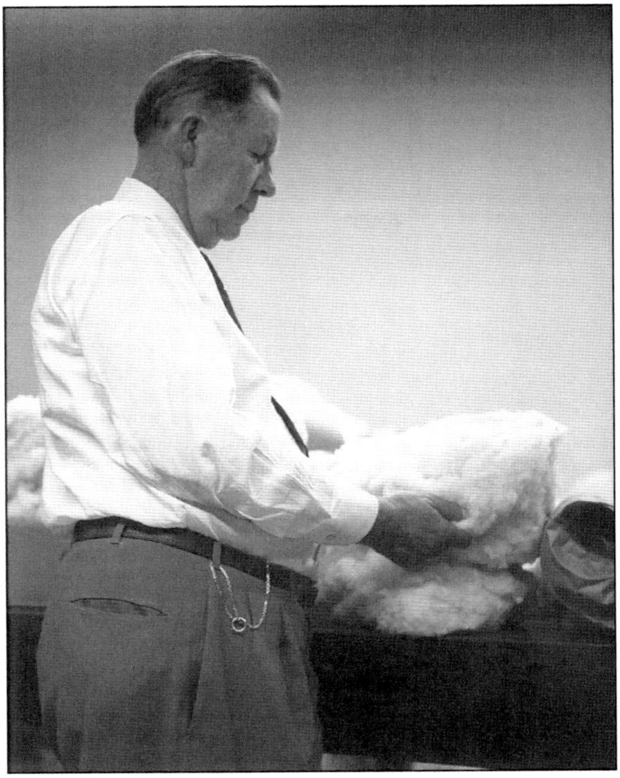

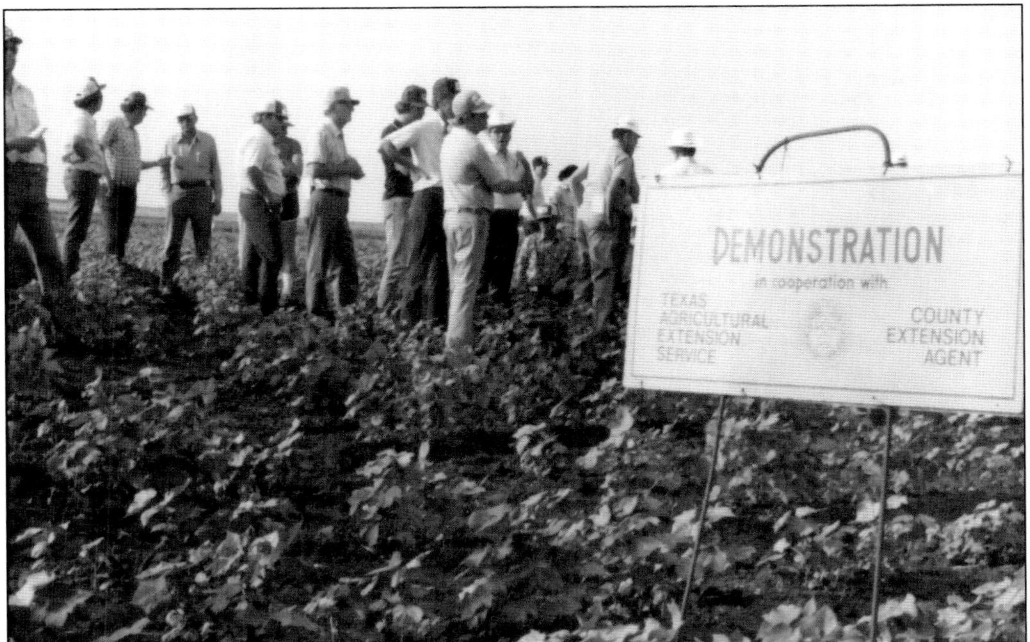

The Texas Agriculture Extension Service has a long history in Hill County of promoting better farming practices, such as the improved cotton varieties being viewed at this demonstration test plot. The first county agent, A.C Bayliss, began work in 1909. Extension work has included livestock and pasture work, improved seeds, and soil conservation.

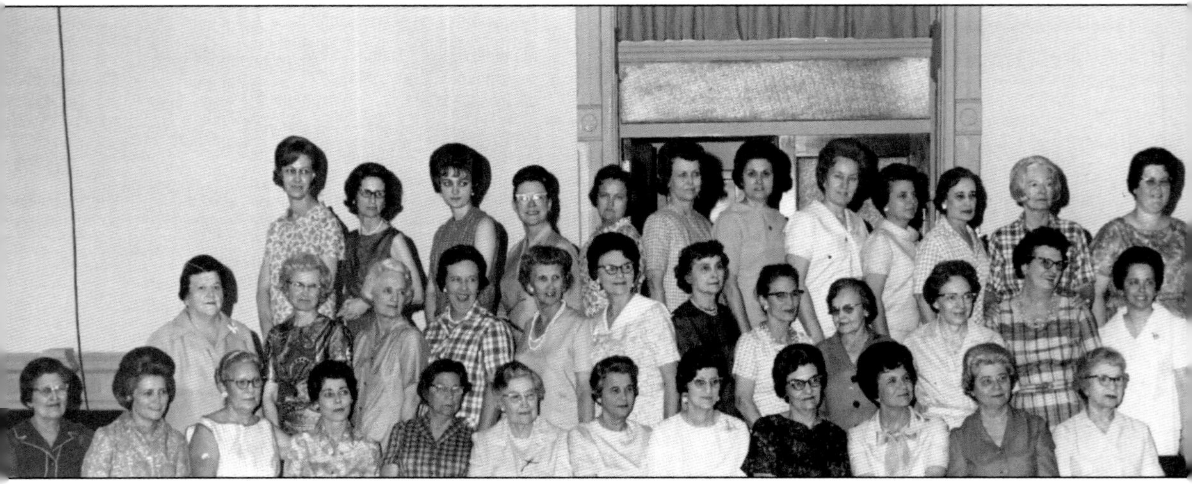

During the time when cotton was king, the female employees of the Hill County Courthouse organized a New Cotton Dress Day. On a specific day in April, they each wore a new cotton dress to work and had a covered dish luncheon. These attendees included, from left to right, (first row) Mary Jackson, Mary Barnett, Dorothy Dudley, Kathleen McCurry, Mattie Boyd, Mary Harvey, Maynett Willis, Ora Mae Bobbitt, Irene King, unidentified, Mary Love Warren, and Catherine Page; (second row) Mattie Crain, Jeanette Barrow, Pauline Martin, Kay Watson, Tommie Beene, Ruth Bottom, Esther Blanchard, Lucille Porter, Clare Dean, Frances Bilbrey, Pauline Mobley, and Betty Ray Dohoney; (third row) Jane Waller, Nita Curlee, Pam Schulz, Alma Spence, Virginia Sullins, Virginia Anderson, Ruby Lewis, Rachael Malone, Ruby Malone, Velma Crabs, Gladys Marshall, and Bobbie Smalley.

Three

How We Got There and Back

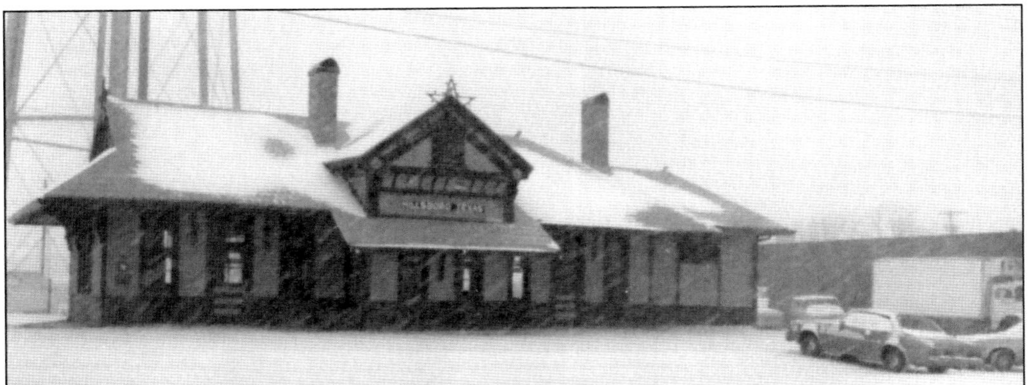

This depot was completed in 1902 to serve the Missouri, Kansas & Texas (MKT) rail line, which reached Hillsboro in 1881. The station features elements of the Eastlake, Victorian, and Prairie styles. Early trains carried materials for the growing town and brought new residents. It also brought such notables as presidents Woodrow Wilson, William Howard Taft, Calvin Coolidge, and Harry Truman. The building was moved to 115 North Covington Street in 1978. Today, it serves as a chamber of commerce office and tourism center.

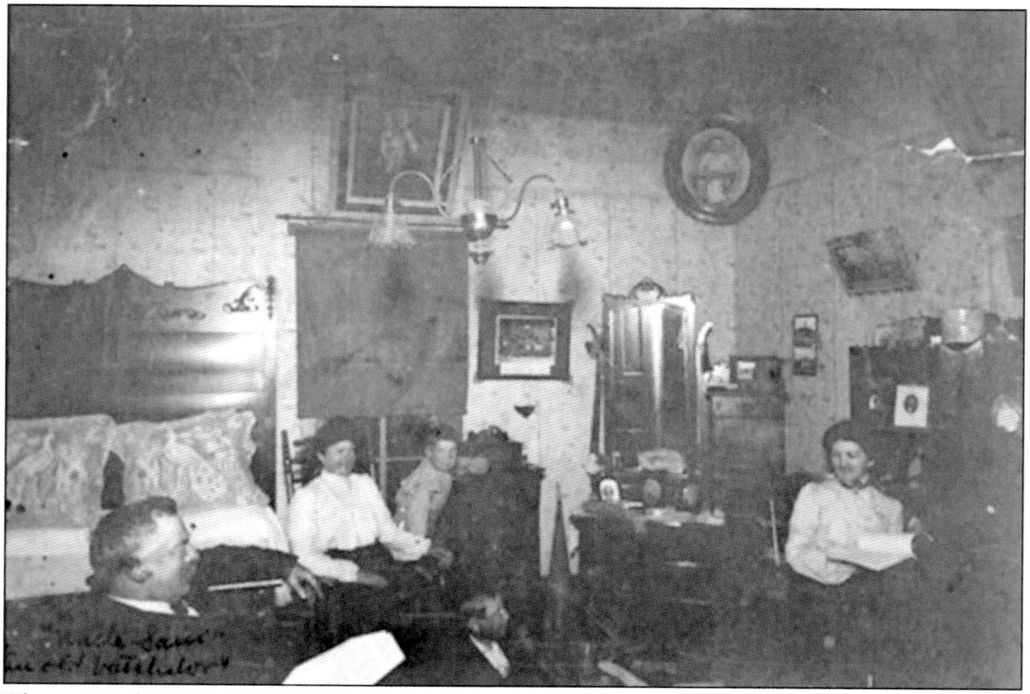

There were hotels in Hillsboro as early as 1856. One of the first was the Nelms Hotel, which was later remodeled and named the Alhambra. School was taught nearby in 1857, and students boarded at the Alhambra. Seen here is the Lawler House, erected by Abner and Amanda Lawler between Church and Gould Streets in 1883 as a hotel and later used as a rooming house.

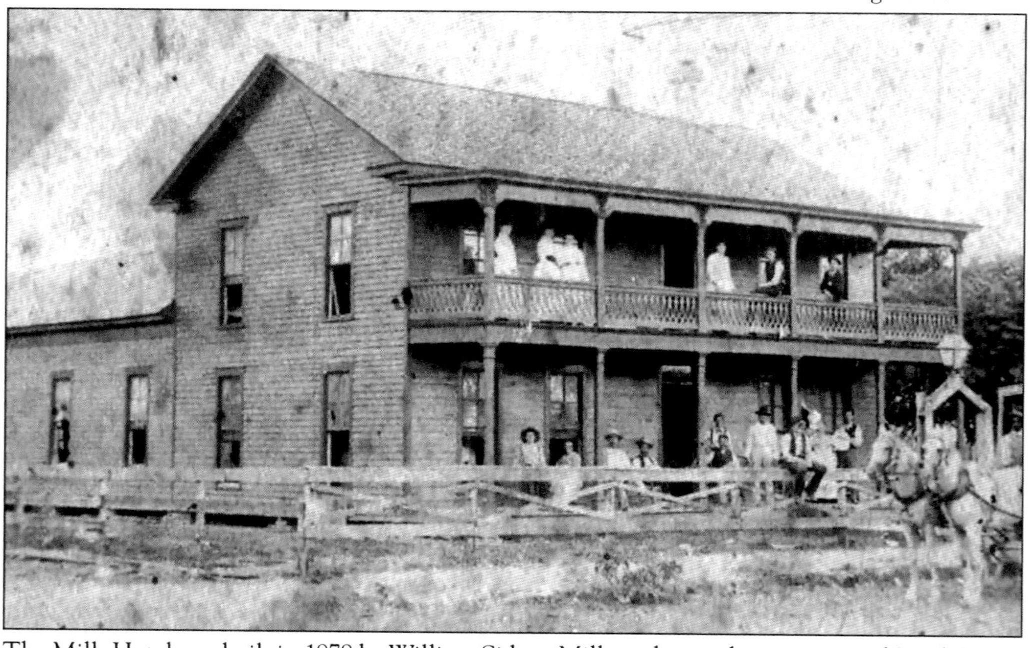

The Mills Hotel was built in 1878 by William Sidney Mills at the southeast corner of South Waco and Gould Streets. The hotel was constructed by J.S. Robinson, and Mills also built a livery stable on the northeast corner. It later operated as the Porter & Crumley barn. The *Hillsboro Mirror*, a local newspaper, was built on the former site of the hotel in 1901. (Erin Russell Ripple.)

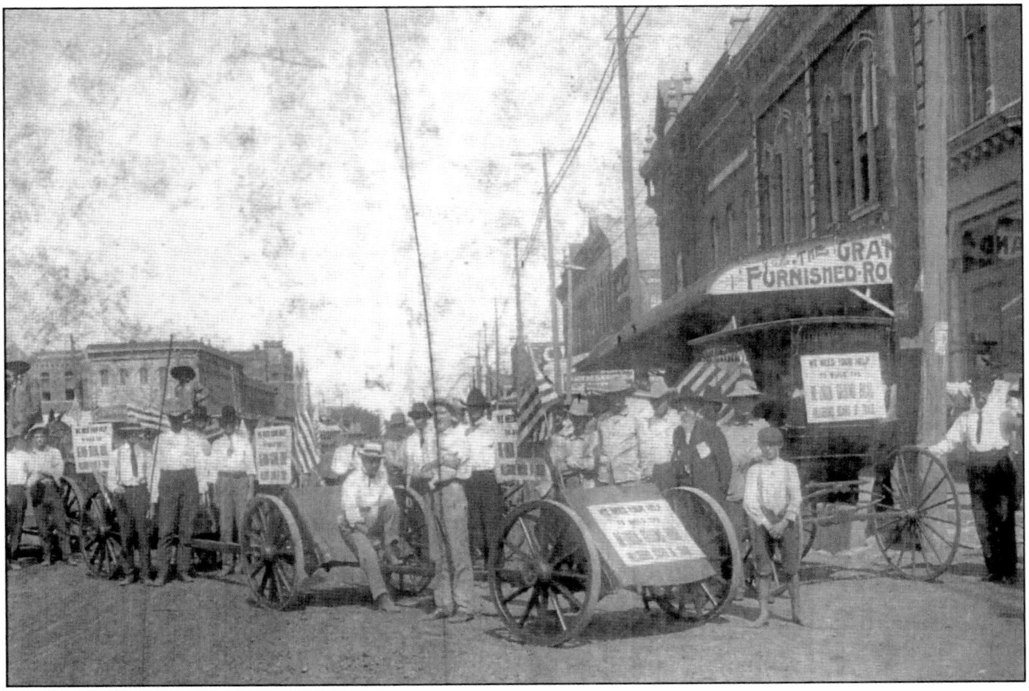

The signs on the back of farm equipment parked at the corner of Elm and Covington Streets read, "We Need Your Help To Build the Reunion Grounds Road, Hillsboro Board of Trade." The farm equipment was used to build the road. The construction of the three-mile road to the facility located southeast of town was facilitated by the solicitation of funds from private citizens. The 1909 campaign raised $750 for the construction of a gravel road.

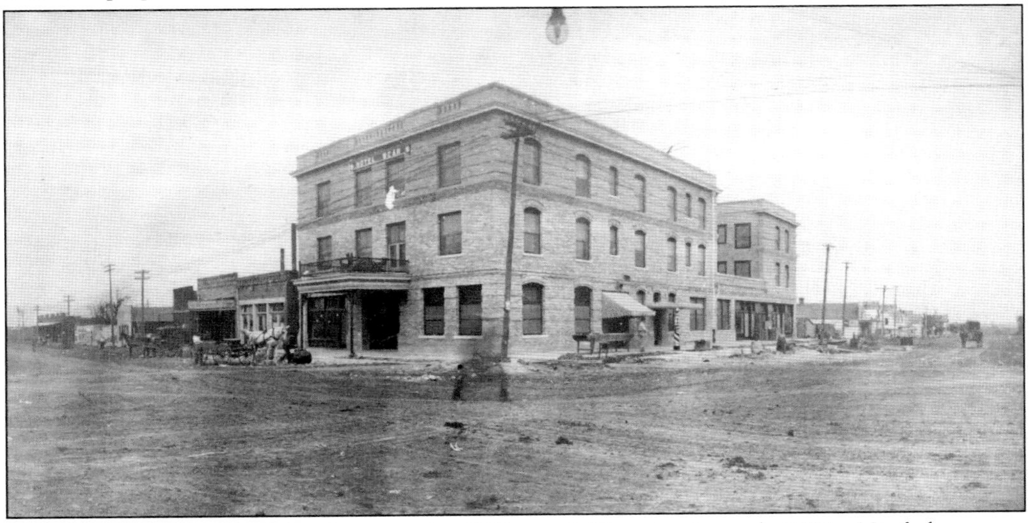

The Wear Hotel was built by district judge William C. Wear in the early 1900s. His father was a Cumberland Presbyterian minister who came to Hillsboro in 1881. Wear worked on the railroad to pay his way through the University of Texas and earn his law degree. Located on the northwest corner of North Covington and West Franklin Streets, the hotel was convenient for railroad and interurban passengers. The hotel had three stories, a barbershop, and a restaurant. It later became the Newman Hotel. In the 1940s, the United Service Organization operated a recreation room for soldiers there.

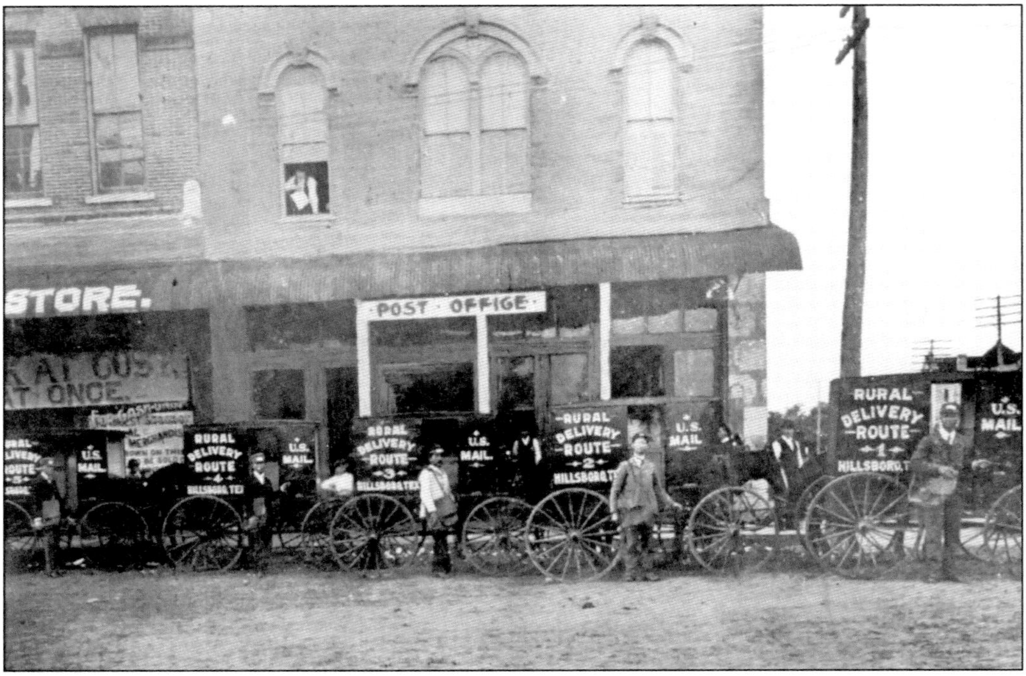

The Hillsboro post office has had several locations since 1854. This photograph from around 1912 shows the post office on the north side of the square, with the Hill County Jail visible in the background. Wagons for rural delivery are in front of the post office. Mail and telegraph messages for city residents were delivered by couriers riding motorcycles, as seen below, from around 1914. In 1884, the post office was located at 110–112 South Waco Street and Herman Eastland Sr. had space in the building for a bookstore. By 1913, the post office was housed in its new facility at 118 South Waco Street, which is now the Hillsboro City Library.

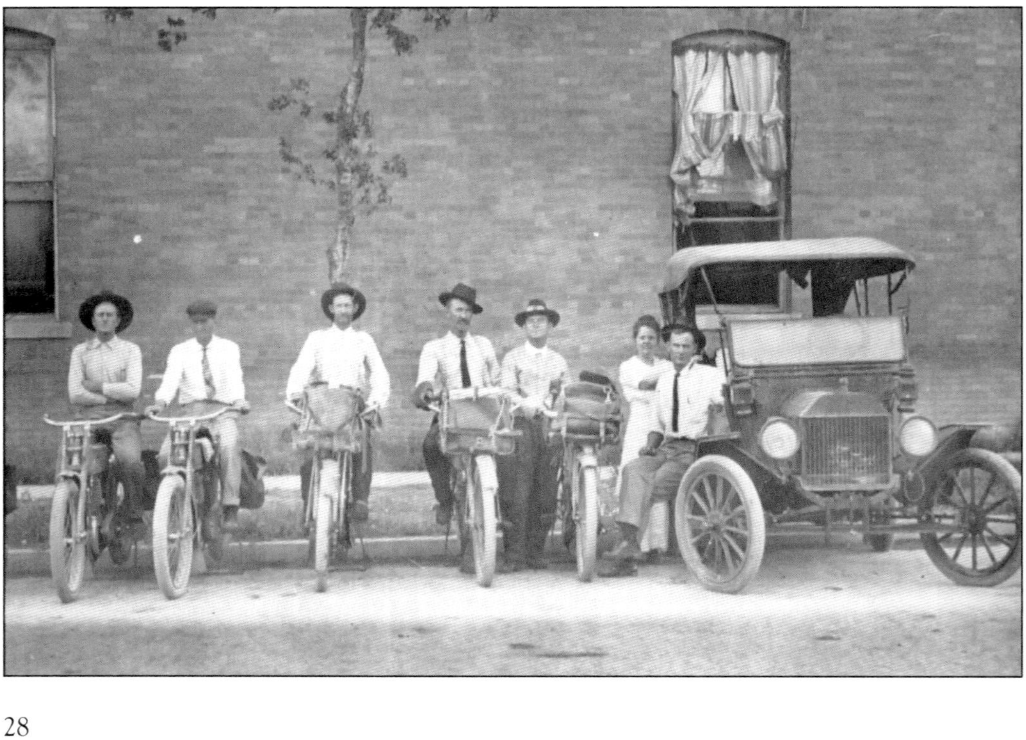

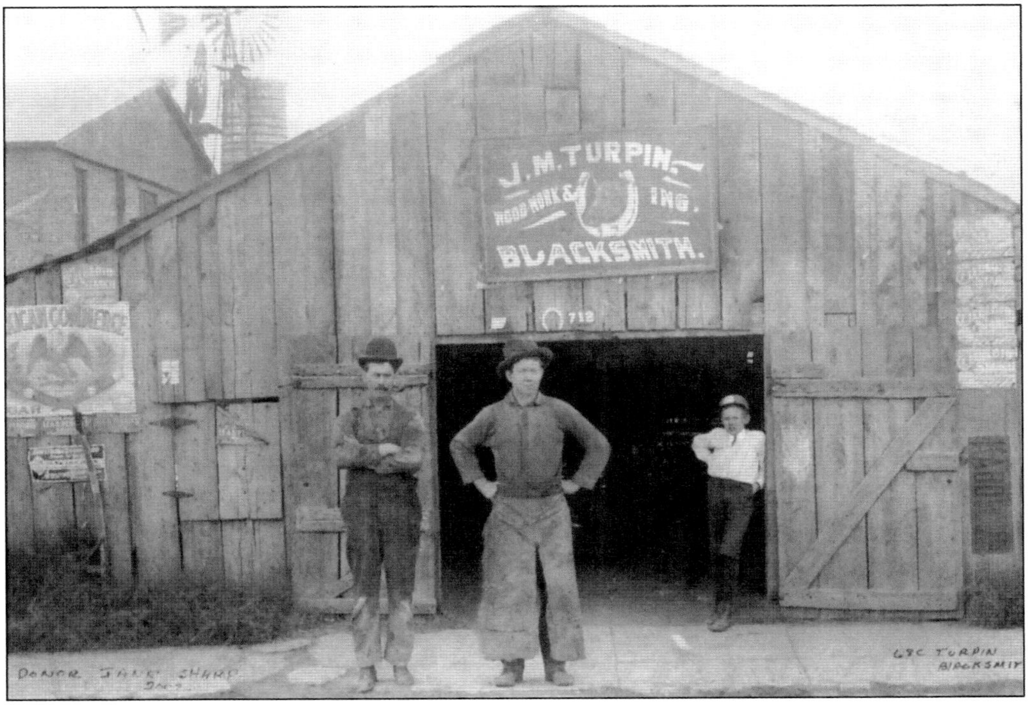

James M. Turpin and his brother Robert Floyd Turpin began working together in the J.M. Turpin blacksmith shop, at 712 Pascal Street, in 1919. With the advent of the motorcar, the shop became Turpin's Welding & Radiator Shop. Robert Floyd Turpin's wife, Addie, was a seamstress who sewed for the public out of their home. During World War II, she and her sister Bertha Wiesen took the interurban to Waco to make Army clothing, according to *Heritage of Hill County*.

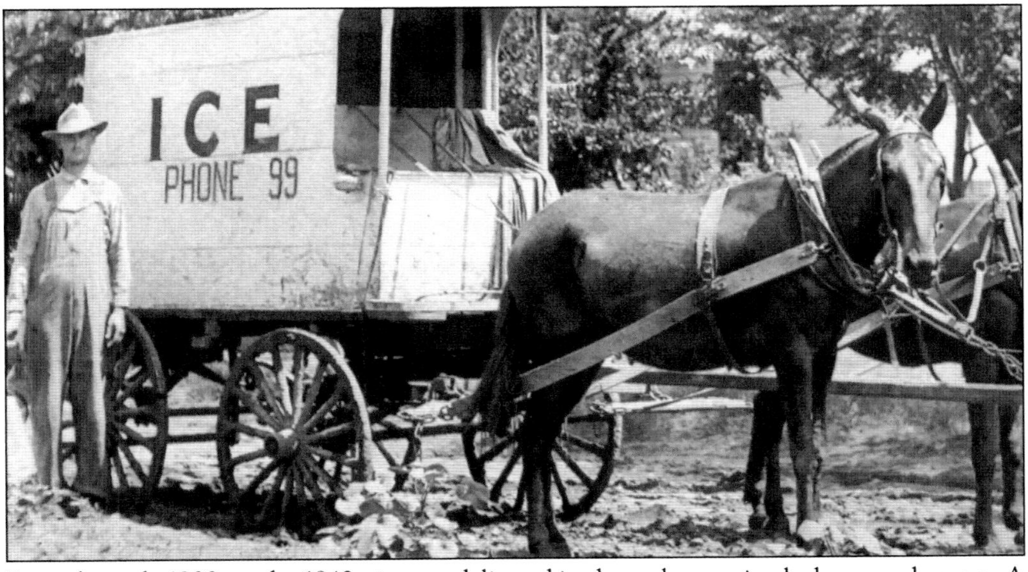

From the early 1900s to the 1940s, ice was delivered in the early morning by horse and wagon. A square card designating the day's order—12.5, 25, 50, or 100 pounds—was placed in the window to inform the driver how much ice to deliver. Local ice companies included Hillsboro Ice on West Franklin Street, Home Ice on South Waco Street at the Robertson Gin, and Hilltex Ice on East Elm Street.

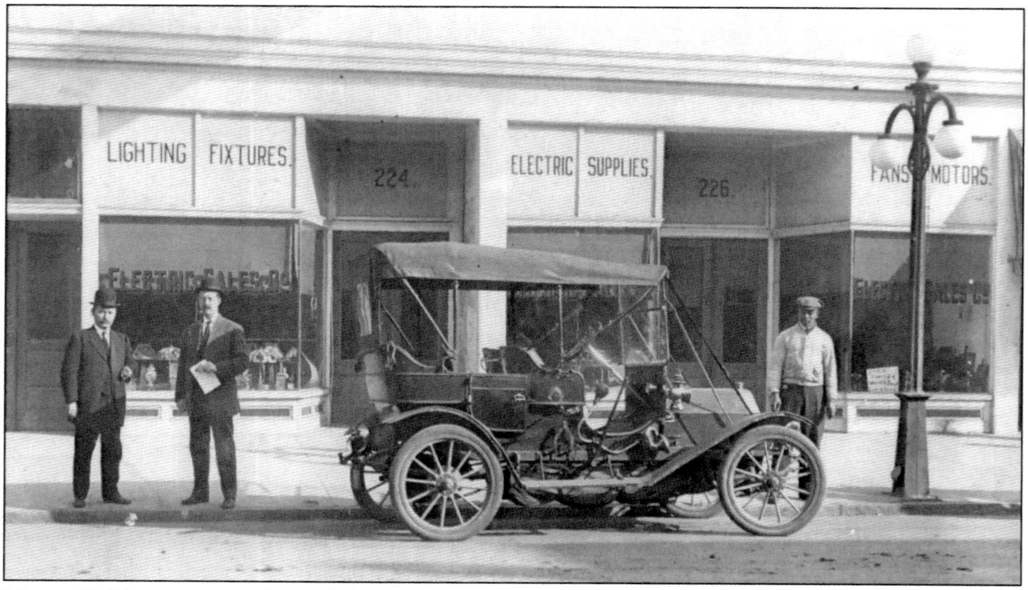

Hattie E. Vance, an early Hillsboro dressmaker, remembers the first automobile seen on the streets of Hillsboro. It caused a sensation, with people running from all directions to see it. The car arrived on an MKT railroad car and was used by the Montgomery Ward Company to deliver catalogues. The second car in Hillsboro was owned by a Mr. Mason. The automobile seen here is a 1912 Ford Model T touring car.

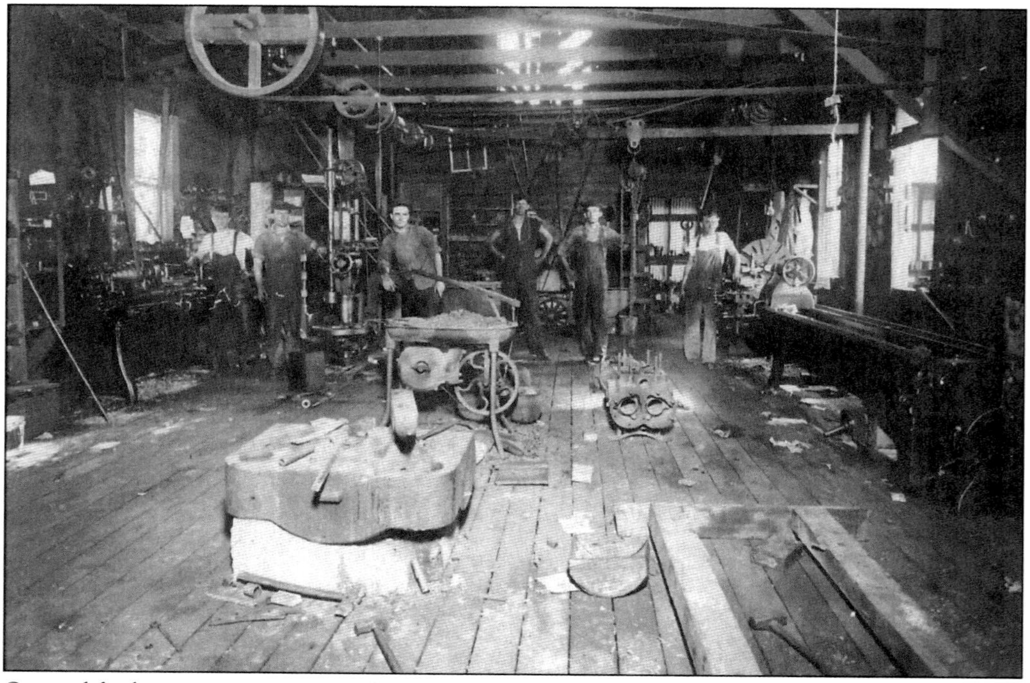

Opened for business in 1908 in a sheet-iron building, Monarch Foundry & Machine Shop built a new brick building at 113 West Franklin Street in 1914 for heavy machinery and automobile repair. When George R. Adams opened the doors for business, there were only two or three automobiles in the county, no paved streets in Hillsboro, and few sidewalks. Adams was a sales agent for Hudson and Essex automobiles, as chronicled in *Heritage of Hill County*.

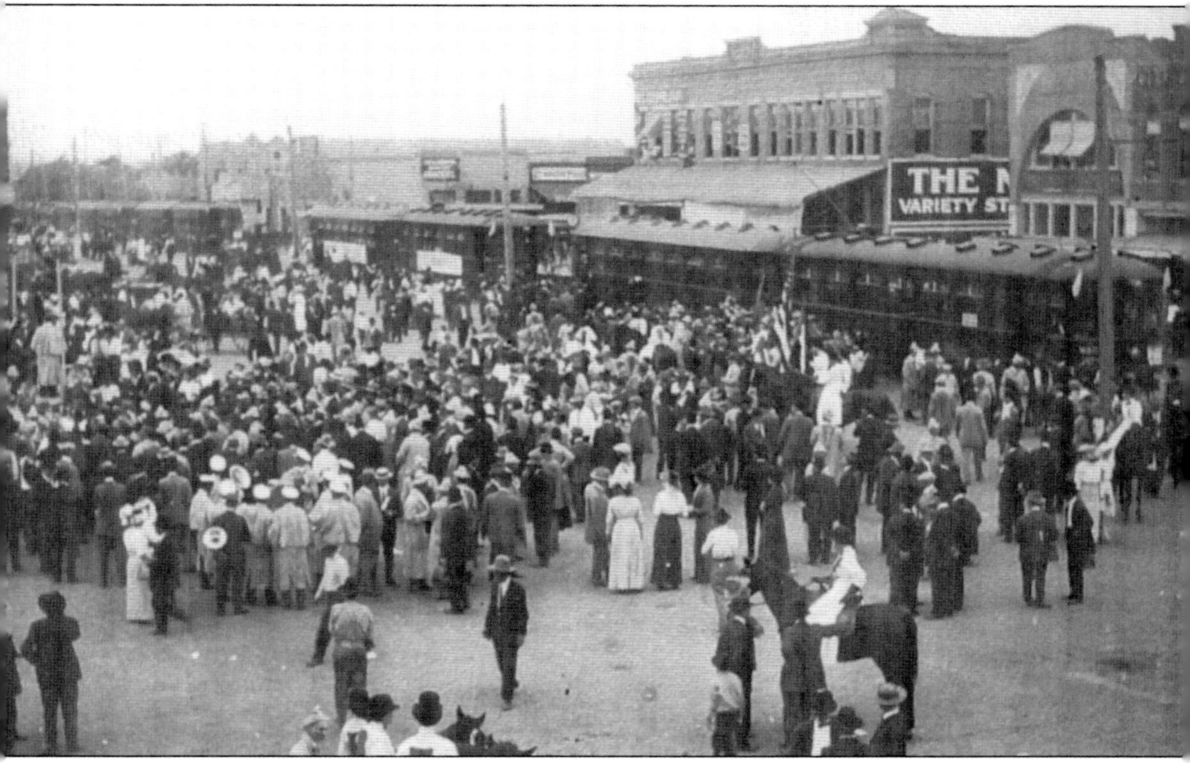

On the east side of the courthouse square, the "home interurban" celebrated the North Meets South Texas Electric Railway stockholders' inspection trip on September 30, 1913. Some Hillsboro residents remember paying a dime to ride a special car to the fairgrounds north of town. From 1913 to 1948, the interurban was an important provider of transportation to and from Dallas and Waco. It offered both passenger and package service. Interurban cars were individually powered by an electric motor and cars were tied to the electric lines with an overhead trolley. The interurban ticket office, waiting room, and sub-station were located at 105–113 North Waco Street.

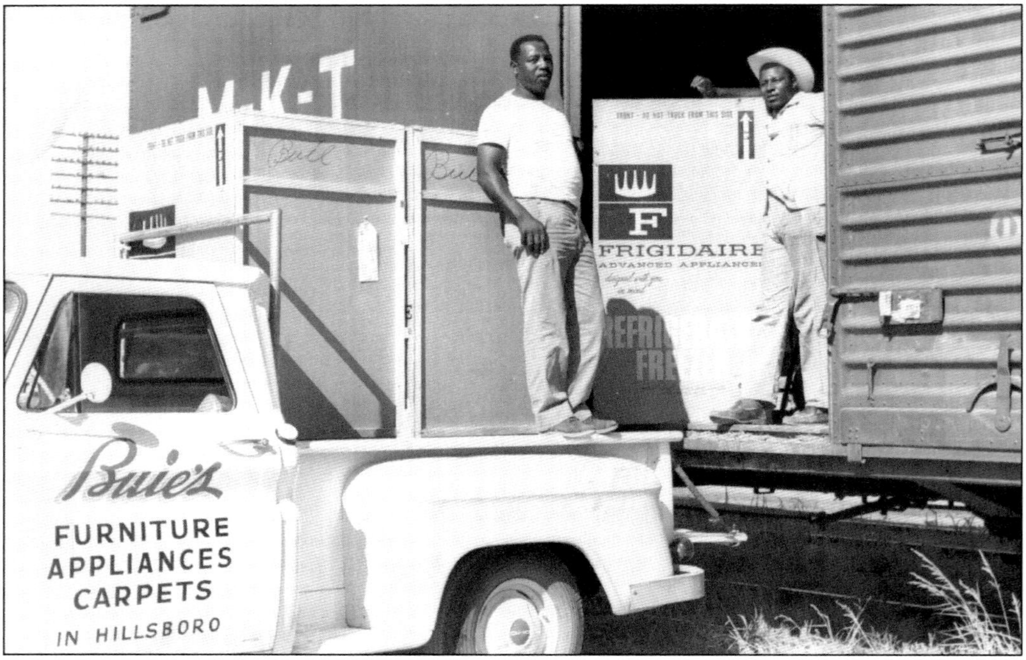

Employees of Buie's appliance store unload merchandise from an MKT railcar. The railroad sidings allowed cotton to be shipped out and goods to be delivered to Hillsboro. A railroad siding like this was the site of the first load of lumber brought into Hillsboro, by A.J. "Johnson" Thompson, who was married to D.L. "Kittie" Brooks. The Thompsons' home was built at 106 Corsicana Street in 1881.

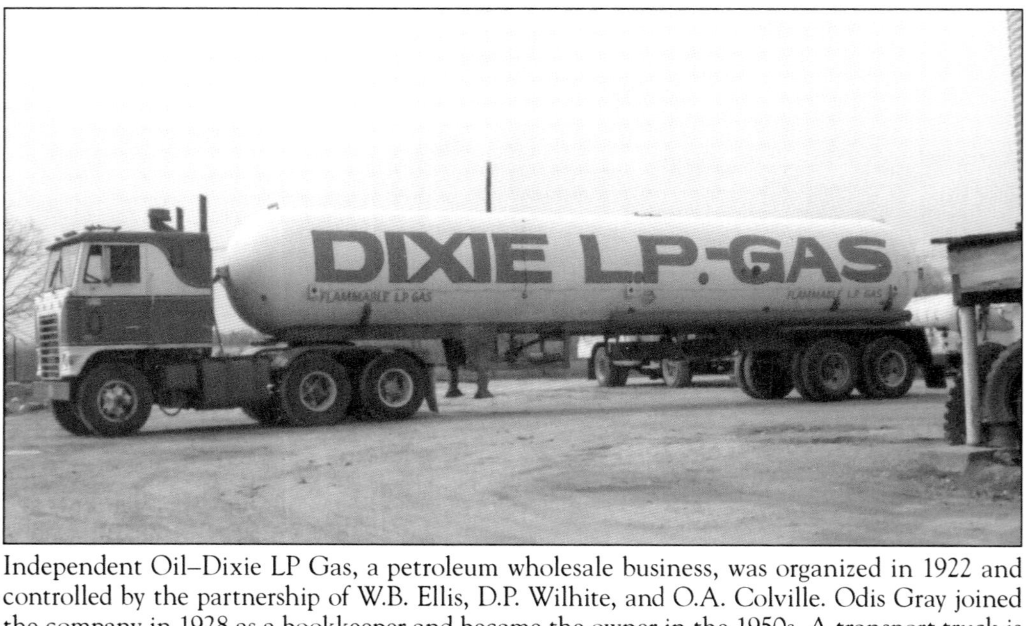

Independent Oil–Dixie LP Gas, a petroleum wholesale business, was organized in 1922 and controlled by the partnership of W.B. Ellis, D.P. Wilhite, and O.A. Colville. Odis Gray joined the company in 1928 as a bookkeeper and became the owner in the 1950s. A transport truck is seen here on the lot at 305 North Waco Street. (Lynn Gray.)

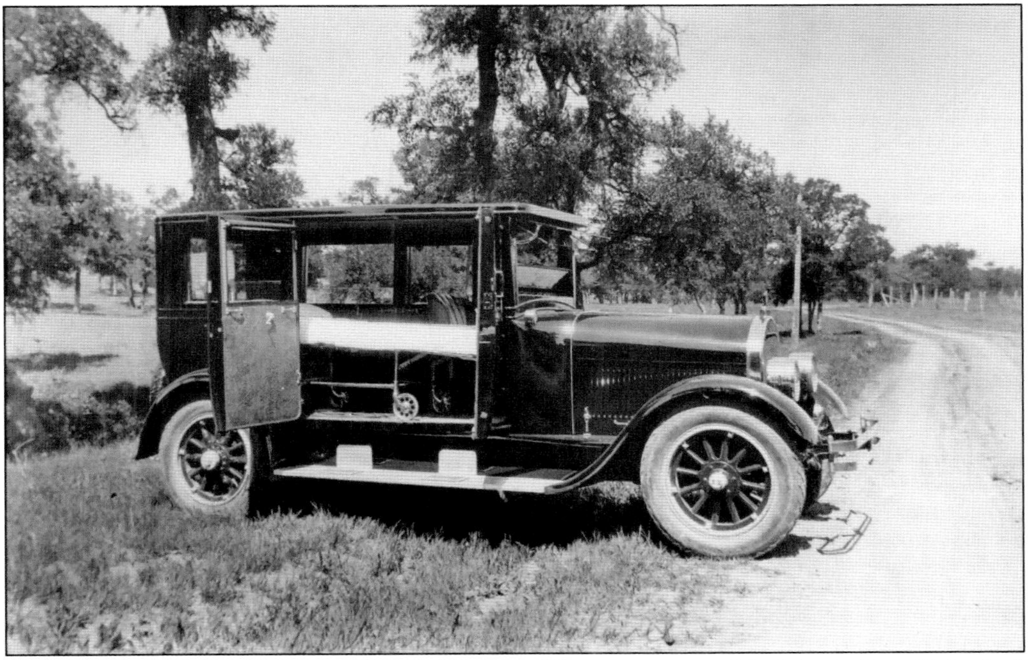

Some early hearses were also used as ambulances. This one was used by Marshall and Marshall Funeral Home, which also operated Marshall and Marshall Ambulance Service, at 200 East Franklin Street. In addition, during the late 1950s and early 1960s, Louie Marshall and C.E. Holloway, both pilots, were pioneer funeral directors who routinely offered air transport. Fred Triplett frequently assisted in these flights. (Marshall and Marshall Funeral Directors.)

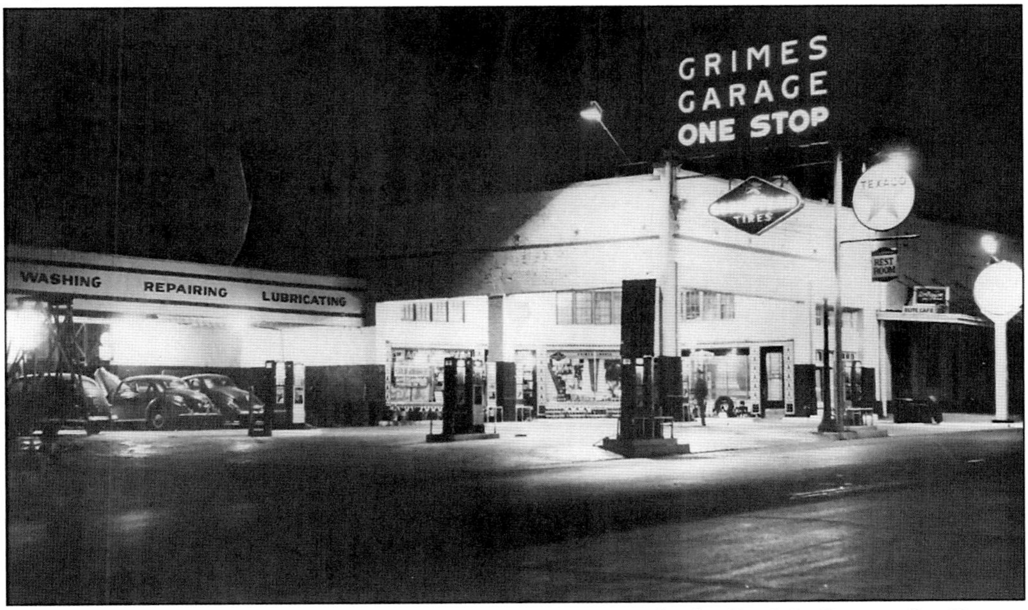

Organized in 1904 by pioneer mechanic and transportation leader Fred O. Grimes Sr., Grimes Garage reflected the early prosperity Hillsboro enjoyed as a major transportation intersection. The garage, credited with having the first wrecker service in Hill County, also furnished the first complete auto service for early vehicles in the area. Grimes was famous for its signs, which were placed along roads all over the country and in Europe and Asia, as stated in *Heritage of Hill County.*

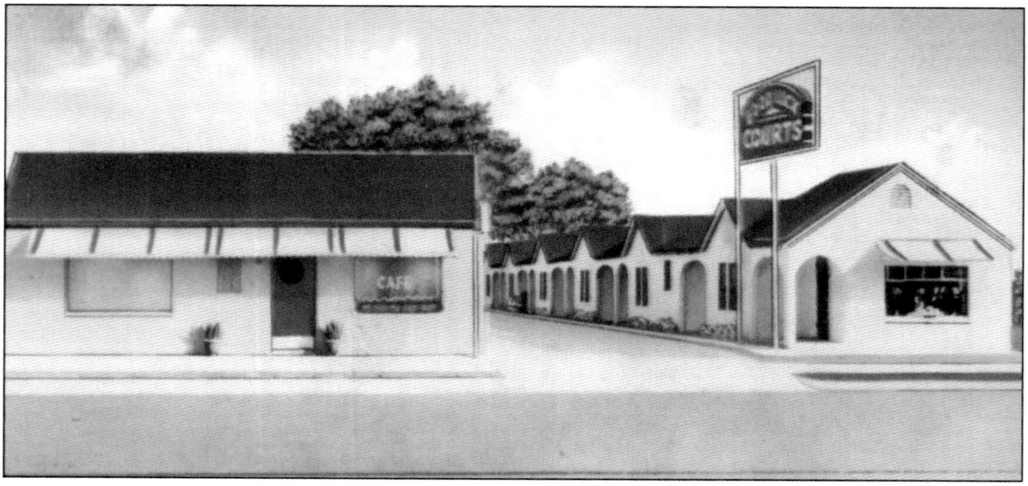

Good Luck Courts was located at 207A South Waco Street, just south of Bob Borden's original Kai-Kai Restaurant, at 207 South Waco Street. Other stops for weary travelers included Melrose Courts and Bluebonnet Courts and Café, located on Rose Hill at 717 Abbott Avenue. The Bluebonnet Café was operated by James T. and Ora Maye Bobbitt.

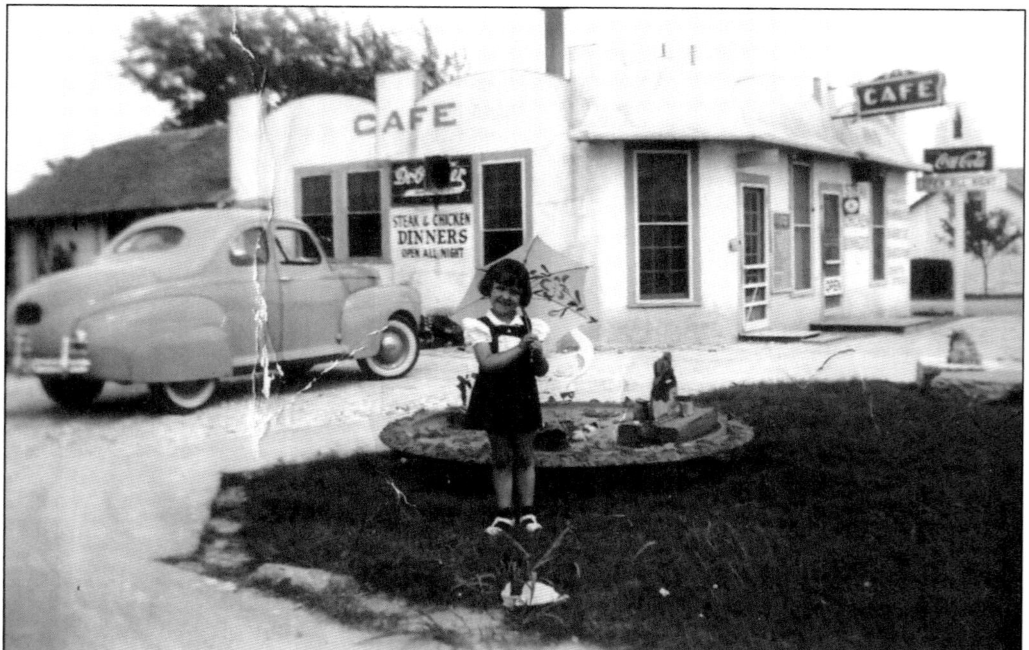

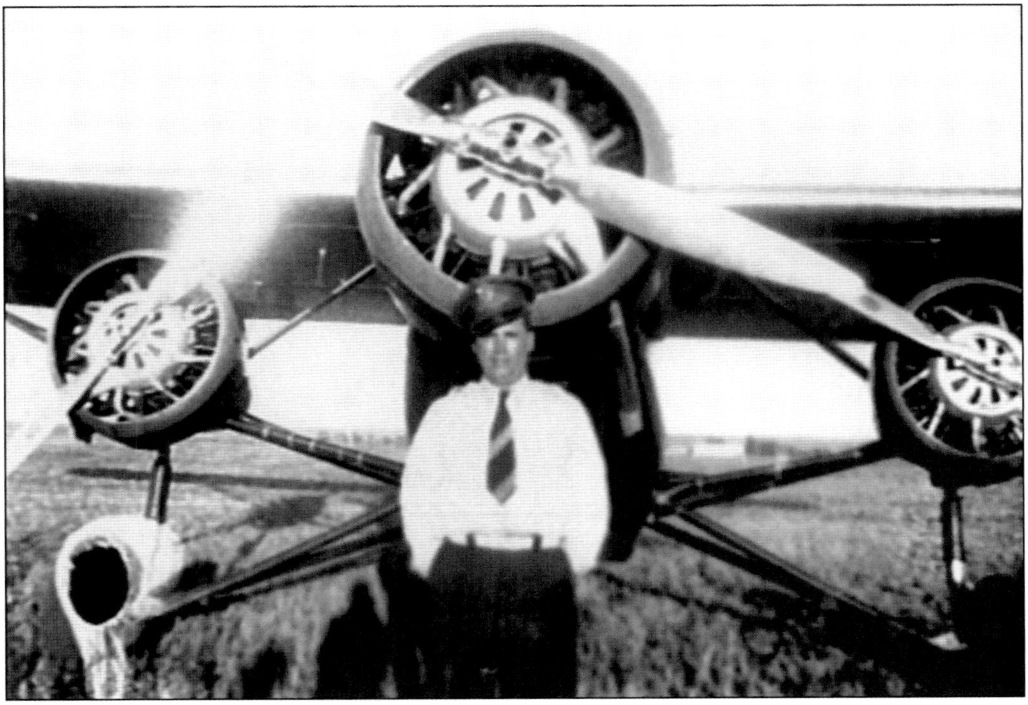

Hillsboro Airport, the first airport to service the Hillsboro area, was located north of town on US 77 on property owned by Senter Blair. In the fall of 1941, Hillsboro Junior College signed a contract with the Army Air Corps to offer cadets pilot training. E.O. Box Jr. ran the ground school and Percy Lee Curtis, seen here, was in charge of the primary flight school at the airport. (Tom Curtis.)

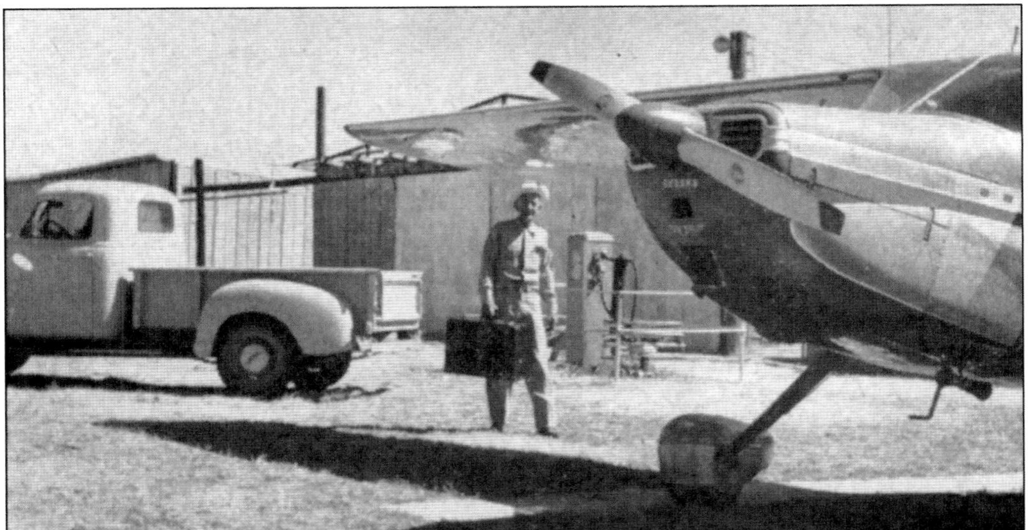

Given the moniker "International Cow Pasture" by members of the National Flying Farmers of America, the second airport to service Hillsboro was south of Peoria on property owned by Fred Triplett. It is seen here in 1954. Townspeople fondly remember contributing a penny per pound for the opportunity to take a flight around town during a mid-1950s March of Dimes fundraiser at the airport.

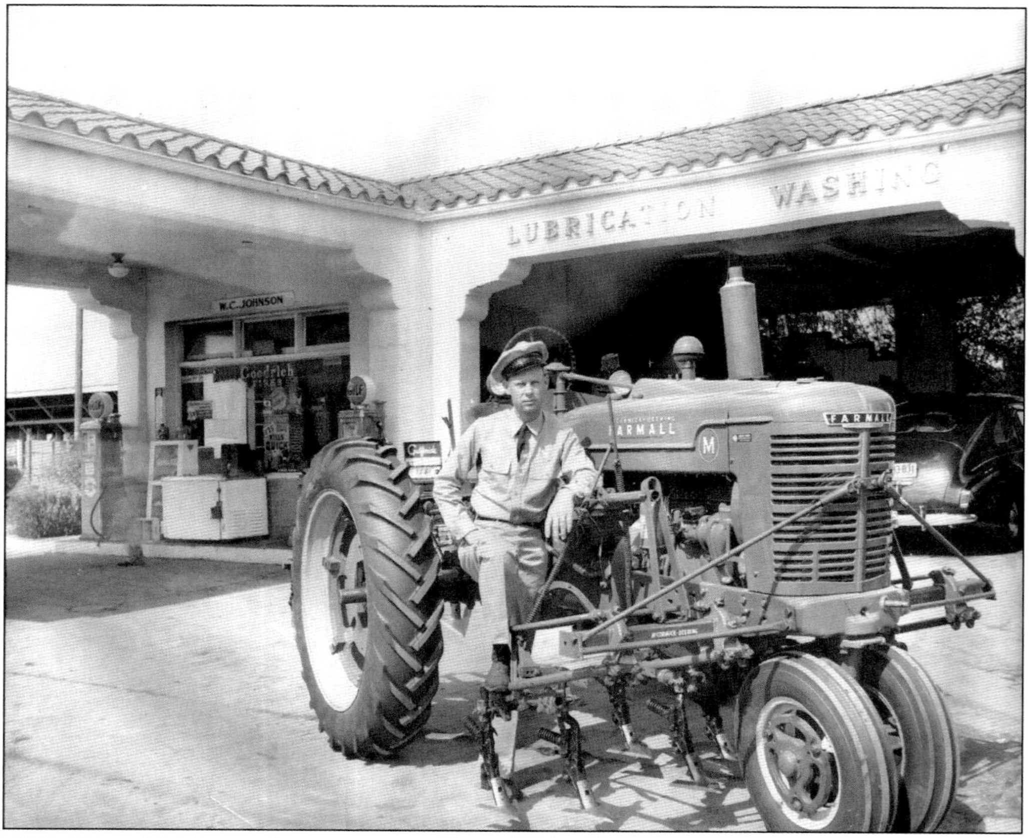

W.C. "Carroll" Johnson leans against a Farmall Model M tractor in front of the Gulf service station at the southeast corner of East Walnut and South Waco Streets in 1926. The station was later used as an official collecting site for rubber during World War II. Lyon-Gray Lumberyard, founded in 1881, can be seen in the background at left.

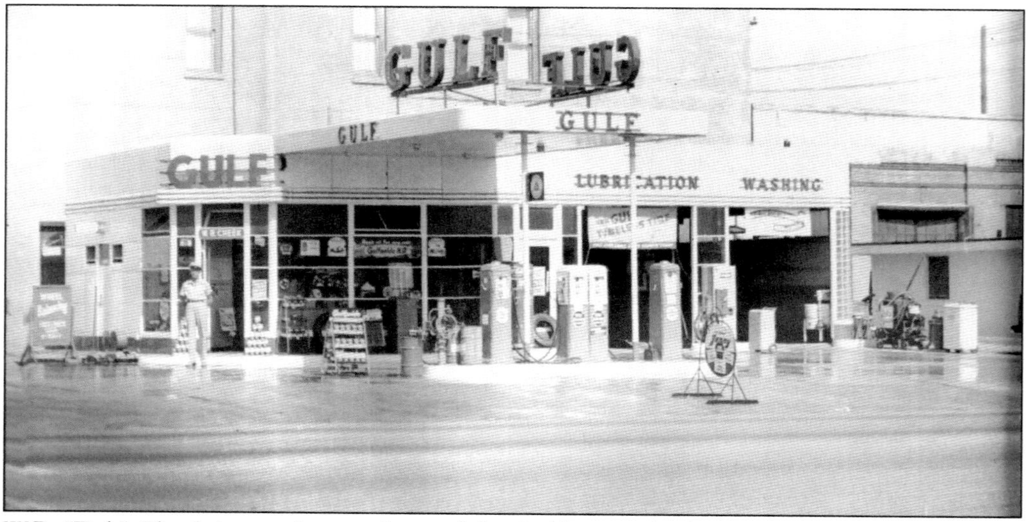

W.B. "Dub" Cheek is seen here in front of the Gulf station he began operating in 1952 at the northwest corner of Franklin and Waco Streets. Cheek let high school boys wash their vehicles in the wash bay on Saturday afternoons.

Four

Downtown and Around

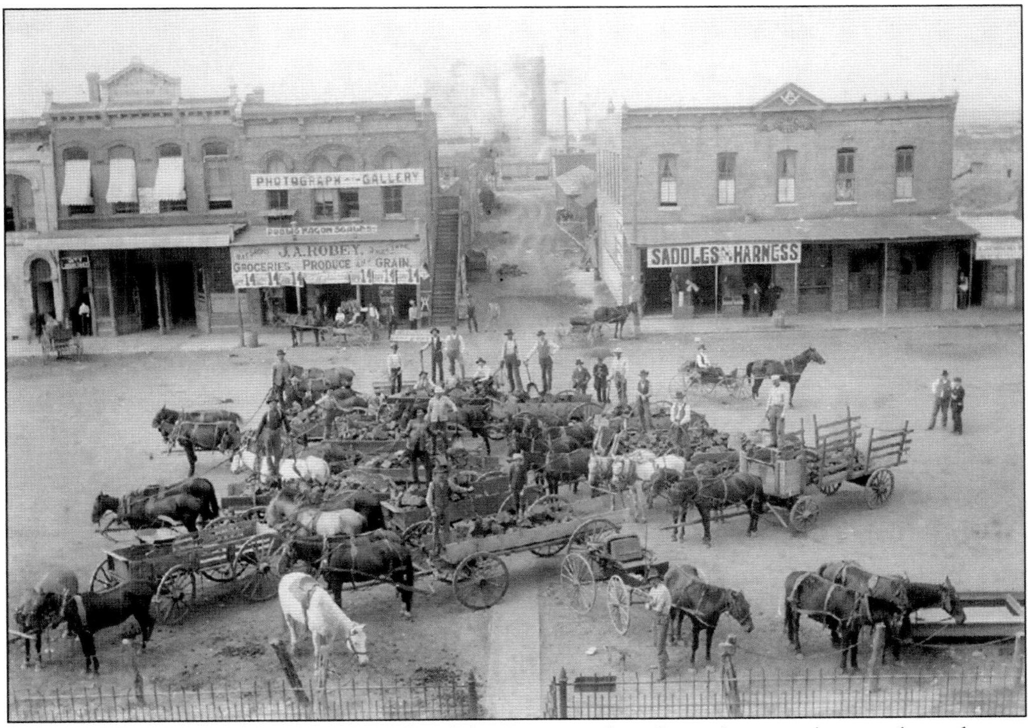

This 1883 photograph of the west side of the square, taken from the courthouse, shows horse-drawn wagons loaded with coal. The Hawkins Hardware building is on the left, and J.A. Robey Grocers is on the corner. A saddle and harness shop was in the building on the right with the Masonic symbol, dated 1883. This building was known as the Patty Building and also housed Harrington Liquors.

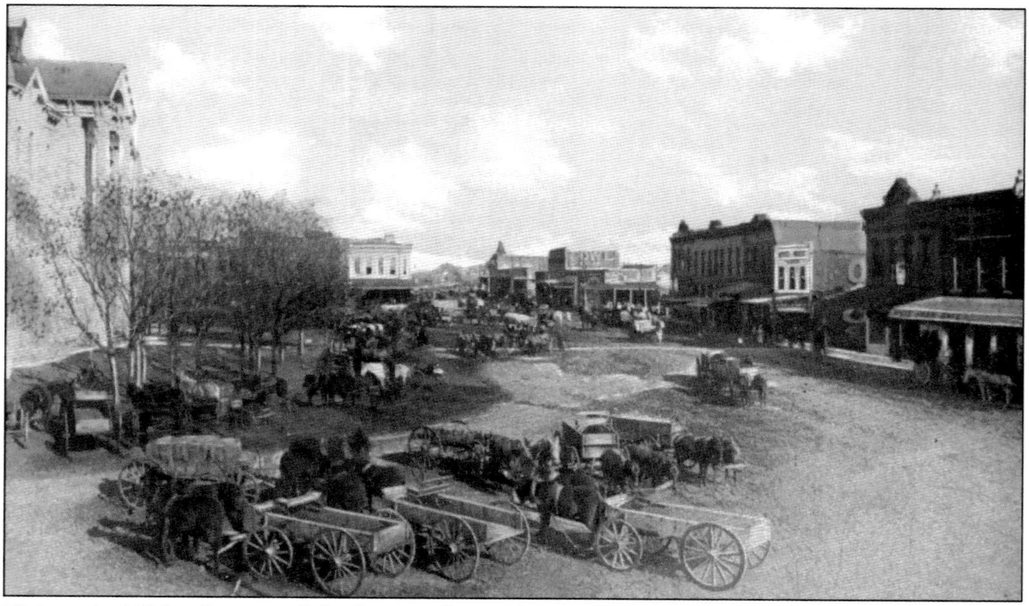

This early 1900s photograph looks east down Elm Street on the south side of the courthouse. Bond's Alley is on the right, where the two buildings divide. The Rock Saloon, built in 1876 at the north end of Bond's Alley, is one of the city's oldest structures, according to *Heritage of Hill County*, and is highlighted by its three white-painted upstairs windows.

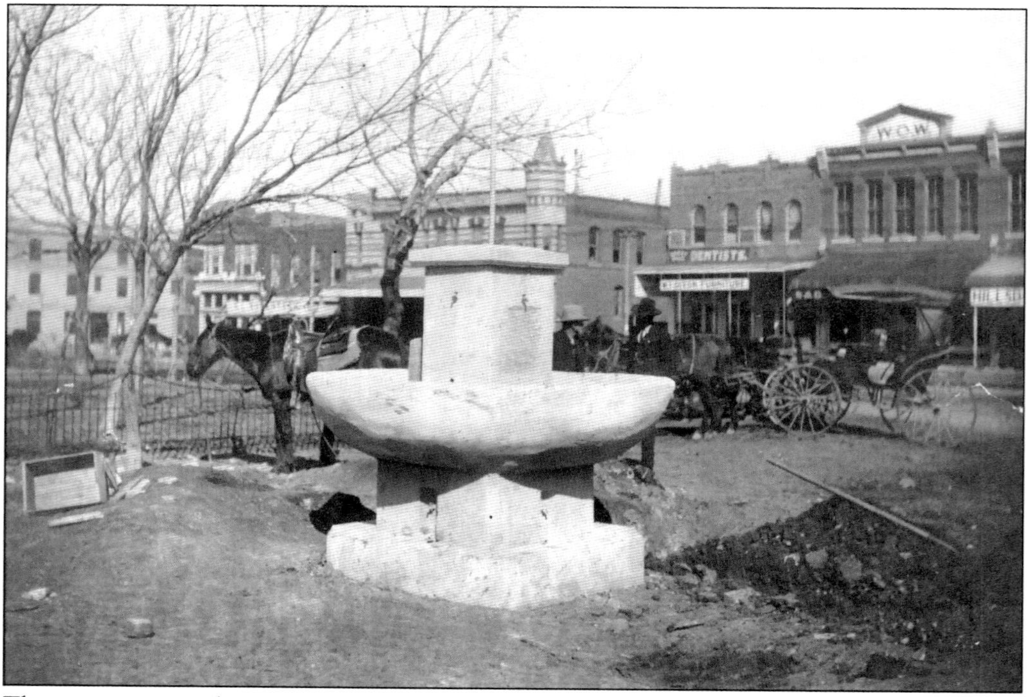

This concrete trough, constructed about 1909, was used to water horses and was located in the northeast area of the courthouse yard. The building with the tower was the original home of the Colonial Trust Company. The iron fence circled the courthouse and was used as a hitching post. The fence was later torn down and replaced, and sections of it can be found around lawns in neighborhoods throughout Hillsboro.

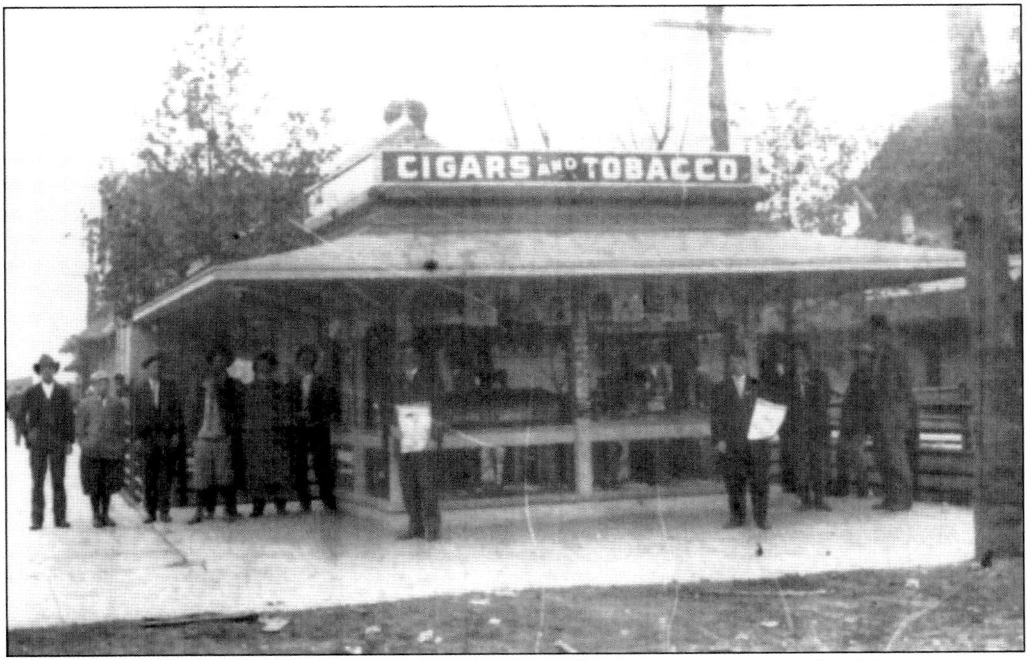

This early newspaper stand was located at the depot for the convenience of Hillsboro residents and arriving and departing railway passengers. Local papers such as the *Hillsboro Reflector* and the *Hillsboro Mirror*, as well as state and national newspapers, magazines, and books provided the main sources of information about the town and the world around it. Other merchandise typical of such a stand included candy, cigars, and tobacco.

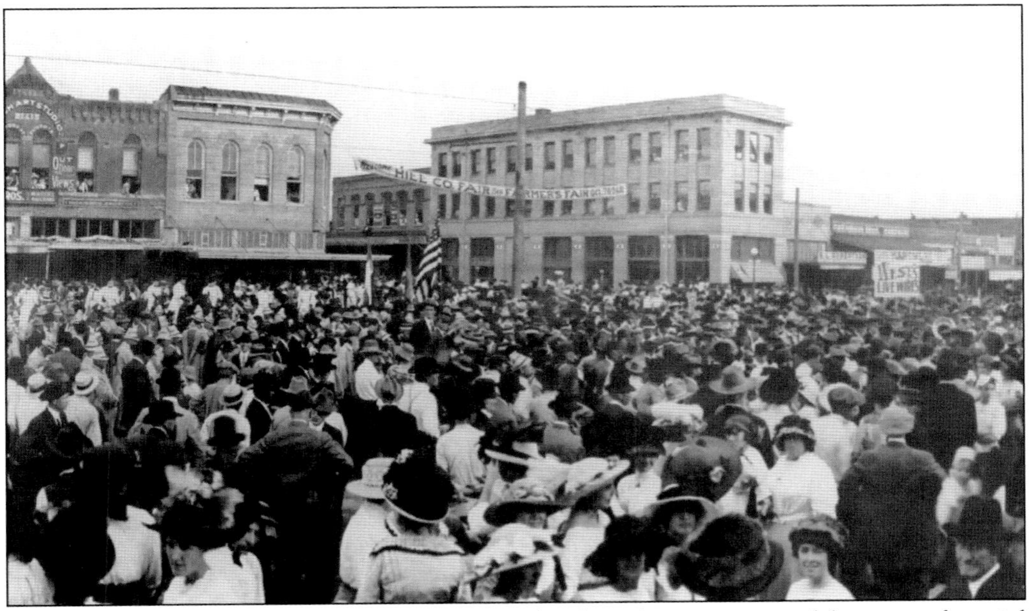

The area around the courthouse and downtown has been host to many celebrations of special times in Hillsboro and Hill County. This crowd, photographed from the courthouse lawn facing the corner of East Elm and South Waco Streets, is gathered for the North Meets South Texas Electric Railway stockholders inspection trip in September 1913. Note the banner across East Elm Street advertising the Hill County Fair.

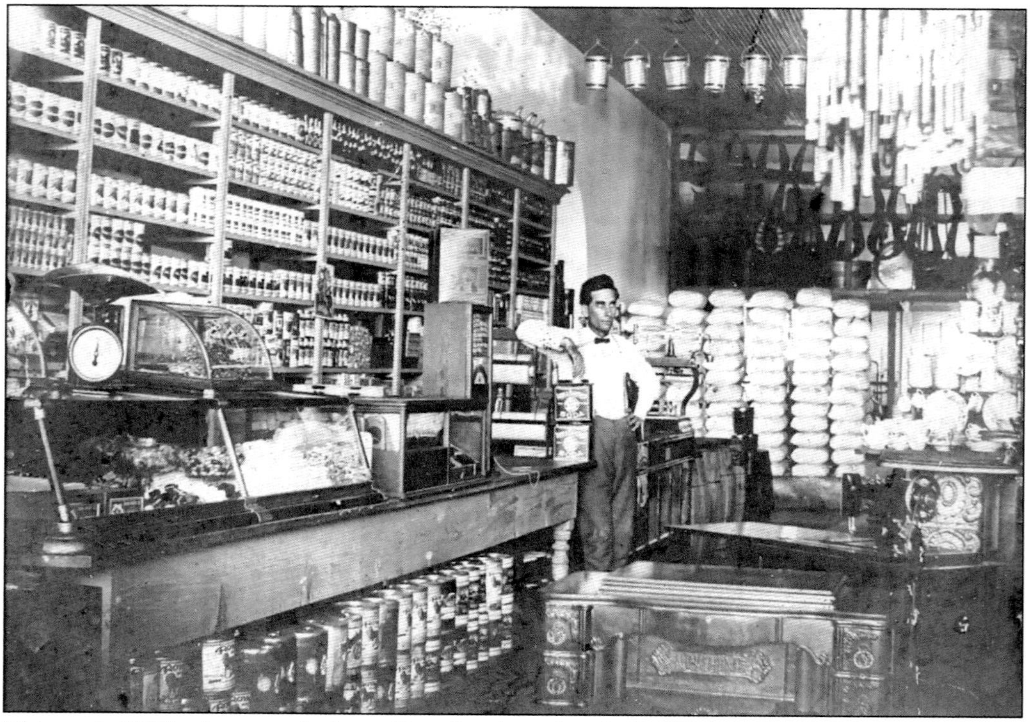

This early 1900s photograph shows Ben Smith in Smith & Tomlinson Hardware, at 123 East Elm Street. T.E. Tomlinson purchased E.B. Stroud's interest in Hawkins Hardware Co. in 1891. In the early 1900s, A.L. Smith became the president of Smith & Tomlinson.

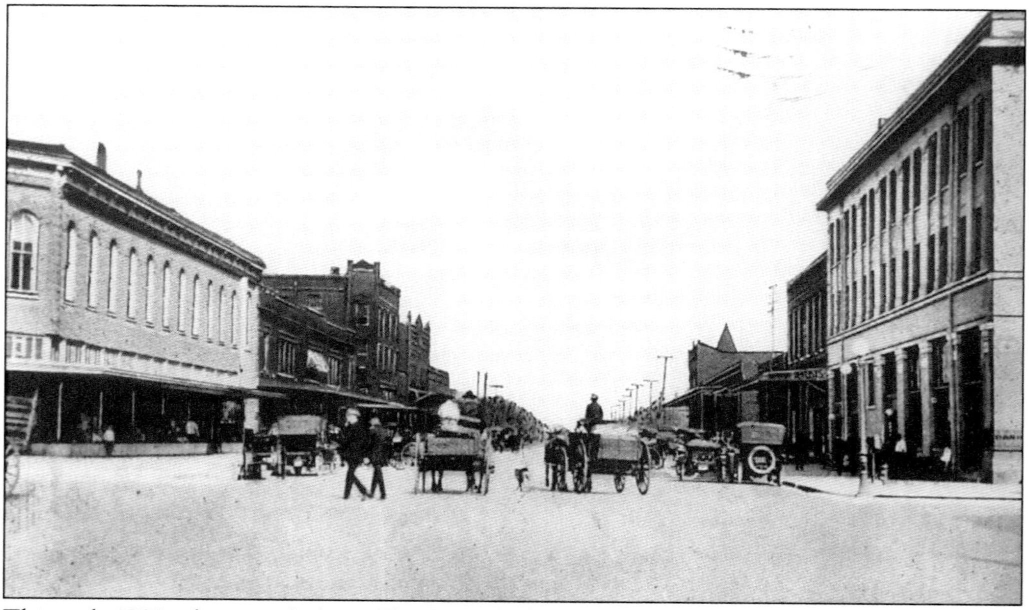

This early 1900s photograph shows Elm Street looking east from Waco Street. Flanagan Brothers Men's Store (later Brown Drug) was on the northeast corner of Elm and Waco Streets, and Graham Department Store (later Martin-McDonald Department Store) was adjacent to the east. On the right, note the spire of Cumberland Presbyterian Church, which was later the location of McCauley's service station and Citizens National Bank.

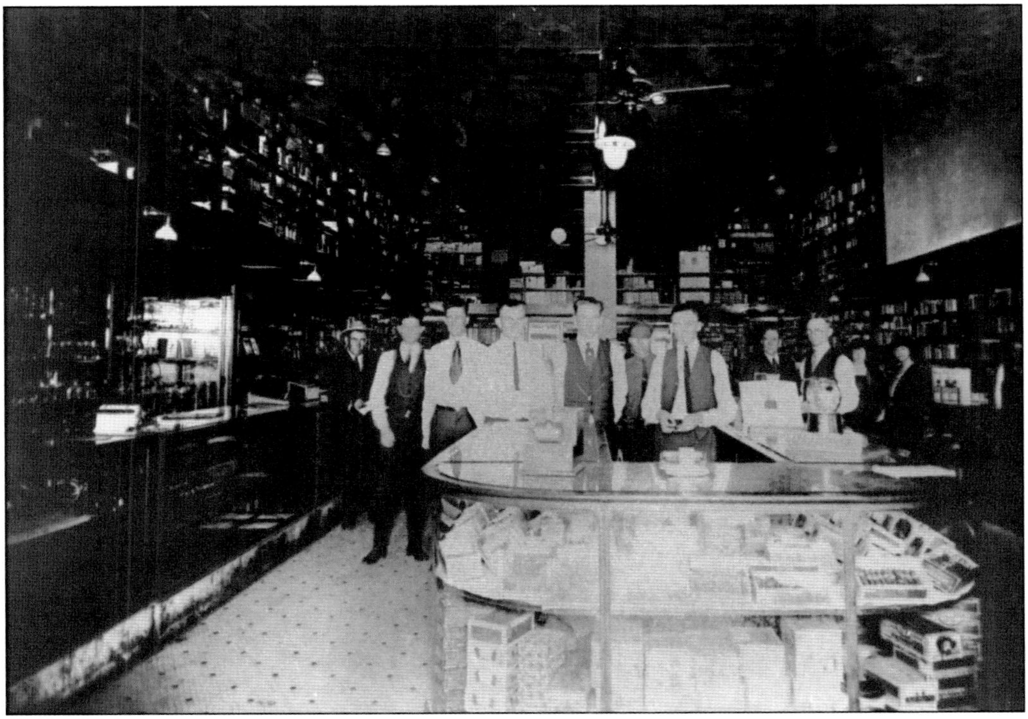

Dr. William M. Bond established a drugstore (pictured) in 1881 at 66 West Elm Street, then moved to 64 West Elm, on the south side of the square. In 1893, it moved to its current location, 60 West Elm Street, at the corner of Bond's Alley. The name changed to T.B. Bond Drug when Dr. Bond's son Thomas Burke Bond took control of the business. It has the distinction of being the oldest continually operating drugstore in Texas.

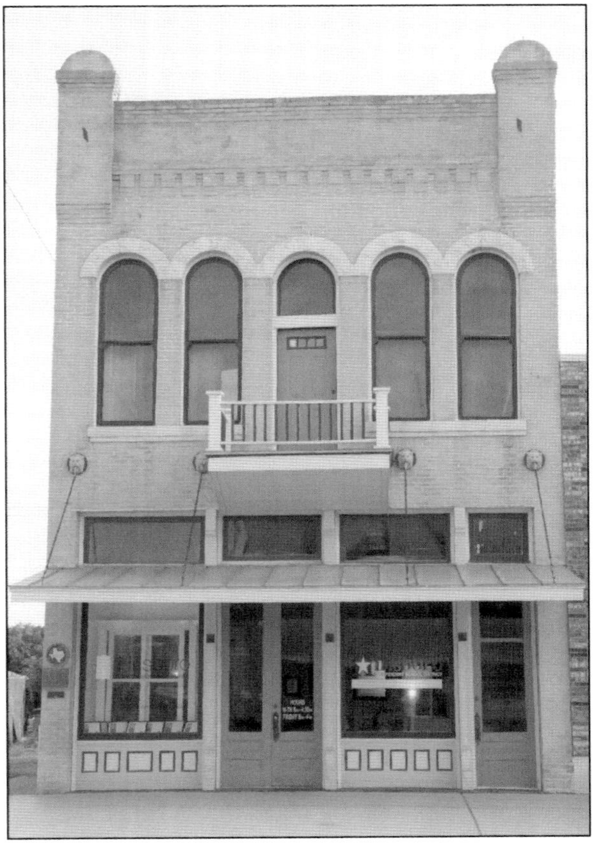

In 1901, German native Charles Gebhardt established Hillsboro's first bakery. He moved his business to this building in 1905, using the second floor as living quarters. The brick commercial structure shows influences of the Romanesque and Italianate styles and features arched second-story windows and decorative brickwork in the cornice and corner turrets. The bakery building was later used as a millinery shop and a barbershop, according to the Historical Commission of Hill County. (Anita Tufts.)

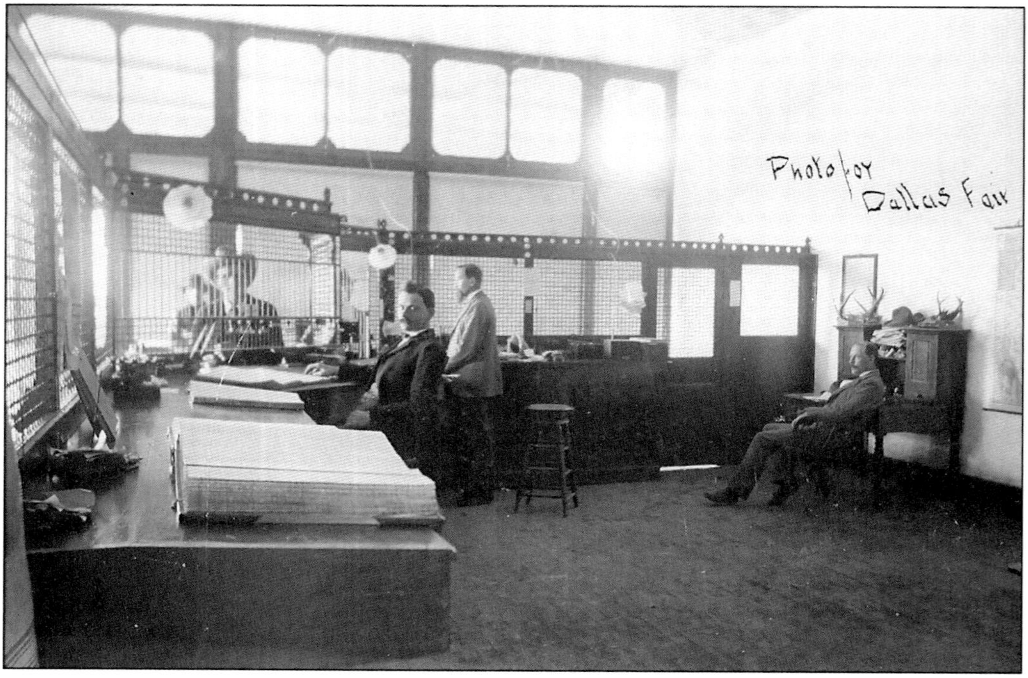

Citizens National Bank was established in May 1893, with directors George Carmichael, Dr. B.H. Vaughan, W.B. Ellington, A.T. Rose, C.F. Graham, O.B. Bowman, E.W. Comfort, H.F. Shelton, and George L. Porter. Sturgis National Bank, established in 1875, consolidated with Citizens National Bank in 1912. The original Sturgis Bank burned in 1882, and a new building took its place on the southwest corner of Elm and Waco Streets. A new facade had been installed by 1912. Citizens National Bank occupied the Sturgis building until December 1965.

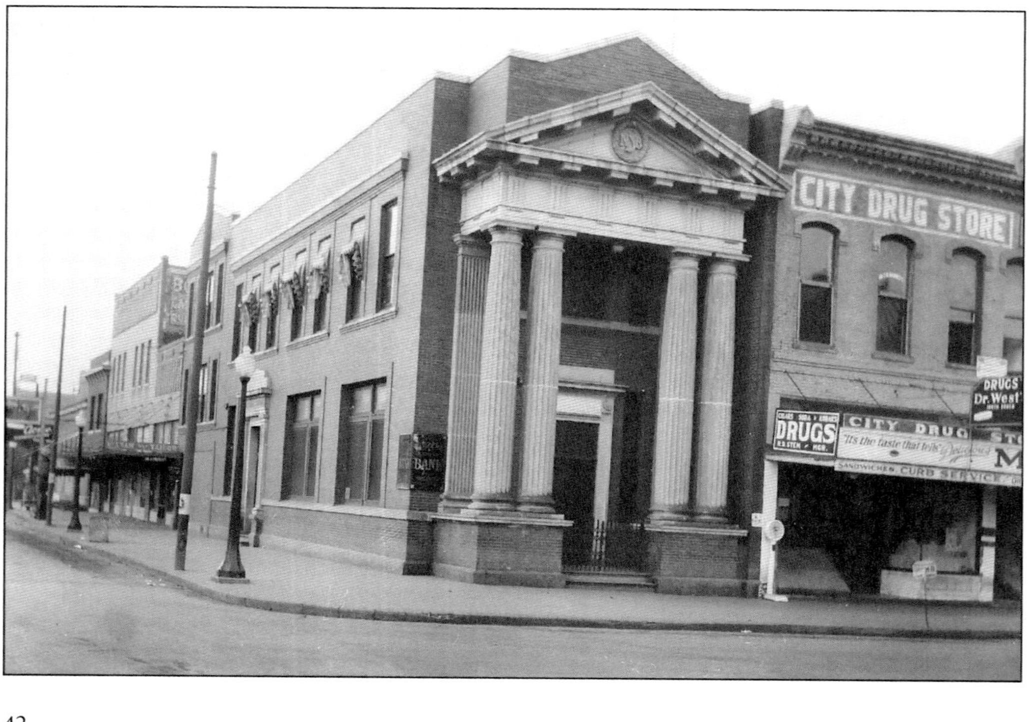

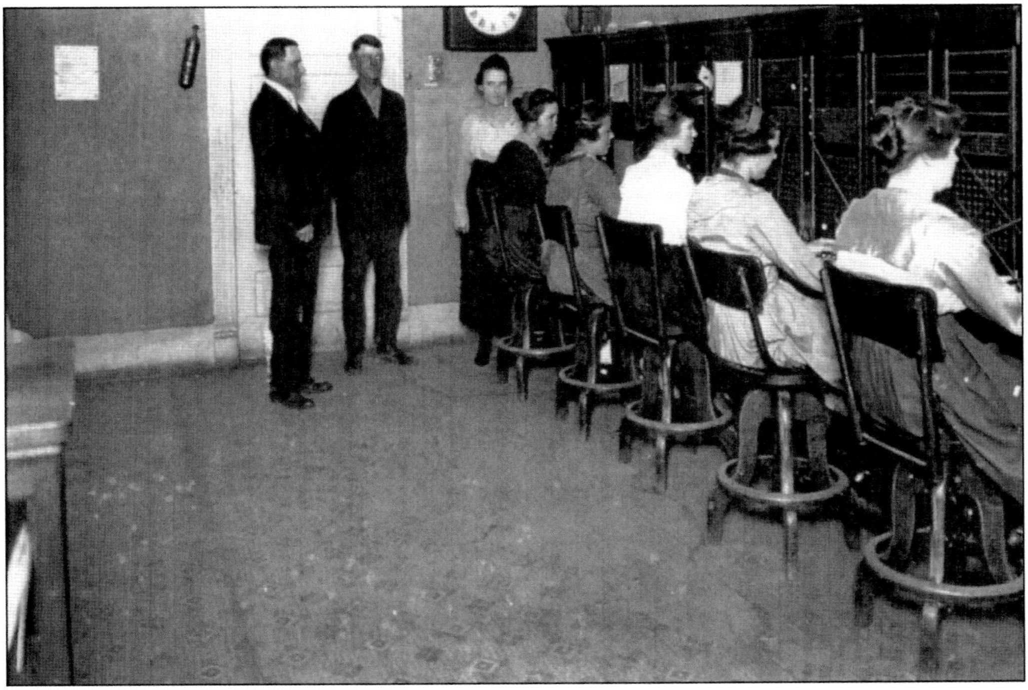

Hillsboro Central Telephone operators worked from the second floor of 81 North Waco Street from 1917 to 1920. Seen here are, from left to right, area manager Allen Chase, C.C. Isbell, Lila McSpadden, Blanch Weir, Stella Wilson Sweeney, Clelia Longino, Mary Lou Blair, and Meg Loftis. Southwestern Bell operators worked from the upstairs of the L. Brin store, on the east side of the square in the Tarlton Block.

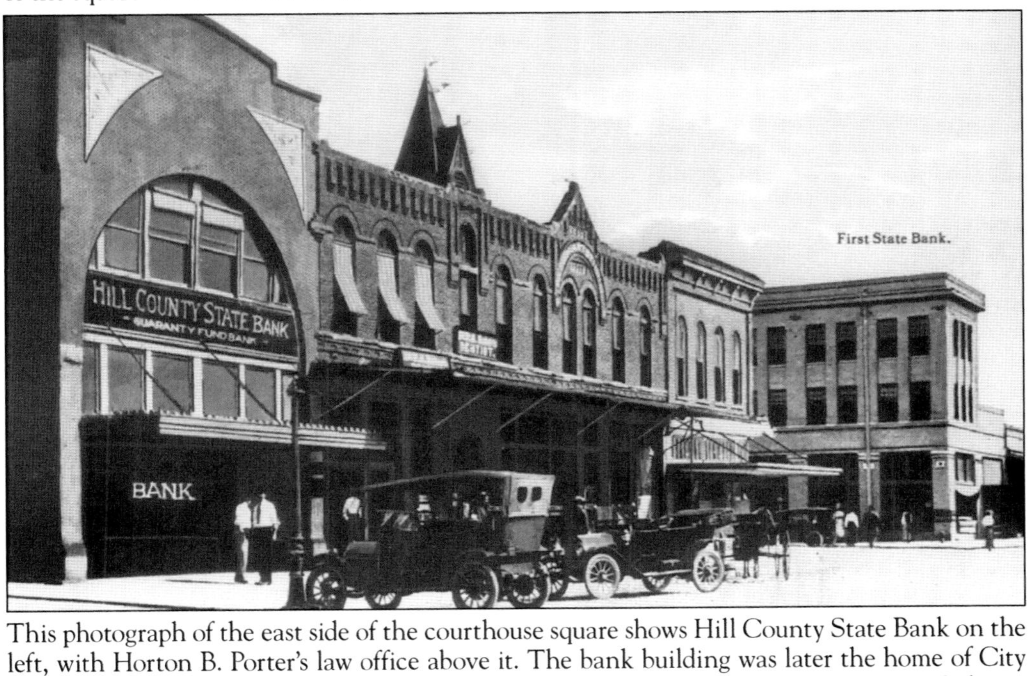

This photograph of the east side of the courthouse square shows Hill County State Bank on the left, with Horton B. Porter's law office above it. The bank building was later the home of City Café and Exchange Barber Shop. The second floor included the offices of dentist Dr. P.A. Roberts, Blanchard Photographic Studio, and, later, Parish Studio.

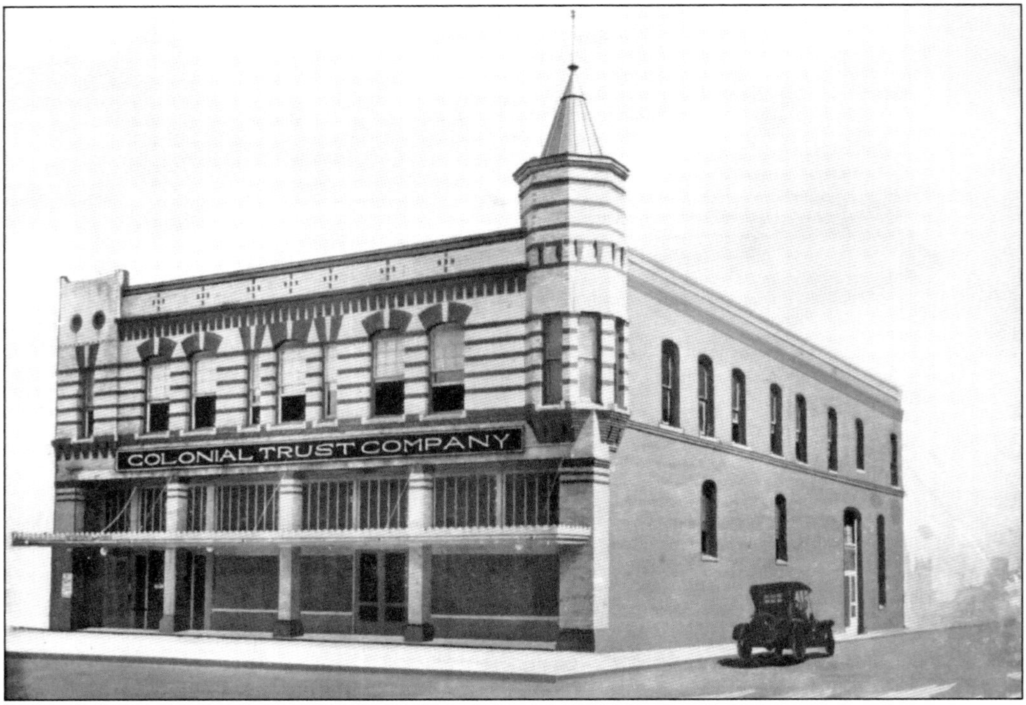

This 1912 photograph of the original Colonial Trust Company shows the distinctive corner tower of the building, located at 59–61 Franklin Street on the north side of the square. The company operated under a special charter granted by the Texas legislature. It moved to the southeast corner of Elm and Covington Streets, to the building once occupied by Farmer's National Bank. This building was remodeled in 1926 by Montgomery Ward.

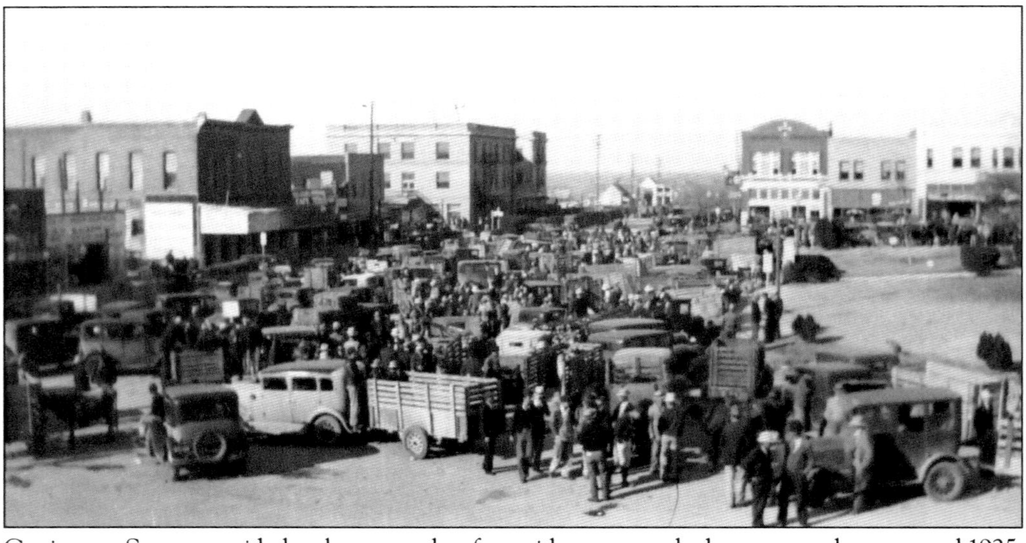

Covington Street provided a place to gather for residents on trade days, as seen here around 1925. Trade days, some more crowded than this one, brought crowds into the courthouse square and the surrounding streets. The days provided not only shopping but also a time of social interaction for the townspeople and area farmers and their families.

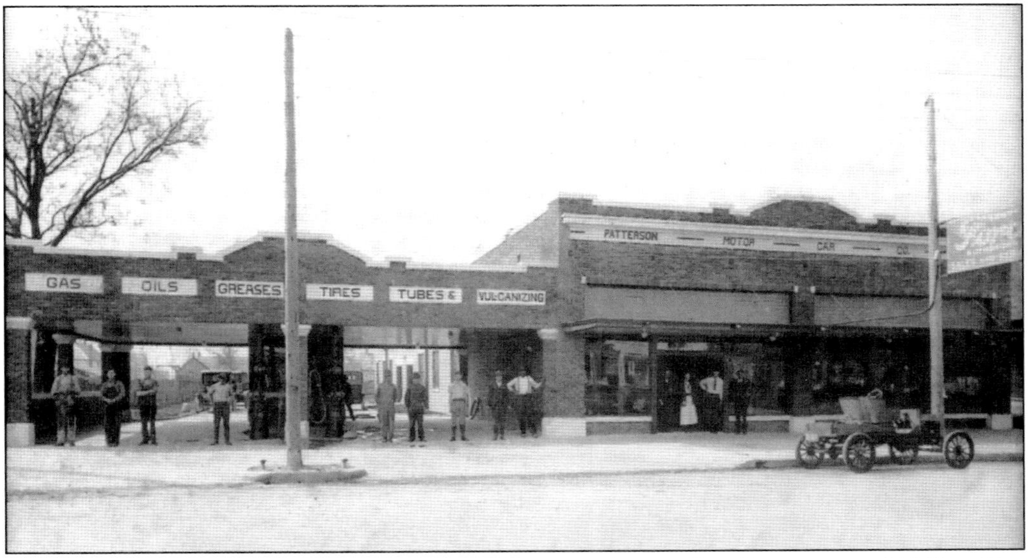

Established in 1912 by Curtis Patterson, the Patterson Motor Car Company, at 214 East Elm Street, sold and serviced Ford vehicles. Patterson's son Joe W. Patterson was the manager of the Ford agency in 1930. Later known as the Campbell & C.A. Ganus Garage, C.A. "Aubrey" Ganus sold the dealership to Jim Carr. Lawrence Cole purchased the Ford agency in 1964, and it is now operated by his son Larry Cole. This photograph was taken about 1920. (Larry Cole.)

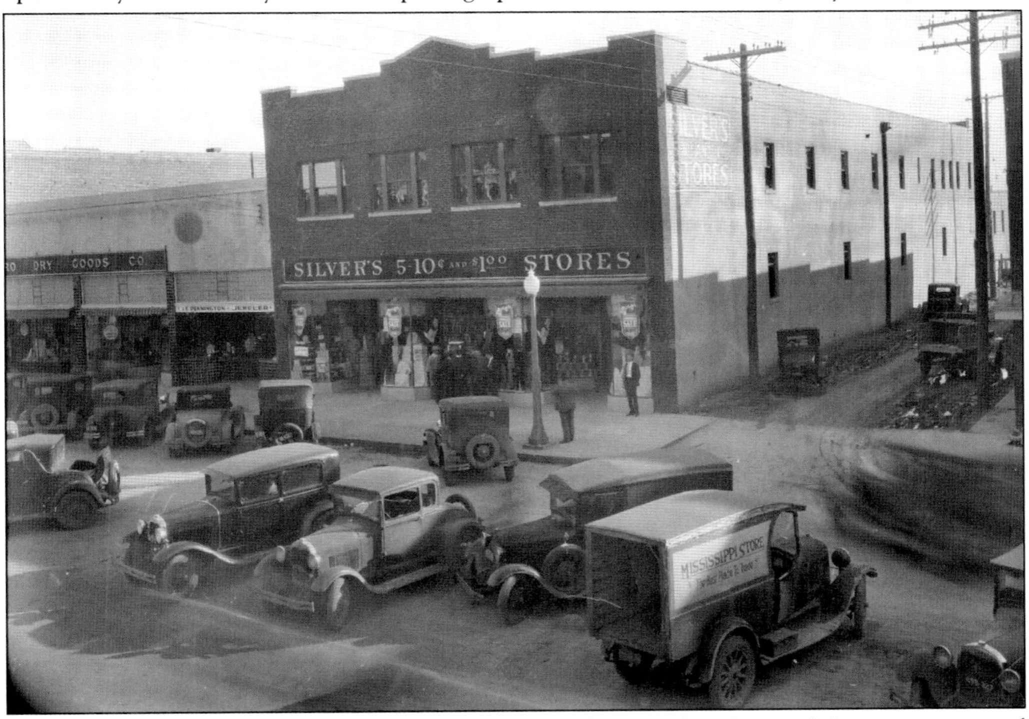

The south side of Elm Street was home to Silver's "racket store," or five-and-dime store, around 1930. In later years, it was the home of McCrory's five-and-dime. Racket stores were discount variety stores with a focus on the smaller, less expensive items used to furnish a home. The name originated from the noise created by the metal pots and pans carried by the tin-peddler carts of old.

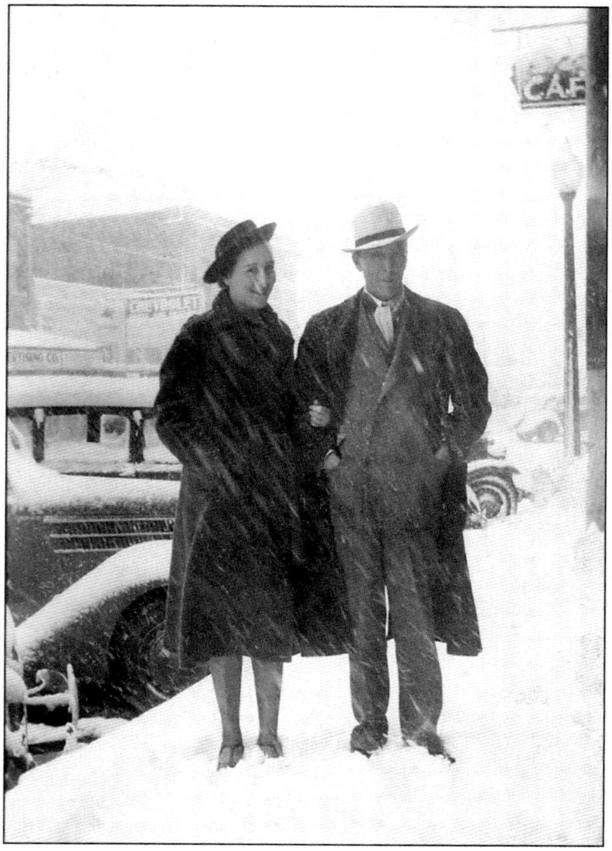

Lon and Maureen Bacon enjoy a rare snowy day on South Waco Street about 1935. Maureen remembers that her coat was a Kelly green wraparound tied with a belt and that her hat and shoes were black. Lon Bacon owned a successful dry-cleaning operation on Franklin Street. (Linda Bacon.)

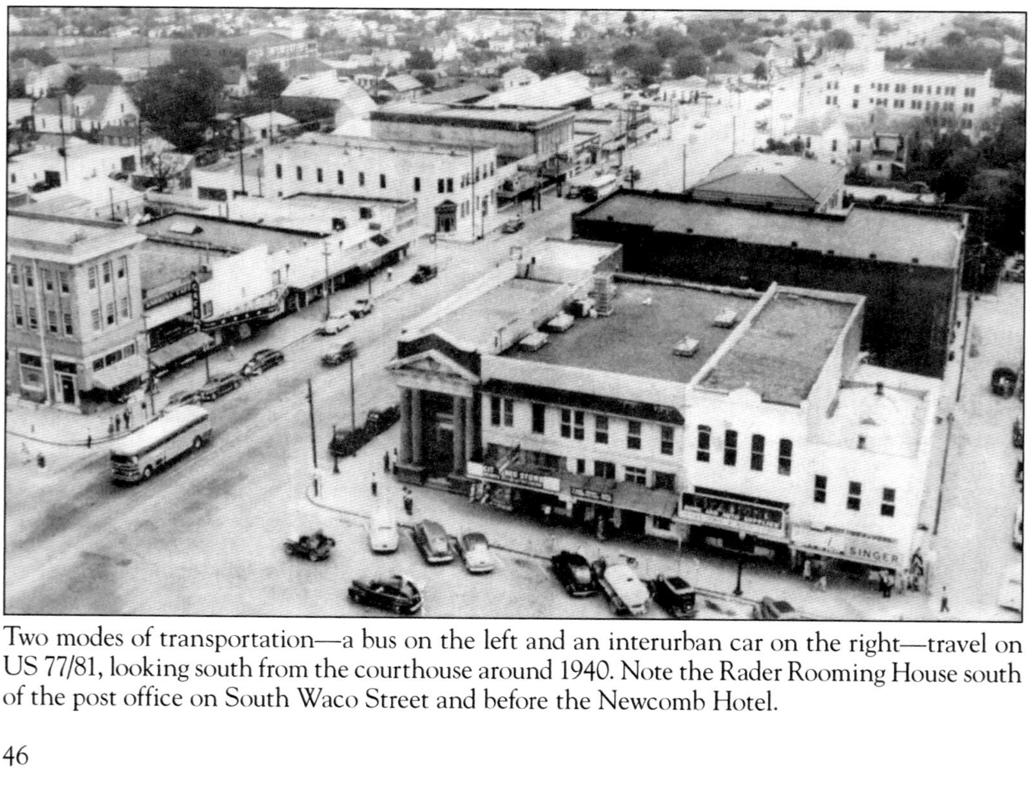

Two modes of transportation—a bus on the left and an interurban car on the right—travel on US 77/81, looking south from the courthouse around 1940. Note the Rader Rooming House south of the post office on South Waco Street and before the Newcomb Hotel.

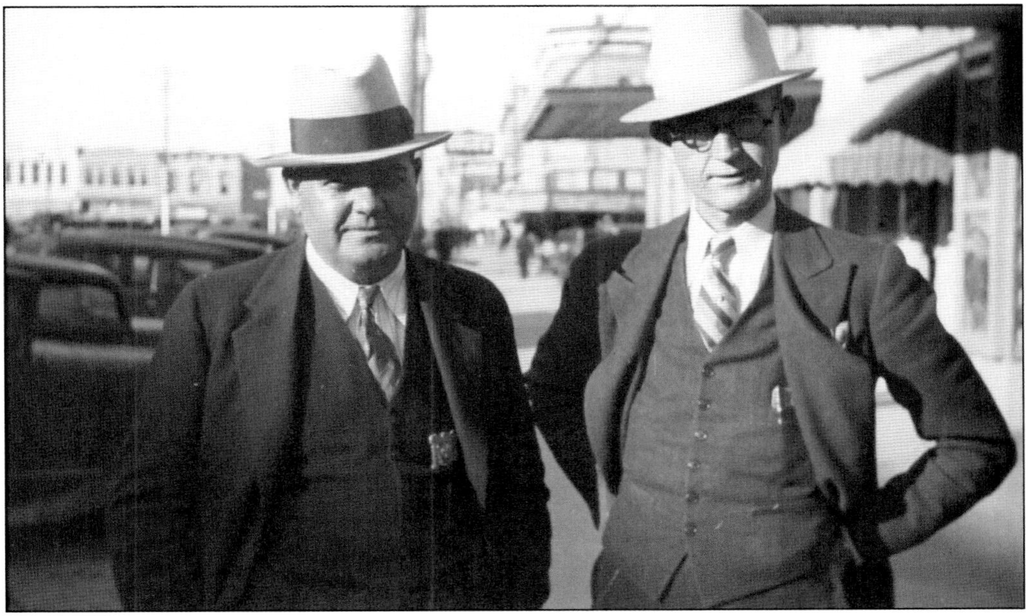

C.W. "Crispy" Taylor (right) came to Hillsboro on May 12, 1926, as the manager of R&R Theaters. He saw the need for an up-to-date theater building and induced R&R to build the Palace Theater on South Waco Street, which opened in December 1926. He also operated the Best Theatre, on the south side of the square. He is seen here with Ed Keeton, the city marshal. Taylor later updated the theaters, renaming them the Texas and the Ritz, respectively.

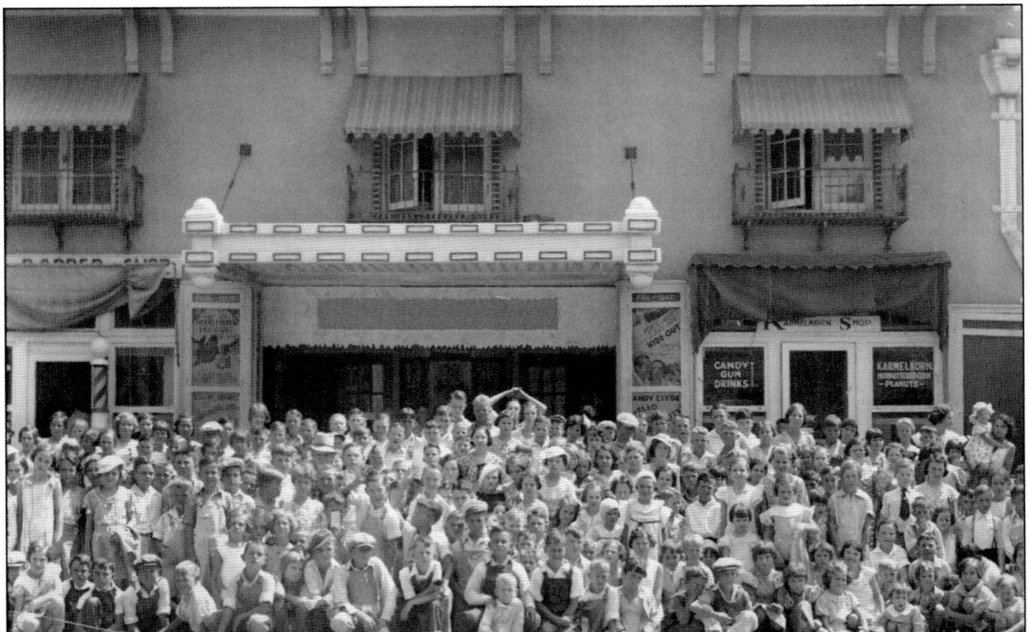

John L. Garner, a local blacksmith, won $350 in 1935 after giving his daughter Earnestine 35¢ to purchase a "bank night drawing" ticket at the theater. It was the winning ticket—and the most money she had ever held in her hand. She had waited to purchase the ticket until the very last minute. This photograph shows the Texas Theater in March 1936, which was showing *A Midsummer Night's Dream*, among other performances.

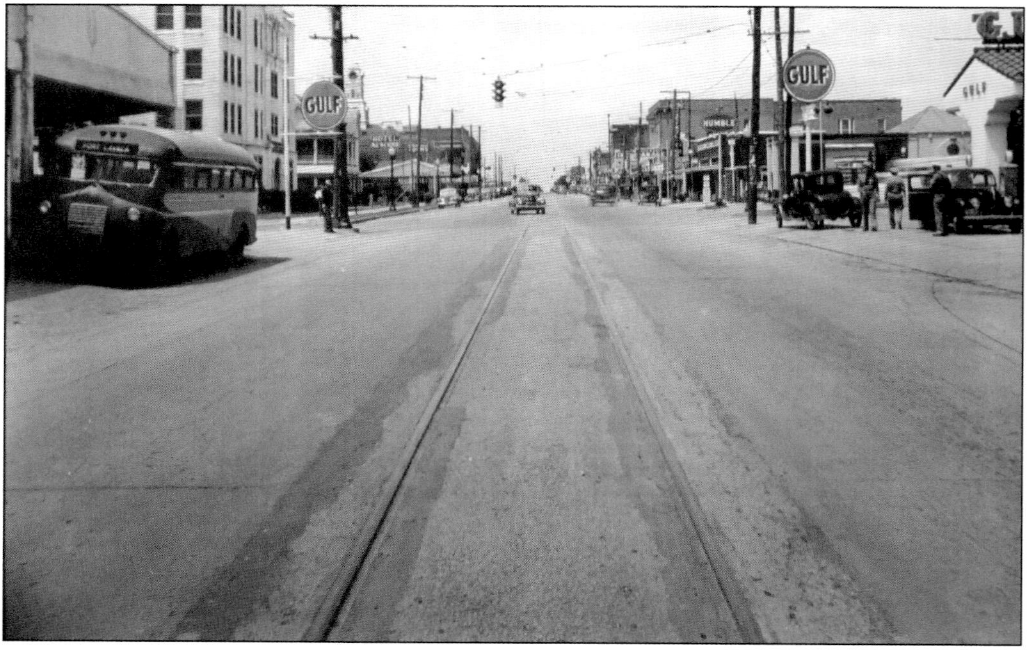

The Hillsboro street scene above shows the interurban tracks on Waco Street. On the left are Renfro's service station and Greyhound bus station at 202 South Waco Street, and the Newcomb Hotel at 140 South Waco Street. On the right are House Chevrolet (later Standefer Chevrolet) at 133 South Waco Street, Shelton-Fawcett's Humble service station at 139 South Waco Street, and W.C. Johnson's Gulf service station at 201 South Waco Street. Pictured below is the "Great White Way" looking north up Waco Street at night after streetlights were installed in the downtown area with assistance from the Lions Club. The tracks in the center of Waco Street are for the Texas Electric interurban.

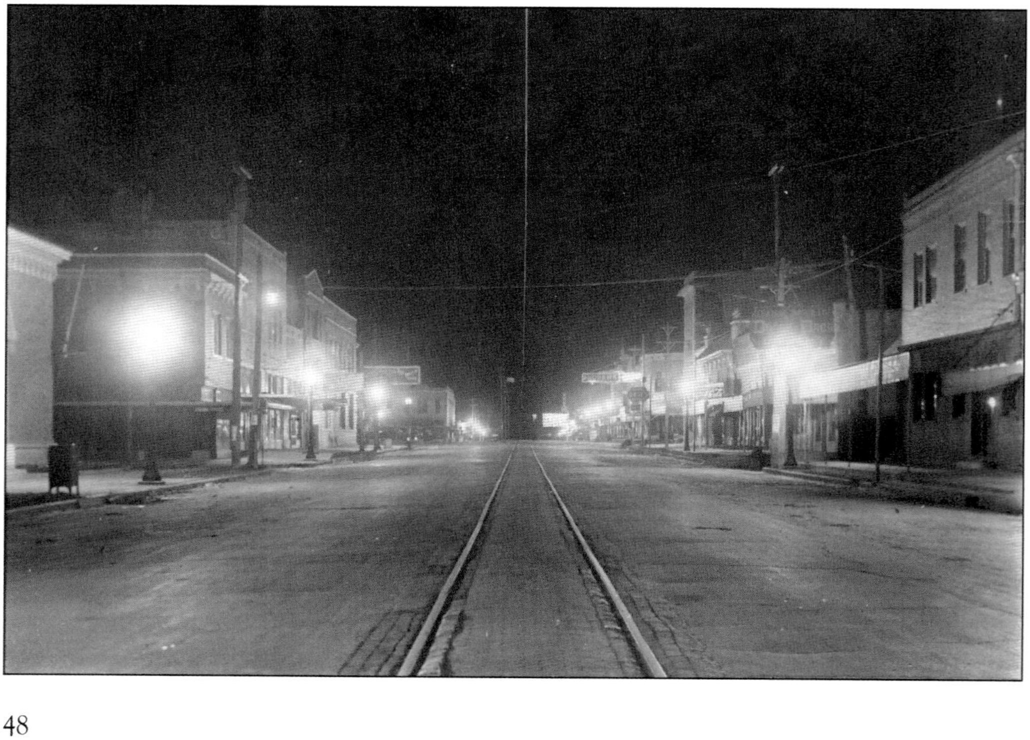

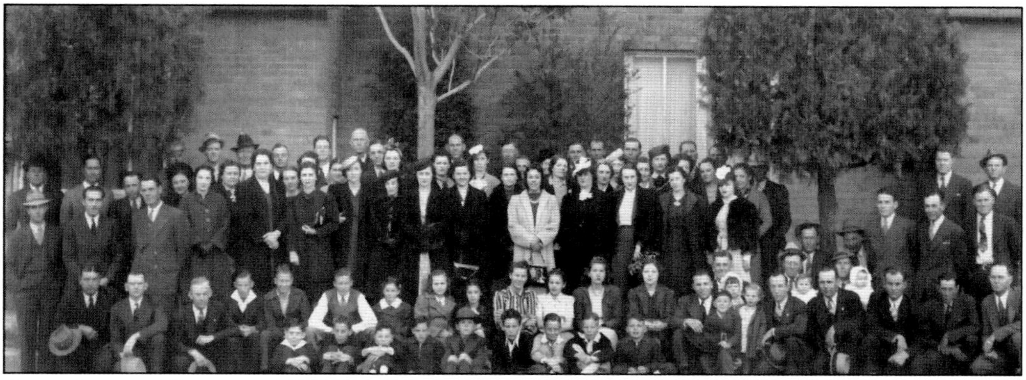

According to *Heritage of Hill County*, in 1904, electric power in Hillsboro was supplied by a 200-horsepower steam engine owned by Hillsboro Electric & Gas Company. In 1912, it became part of Texas Power & Light and had a business office at 205 East Elm Street before moving to 121 East Franklin Street. This employee and family photograph was taken at the side of Parish Studio, at 201 East Franklin Street, in 1934.

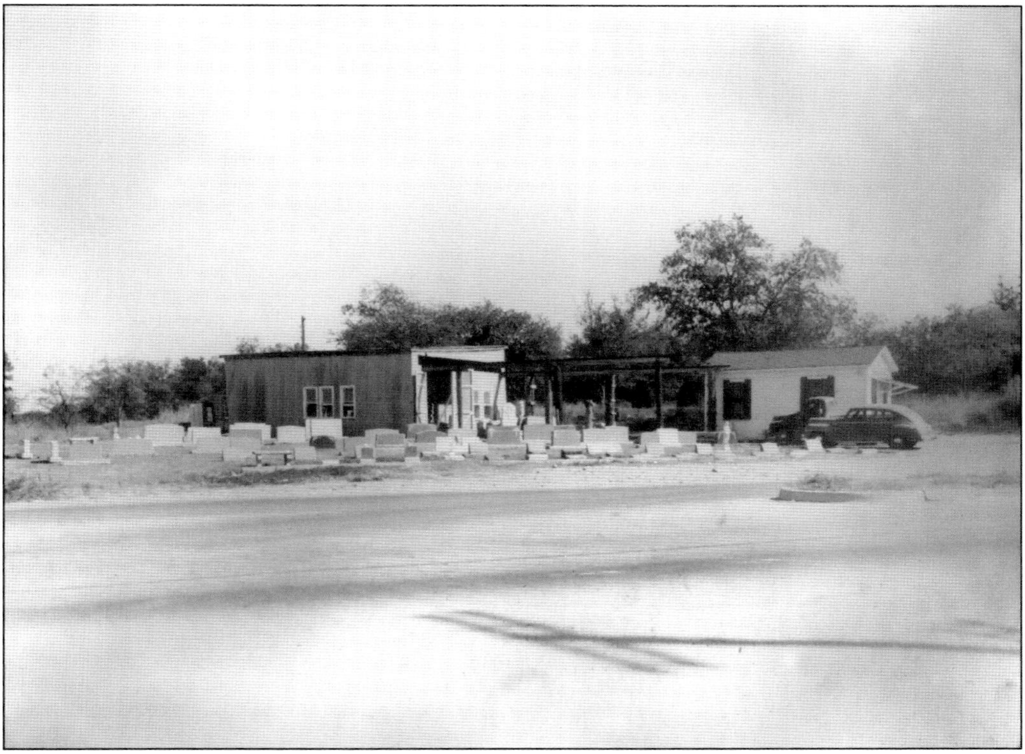

Hillsboro Monument Works was established in 1916 at 314 North Waco Street. John W. Pauling purchased the business in March 1926. He spoke German and assisted in translating documents for those in the German community. He also organized bus trips to Washington, DC, for veterans in the American Legion post. The company made the memorials for noted humorist Will Rogers and famous blues guitarist Stevie Ray Vaughan. (Sandra McCown.)

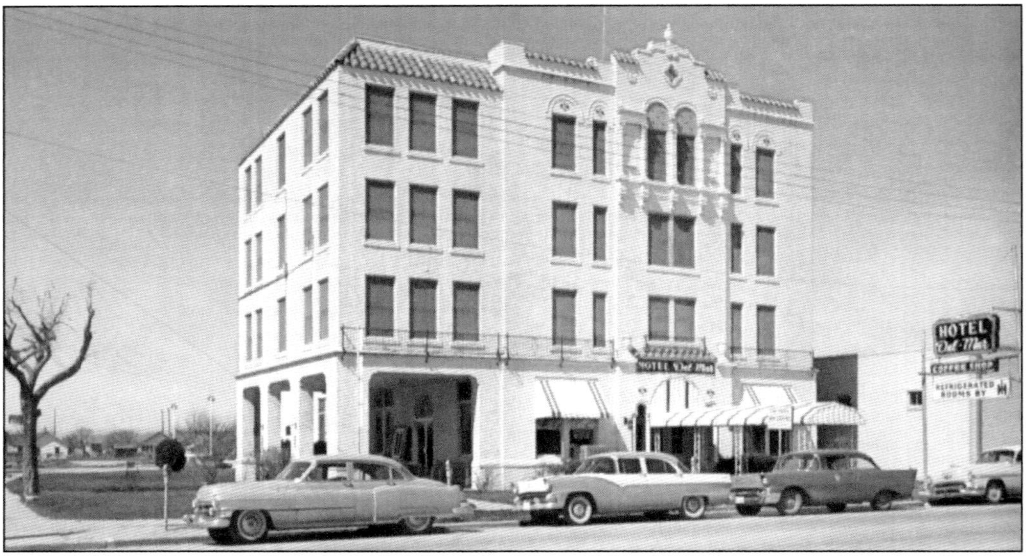

The Newcomb Hotel stood at the northwest corner of West Walnut and South Waco Streets. Miss Willie Helm, the head of the history department at Hillsboro Junior College, lived at the hotel when it was known as the Johnson Hotel. The popular hotel was later known as the Del Mar Hotel and was a meeting place in the 1940s and 1950s for the Lions, Rotary, and Kiwanis clubs.

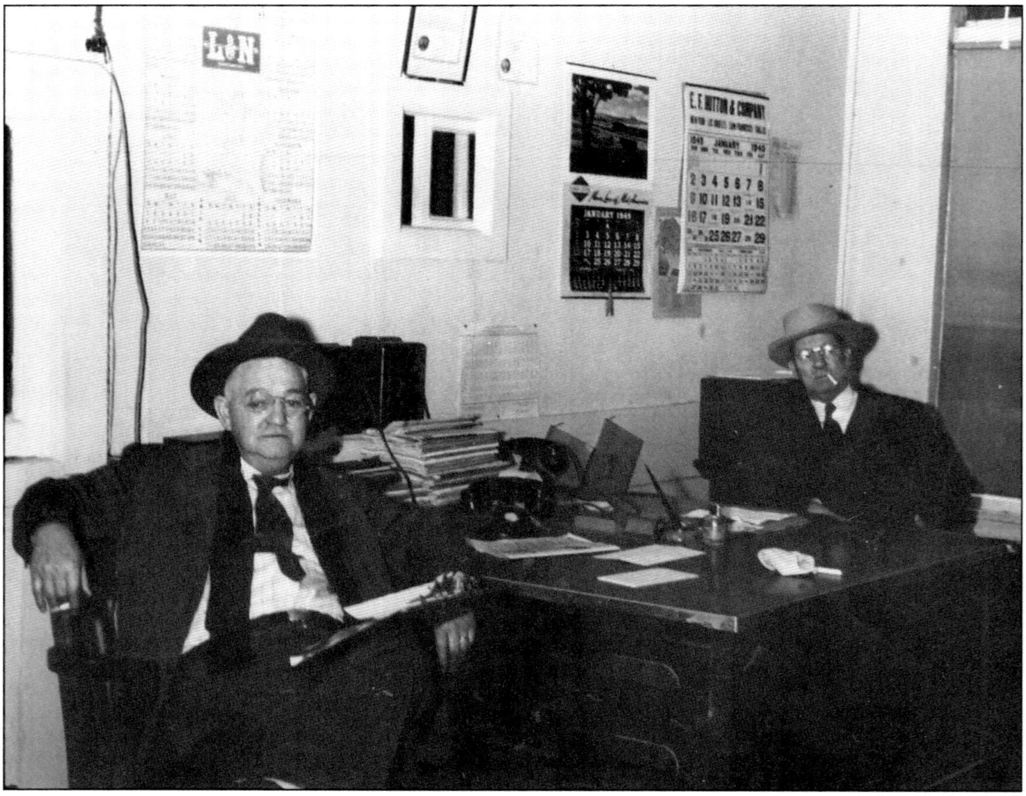

Hugh Miller visits with cotton buyer Cecil Stubblefield in Stubblefield's office at 103 ½ West Elm Street in 1949. Miller was the owner of the largest coal yard in Hillsboro, Miller Miracle Mills, located at 140 South Covington Street. (C.H. Stubblefield.)

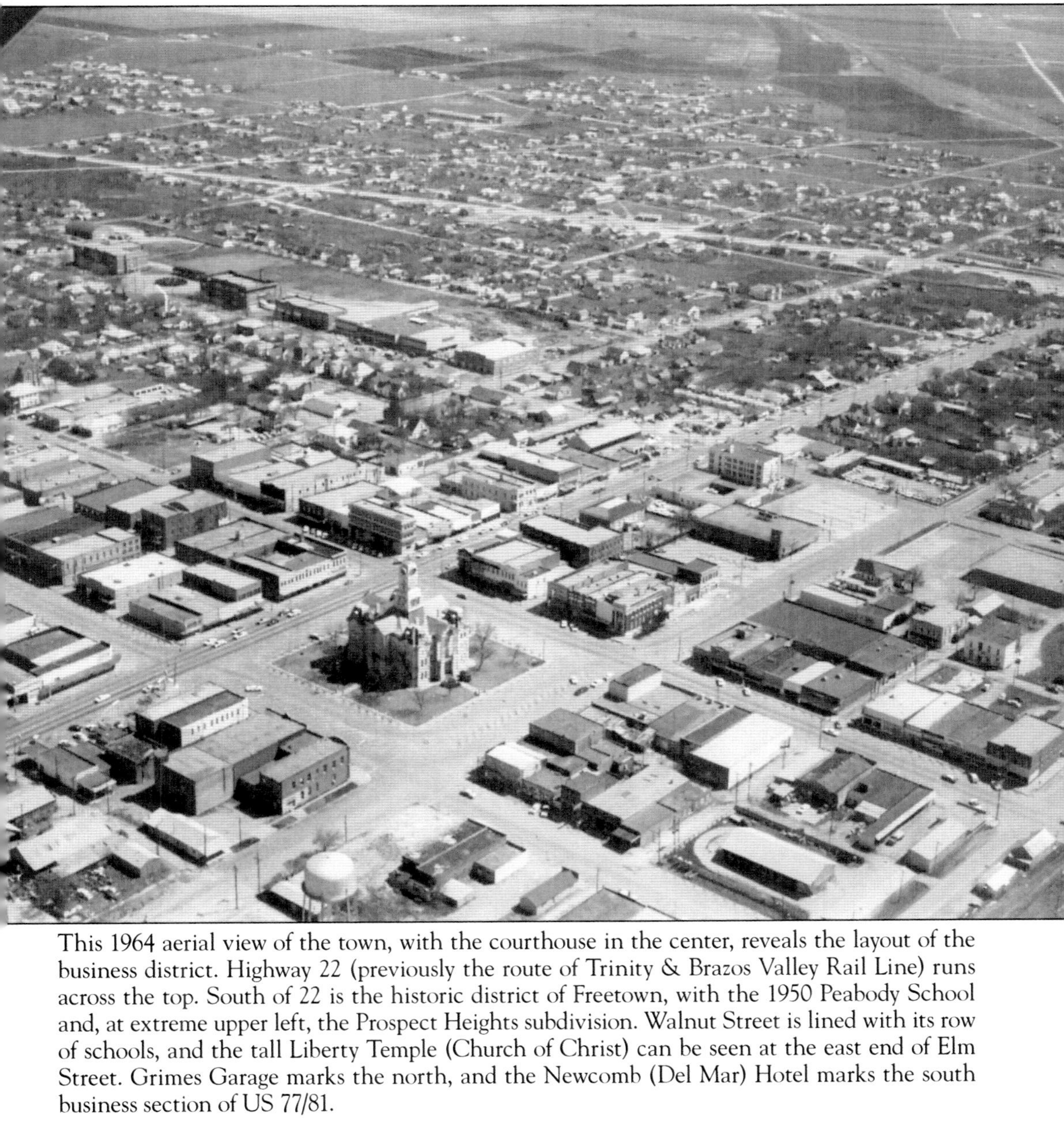

This 1964 aerial view of the town, with the courthouse in the center, reveals the layout of the business district. Highway 22 (previously the route of Trinity & Brazos Valley Rail Line) runs across the top. South of 22 is the historic district of Freetown, with the 1950 Peabody School and, at extreme upper left, the Prospect Heights subdivision. Walnut Street is lined with its row of schools, and the tall Liberty Temple (Church of Christ) can be seen at the east end of Elm Street. Grimes Garage marks the north, and the Newcomb (Del Mar) Hotel marks the south business section of US 77/81.

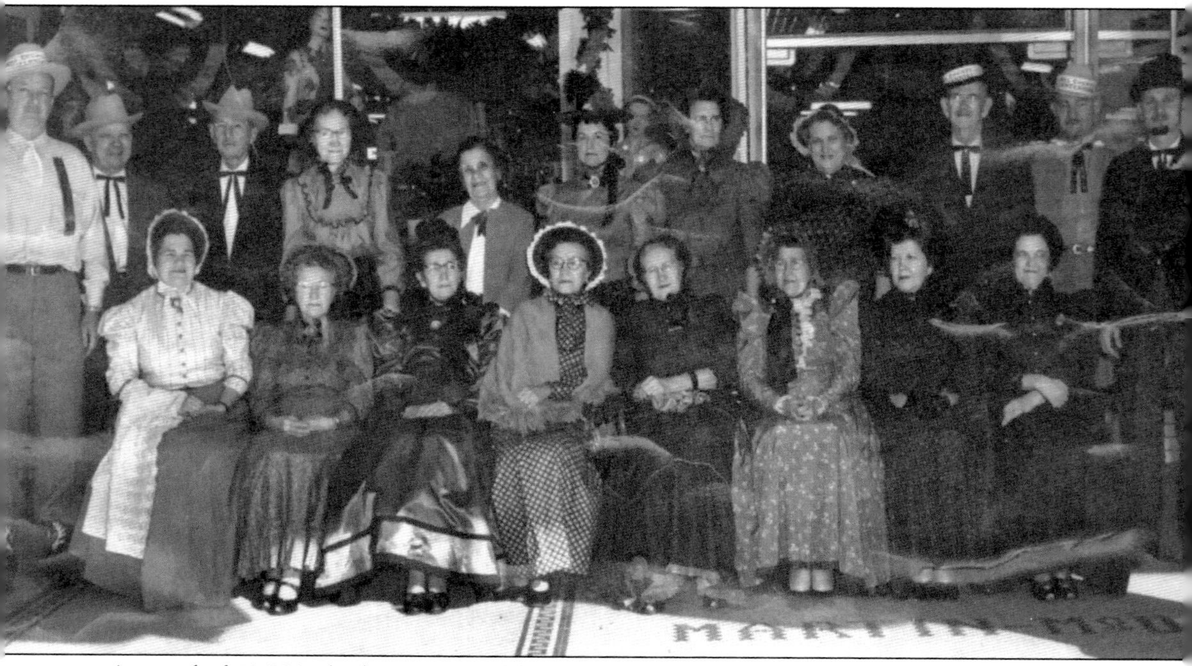

A crowd of 40,000, the largest in Hillsboro's history, lined the streets to watch the gigantic Hill County centennial parade on November 14, 1953. The crowd was thickest around the courthouse square, although it lined every street for blocks around the courthouse. Seen here in front of Martin-McDonald Department Store, at 113 East Elm Street, are employees in period dress. They are, from left to right, (seated) Christine Pace, Edith Leverett, Ruth Brooks, Oneta Head, Ethel Johnson, Ina Curtis, Laurene Hord, and Grace Cantrell; (standing) Bill McDonald, William McDonald, Luther Neal, Sammie Wilkerson, Ann Hill, Loraine Edens, Carrie Lee King, Irene Black, George Echoles, Ned Beavers, and Wyndell Greenhill.

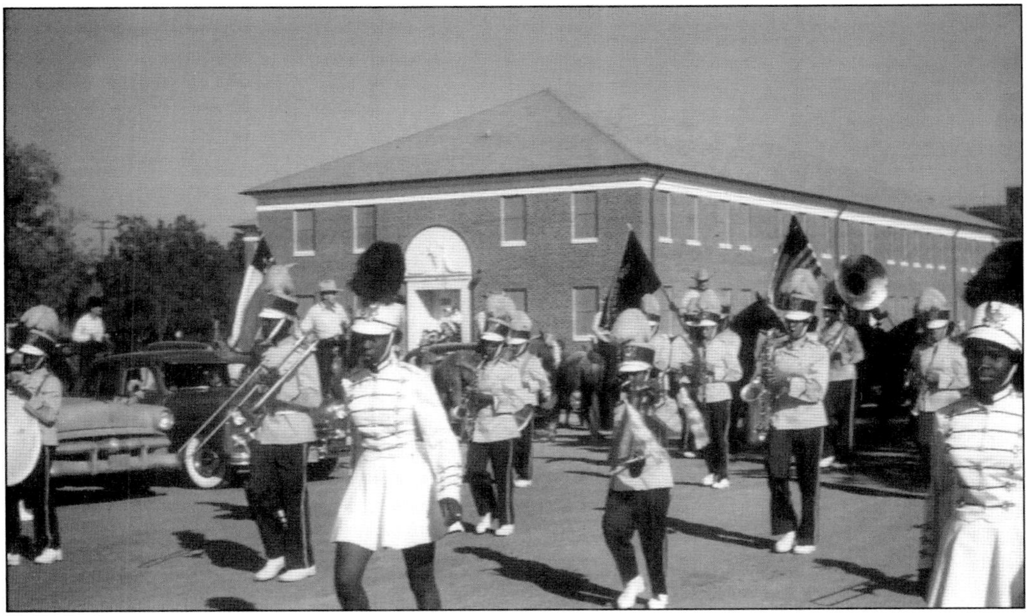

Above, the Peabody School band participates in the 1953 centennial parade. In 1998, an organization called New Beginnings for Peabody sought to revitalize the vacant school building to provide a centralized location for community support. The building burned in 2005, but Peabody School remains a source of pride for Hillsboro residents. An official Texas Historical Marker was dedicated in 2009. Seen below at the marker dedication are, from left to right, Norman Baker; Billye Demerson, president of New Beginnings for Peabody; and Anita Hill.

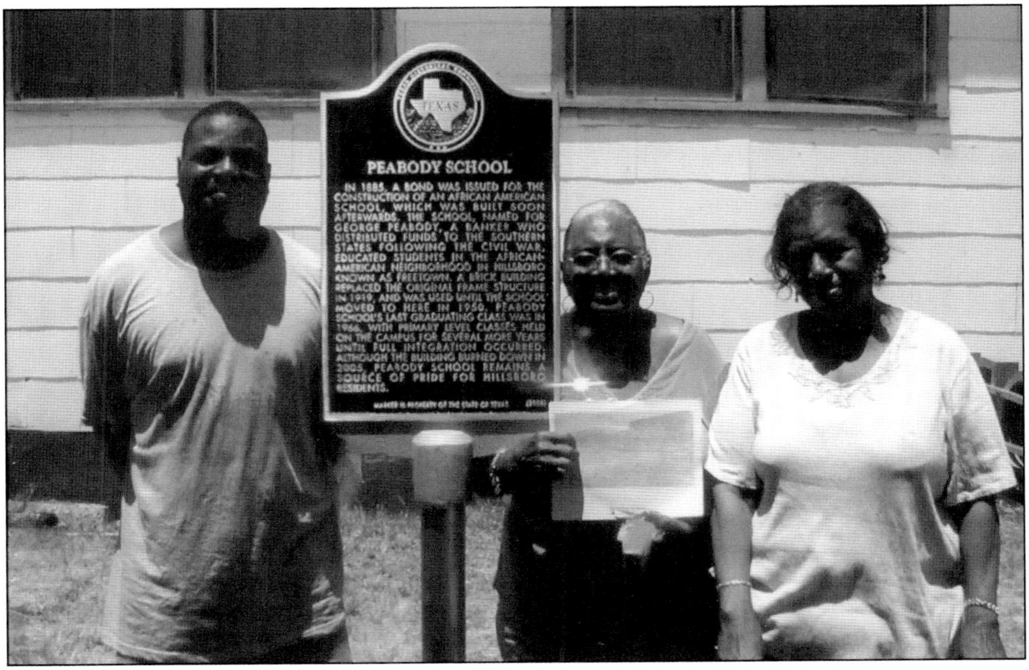

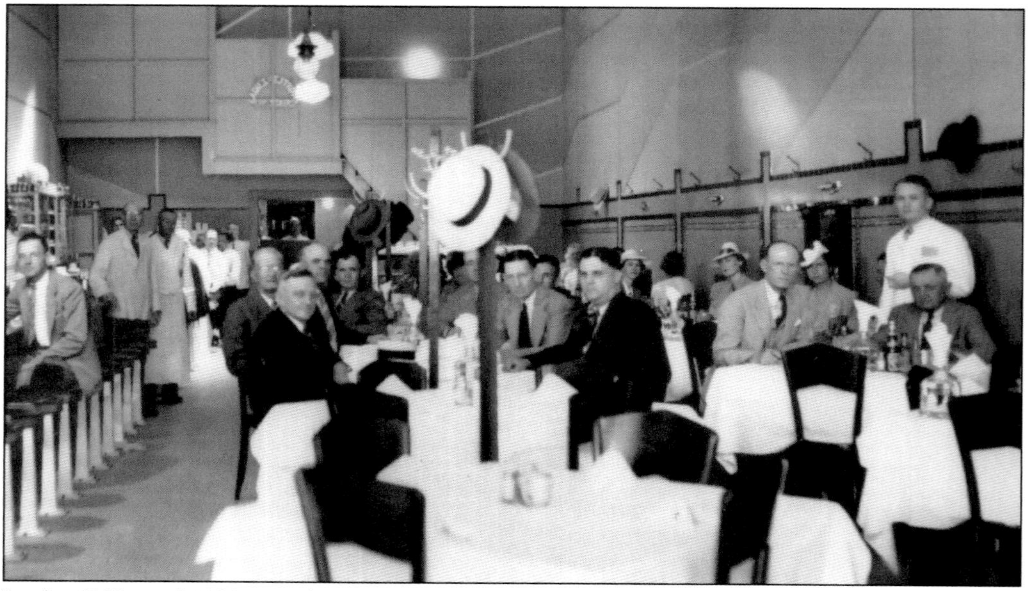

In the 1920s and 1930s, Andrews Café was open around the clock to serve customers traveling through Hillsboro on US 77/81. It was frequently the site of political planning and discussions. Among the customers are Guy West, of Citizens National Bank; Olin Culberson, state railroad commissioner; Ed Hamilton, state representative; and Burris Jackson, postmaster of Hillsboro and Democratic Party Executive Committee leader. (Catherine Andrews.)

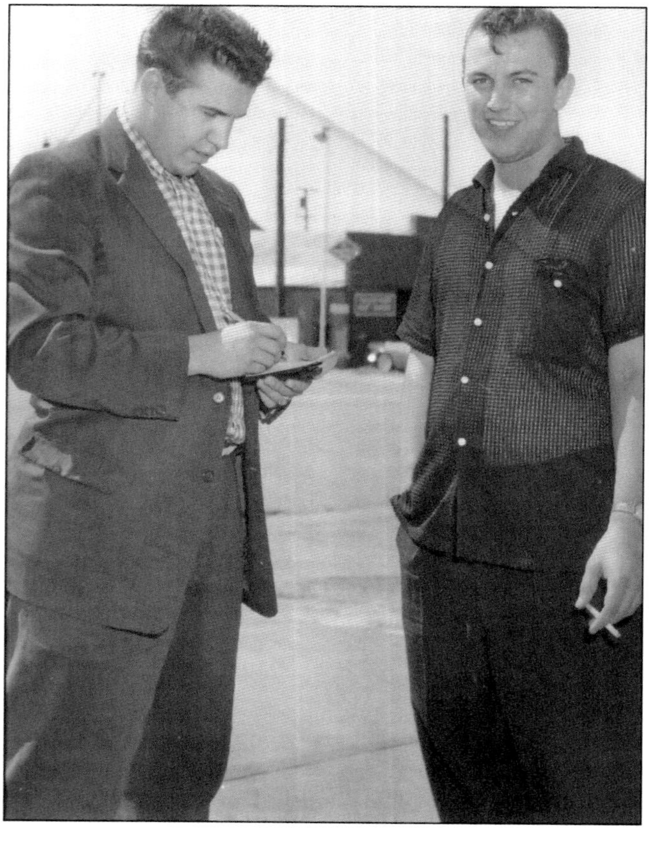

When US 77/81 passed through downtown Hillsboro as the major route between Dallas–Fort Worth and Austin, residents often caught glimpses of celebrities, politicians, sports figures, and entertainers stopping to eat or purchase gas. Here, *Hillsboro Evening Mirror* reporter Jack Loftis (left) interviews rock n' roll singer Bobby Charles, of "See You Later, Alligator" fame. In 1958, hysteria erupted when Elvis Presley dined at Andrews Café. (Jack Loftis.)

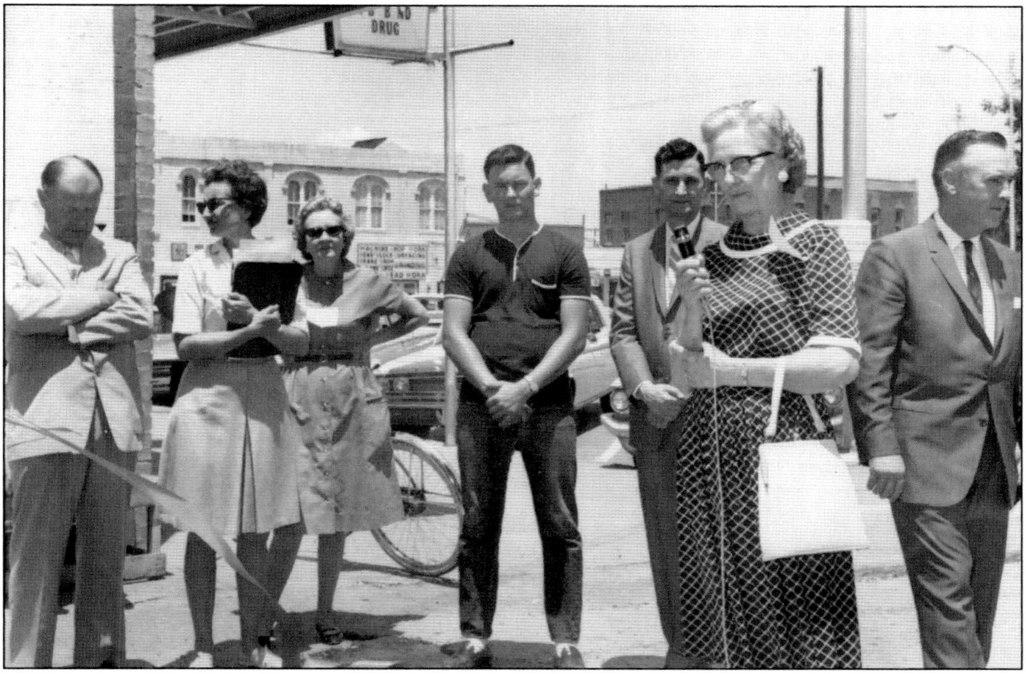

Bond's Alley is named after Bond's Drug Store, which was established in 1881. The alley was a local site for politics, peddler's shows, whittling, cockfights, and fisticuffs. Among the first to occupy the benches of Bond's Alley were Civil War veterans. An annual arts and crafts show in the alley began in June 1964 and raised funds for the Hillsboro City Library and the MKT depot. Seen above at a ribbon-cutting ceremony are, from left to right, Dr. Julius Zhohar, Scottie Cason, Maurine Harvey, Lynn Gray, Hillsboro mayor LaVerne Jobe, Lil Eastland (at the microphone), and master of ceremonies Dr. W. Lamar Fly.

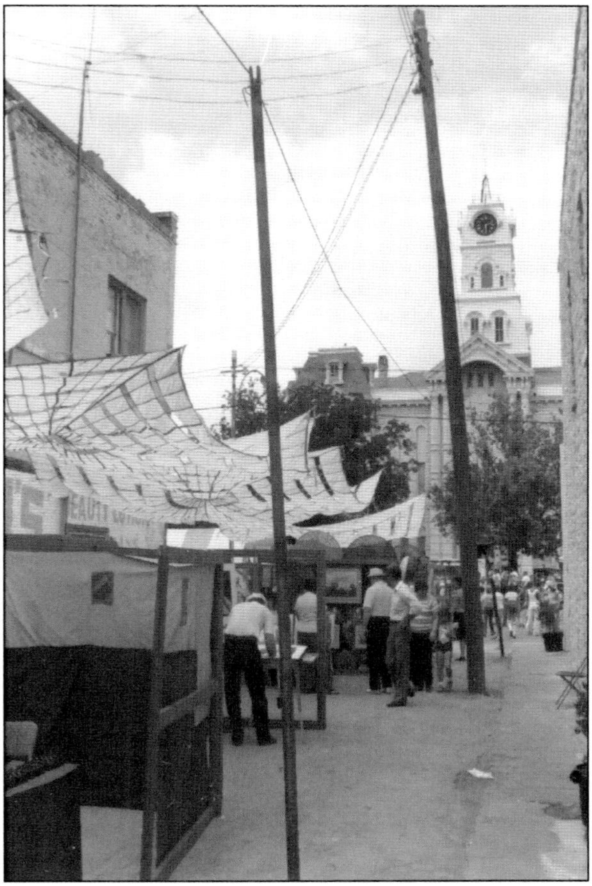

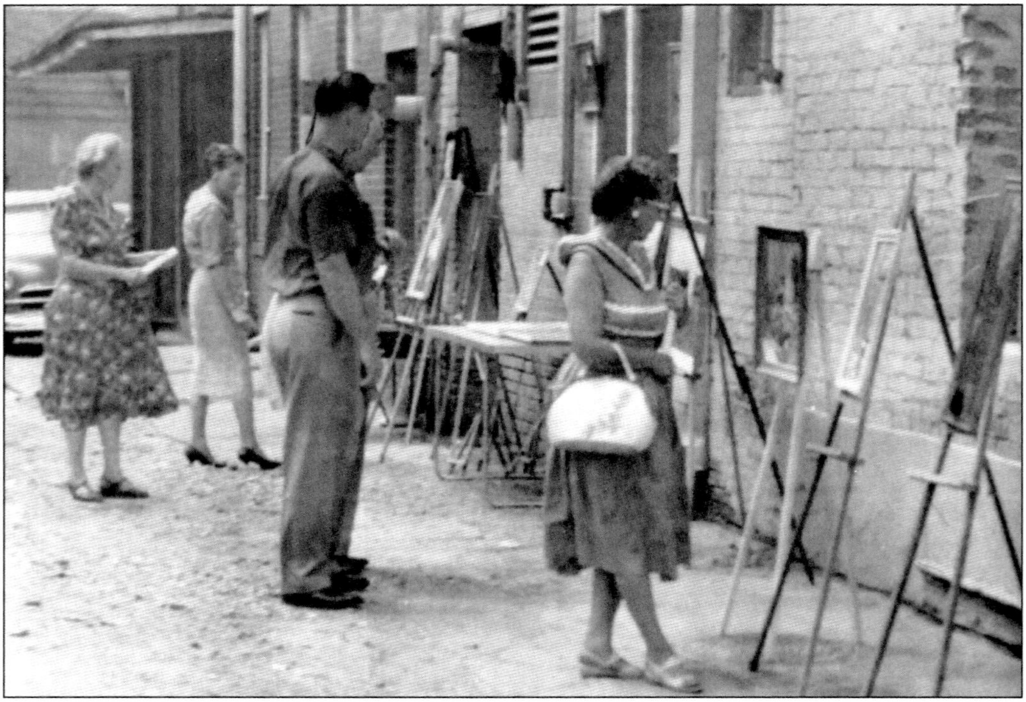

Arts and crafts enthusiasts browse the stalls in an early Bond's Alley arts and crafts show. The show soon outgrew Bond's Alley and moved into the courthouse square. Live entertainment and food booths were set up around the square.

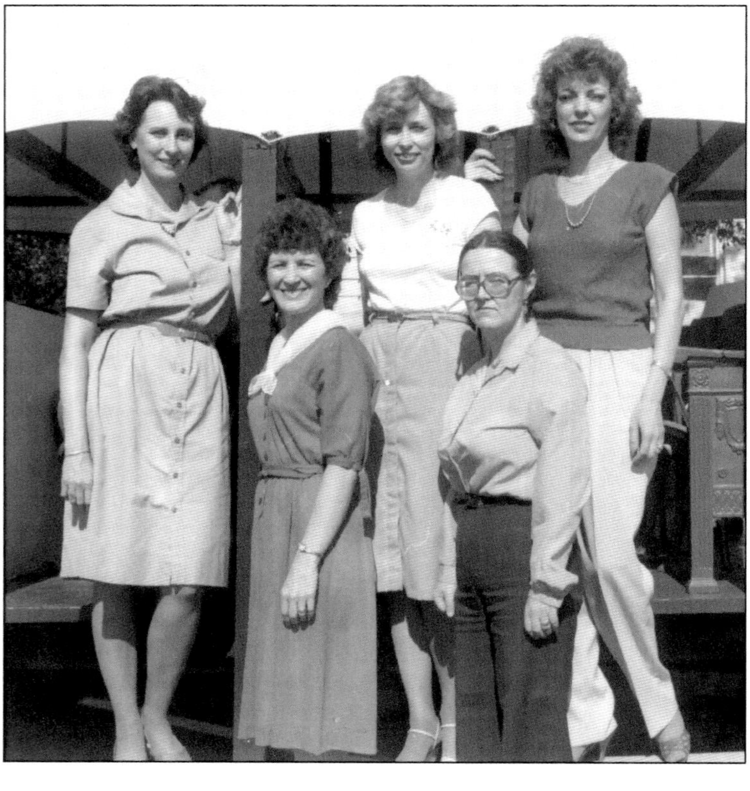

A popular place to meet and eat during Bond's Alley weekend was the Courtyard Café, located in a shady nook off the alley. The conversation centered on the artwork and entertainment lining the alley and the courthouse square. The café was staffed by volunteers; the 1984 committee members are seen here. They are, from left to right, (first row) unidentified volunteer and LaDonna Lewis; (second row) Susan Bacon Williams, Linda Markwardt Neal, and Mary Ann Coutret Schneider.

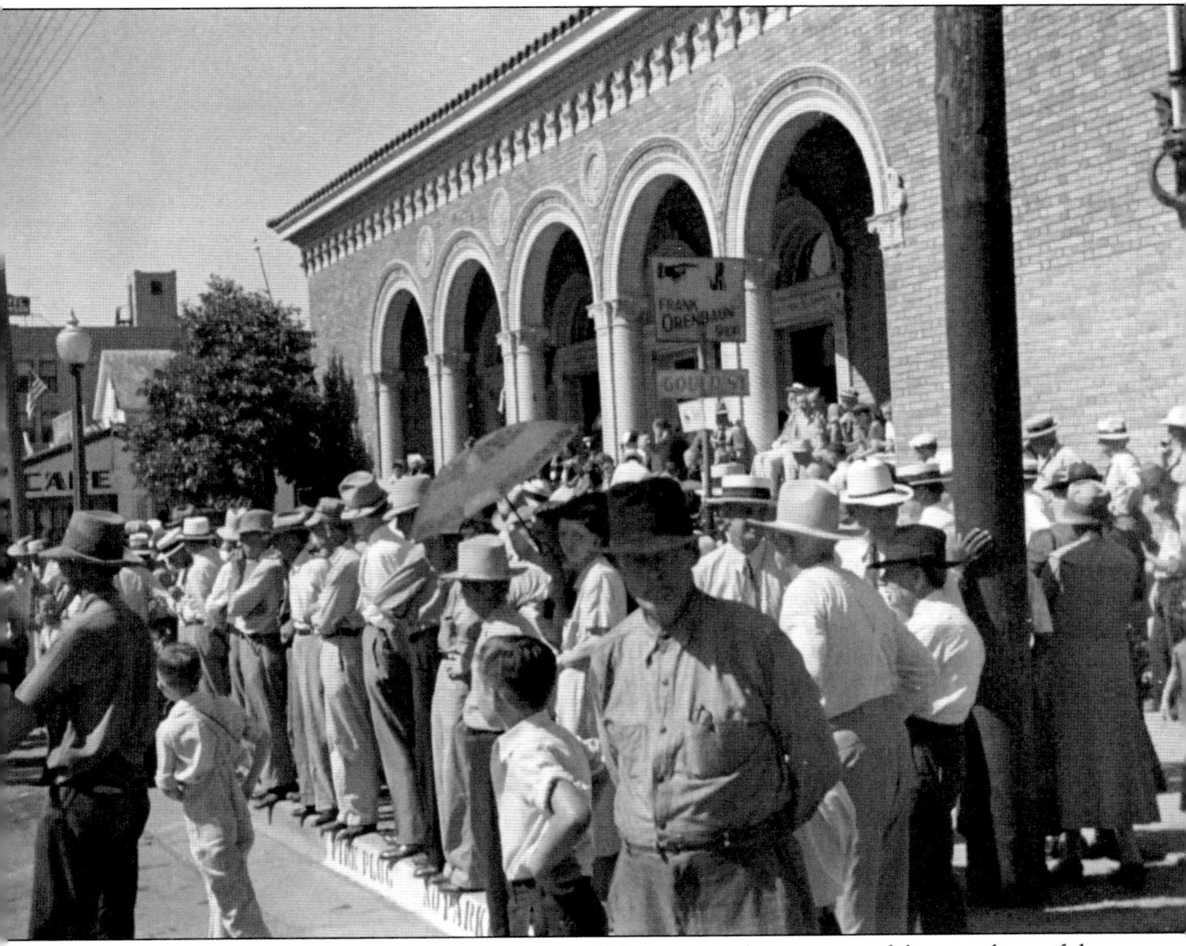

Built between 1912 and 1915 as a post office, the Hillsboro City Library is one of the most beautiful buildings in Hillsboro. An adaptation of the Foundling Hospital for Children in Florence, Italy, architect James Knox Taylor's design includes a tiled roof, an ornate arched entrance arcade, and elaborate detailing of terra-cotta and stone. The Mediterranean Revival–style building is located at 118 South Waco Street. The crowd in this photograph had gathered for a speech by Vice Pres. John Nance Garner.

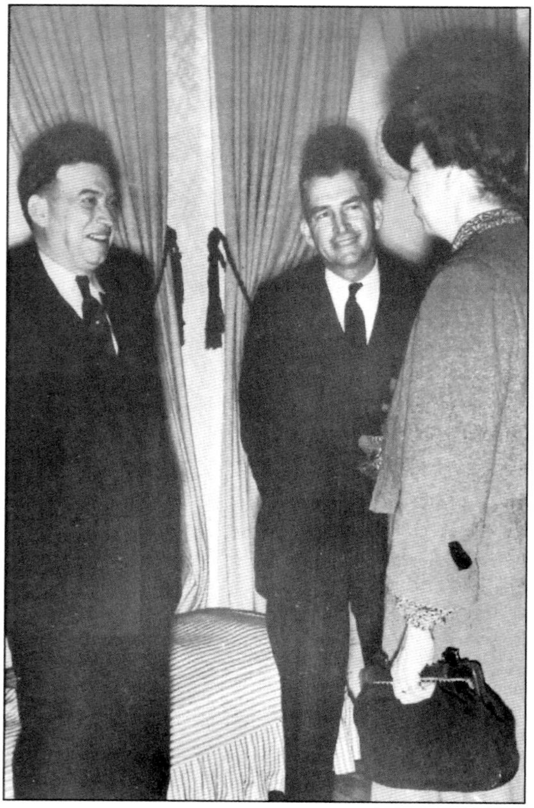

First Lady Eleanor Roosevelt visited Hillsboro in March 1939. She is seen here with Joe W. Patterson, the president of Hillsboro School Board, at one of the two National Youth Administration (NYA) centers in Hillsboro. The NYA community center was located at 509 Abbott Avenue, and the NYA resident center was at 937 East Franklin Street. (Hillsboro Independent School District.)

The view below, of Elm and Waco Streets around 1944, looks from the southeast corner of the courthouse lawn towards Hillsboro State Bank, on the right, and Brown Drug, on the northeast corner in the old Flanagan Brothers building. The soda fountain at Brown Drug was a popular spot for residents and visitors to Hillsboro, as US 77/81 passed through Hillsboro's downtown. (Johnson Studios.)

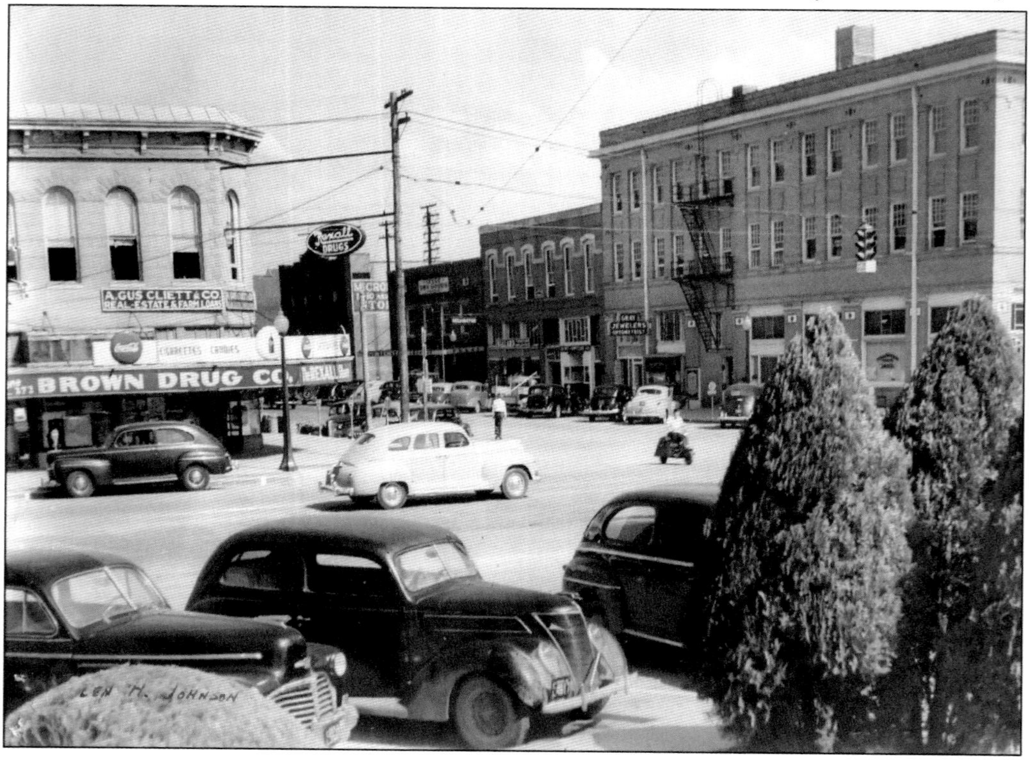

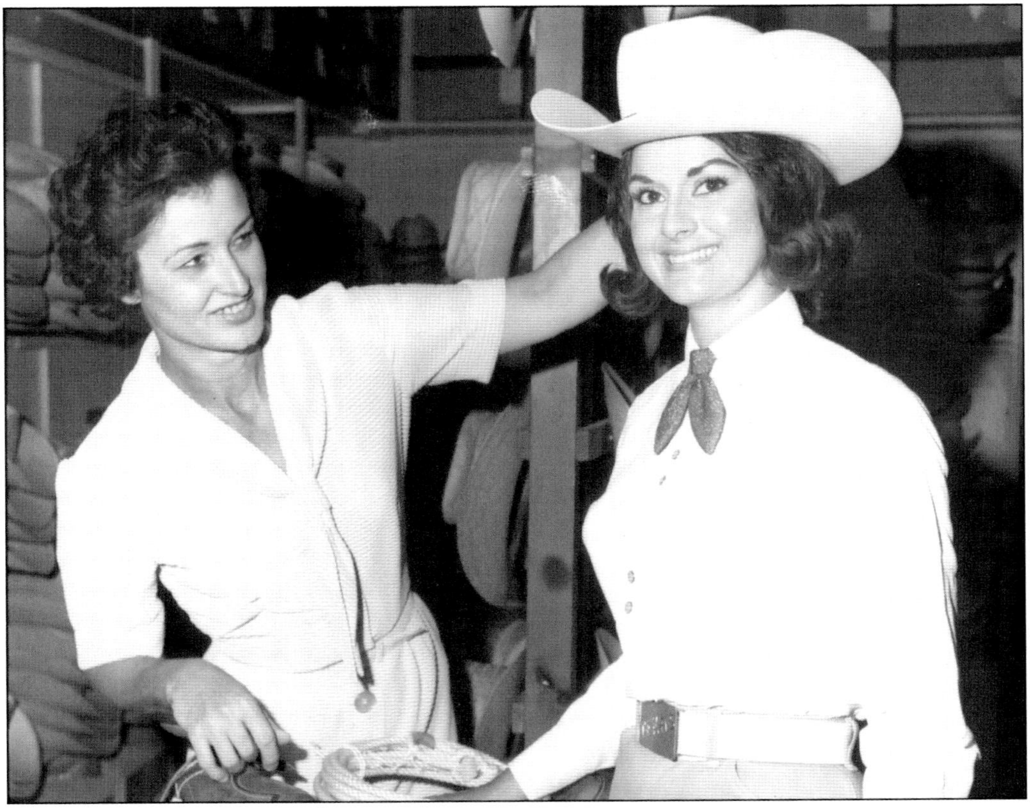

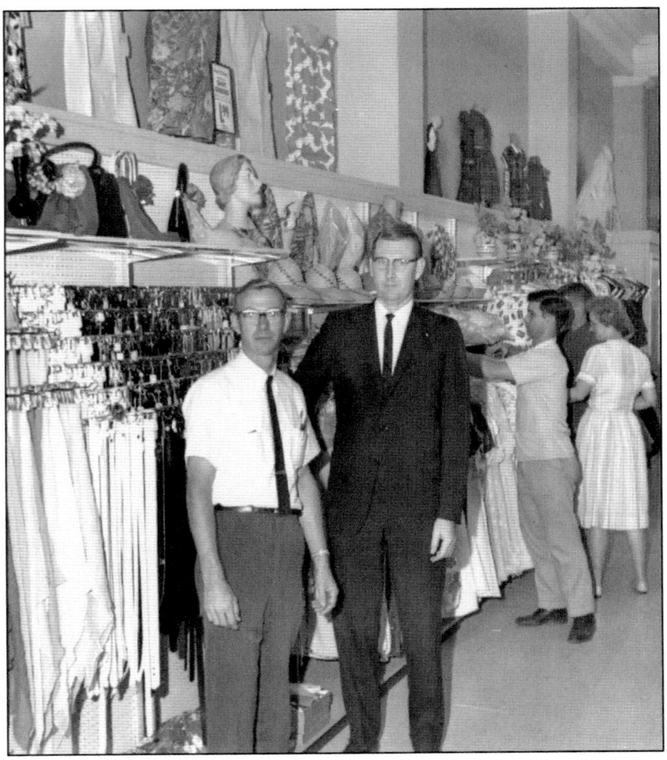

Shoppers from the area found a wide selection of shops in downtown Hillsboro. The 1884 Hillsboro Business Directory listed advertisements for nine dry goods stores, three hardware stores, ten grocers, three drugstores, two furniture stores, two watchmakers/jewelers, two bookstores, and two millinery shops. Through the years, shops such as Young's Style Shop, L. Brin Dry Goods, the Mississippi Store, S.H. Kress Company, Martin-McDonald Department Store, J.C. Penney, Swartz Department Store, Texas Dry Goods Company, Flanagan Brothers, Hillsboro Dry Goods Company, The Hitch'n Post, Herrings Men's Store, and Smith & Tomlinson were favorites among local shoppers.

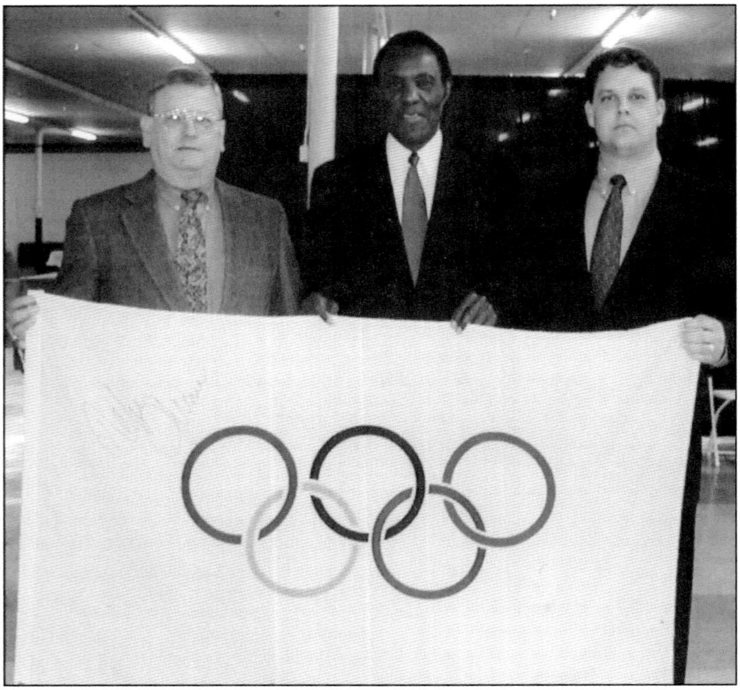

Rafer Johnson (center) presents an Olympic flag to Lynn Gray (left) and Chad Gray (right) upon his 2003 induction into the Hillsboro Chamber Hall of Fame. Born in Hillsboro in 1935 to Lewis and Alma Johnson, Rafer Johnson won the decathlon in the 1955 Pan-American Games, a silver medal at the 1956 Melbourne Olympics, and the gold medal—setting a world record in the process—at the 1960 Rome Olympics. (Lynn Gray.)

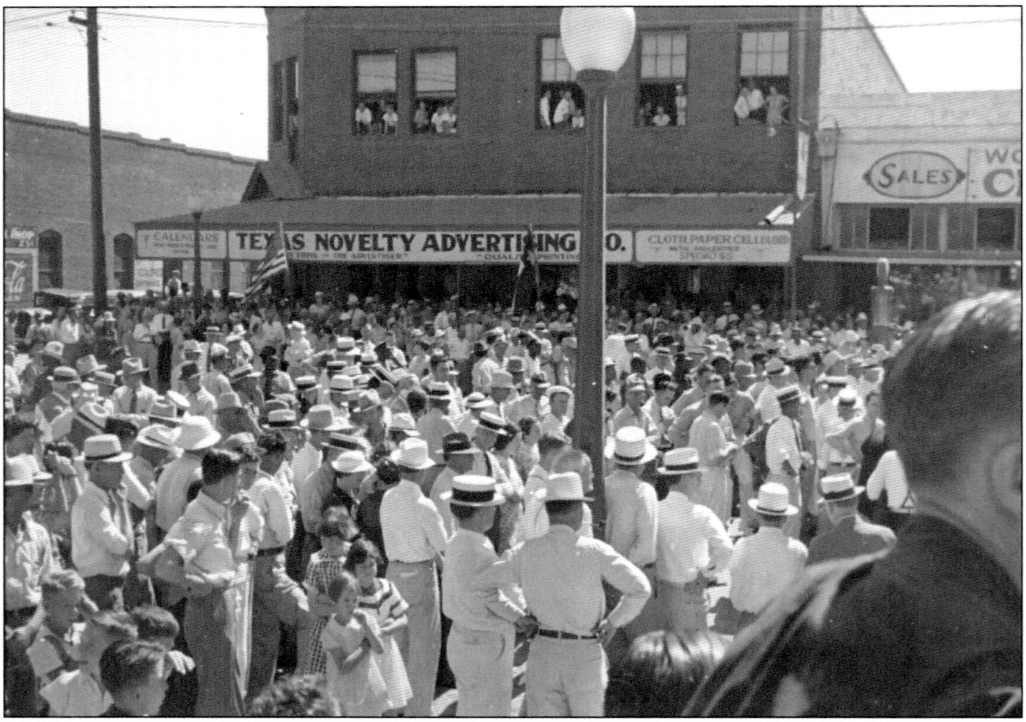

Throughout Hillsboro history, political campaigns and personalities have been popular crowd-pleasers for local residents. Here, in 1936, a crowd gathers to welcome Vice Pres. John Nance Garner to Hillsboro. Election results were posted at the *Hillsboro Mirror* and always drew large crowds eager to see the tallies. The Hillsboro Mirror Building was erected in 1901 on the site of the 1876 Mills Hotel at the southeast corner of Waco and Gould Streets.

Five

Service to Community and Country

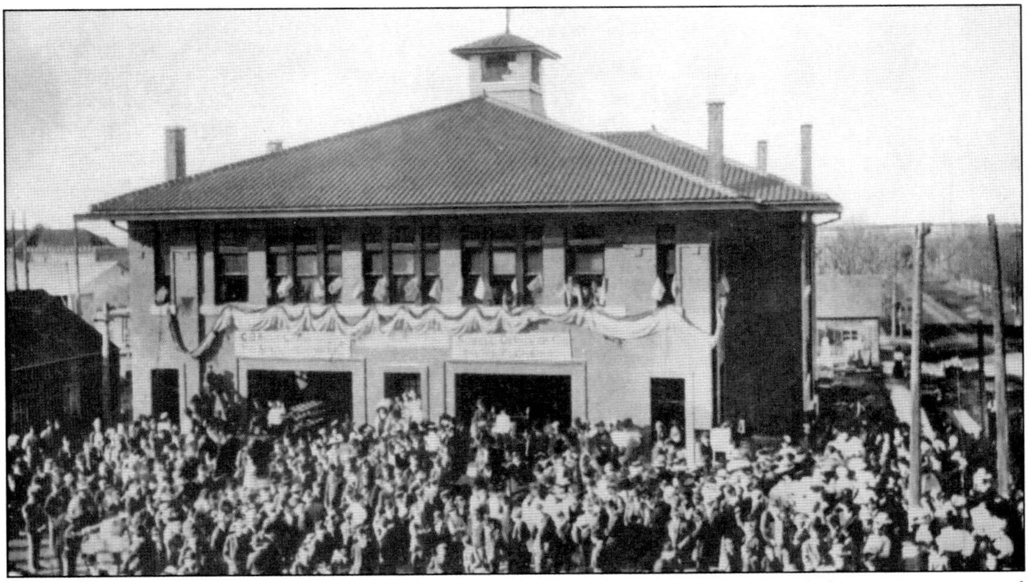

A large crowd was on hand in 1909 for the laying of the cornerstone of the new municipal complex, which included city hall, the fire station, and the police station. It was built at 127–129 East Franklin Street and has currently been restored as Historic City Hall. Ed Woodall was the mayor at the time, and the town aldermen were W.A. Alderson, D.C. Denman, W.F. Dixon, W.C. Elliot, Pat Flanagan, L.C. Hill, W.C. Robertson, and J.W. Young.

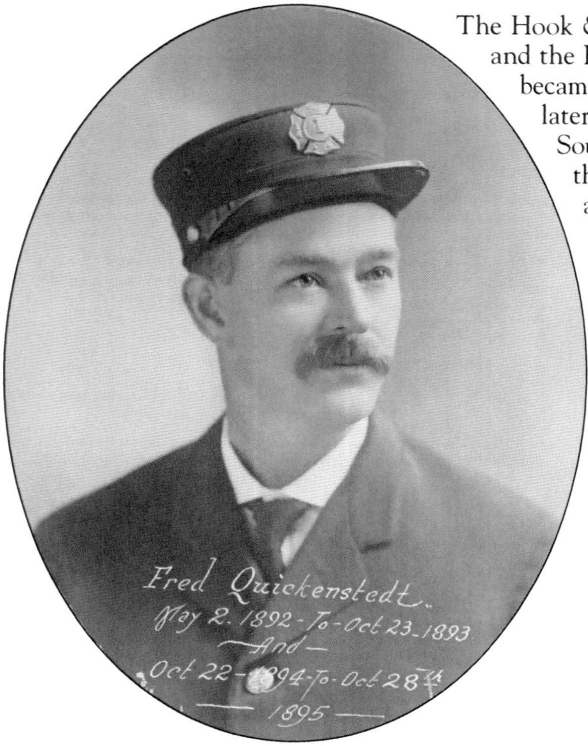

The Hook & Ladder Company organized in 1883, and the Engine Company organized in 1885 and became the Hillsboro Volunteer Fire Department later that year, with a firehouse built at 118 South Waco Street and H.P. Harrington as the first fire chief. An 1894 list of officers and members included Fred Quickenstedt, seen here, who served as fire chief in the early 1890s. He was mayor from 1896 to 1902 and then served two more terms starting in 1904, according to *Heritage of Hill County*.

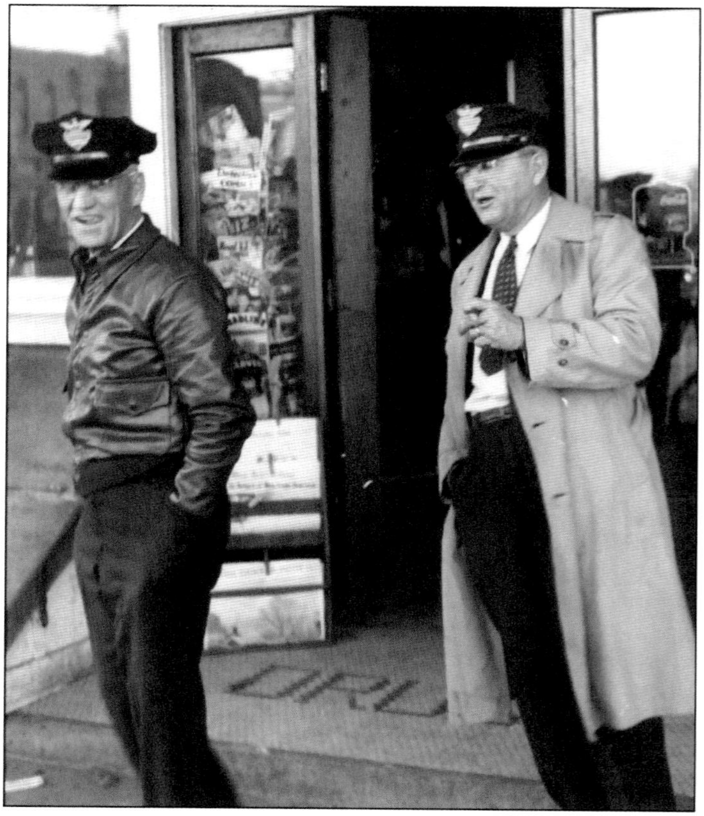

Hillsboro police officer Ed Little and chief of police Will T. Galiga stand in front of City Drug Store around 1946. Little's brother Will Little also served on the police force, and the three made up the entire police department in the 1930s and 1940s. City Drug Store, owned and operated by Bascom Turk and R.D. Stem, was on the south side of the square, adjacent to the Citizens National Bank. (Bill Galiga.)

John G. Abney was elected mayor in April 1882 and served one term. In November 1888, he was elected county judge, and served two terms. During his tenure as county judge, the 1890 Hill County Courthouse was constructed. Abney was born in Harrison County, Texas, and moved to Hillsboro in February 1880. He studied at the University of Virginia and was admitted to the bar in 1875.

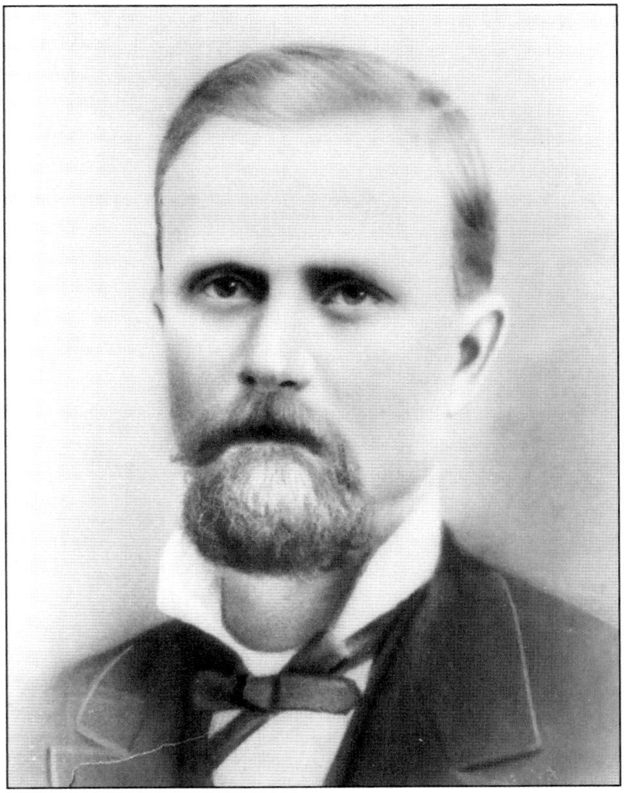

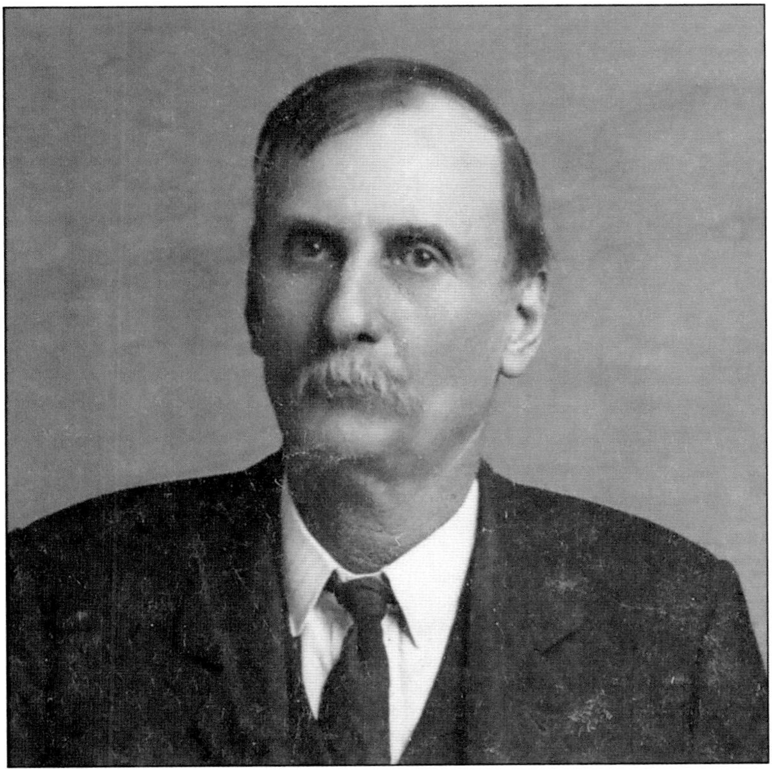

After winning a hotly contested race against two other candidates, John E. Ballard served as mayor from 1891 to 1893. Ballard gave strong support to the bond election for the construction of Central School, and, as county commissioner of Precinct 1 in 1887, worked to support the construction of a new county jail, which was eventually built in 1893. Ballard served several terms as an alderman for Hillsboro and was a saloonkeeper at Old Rock Saloon.

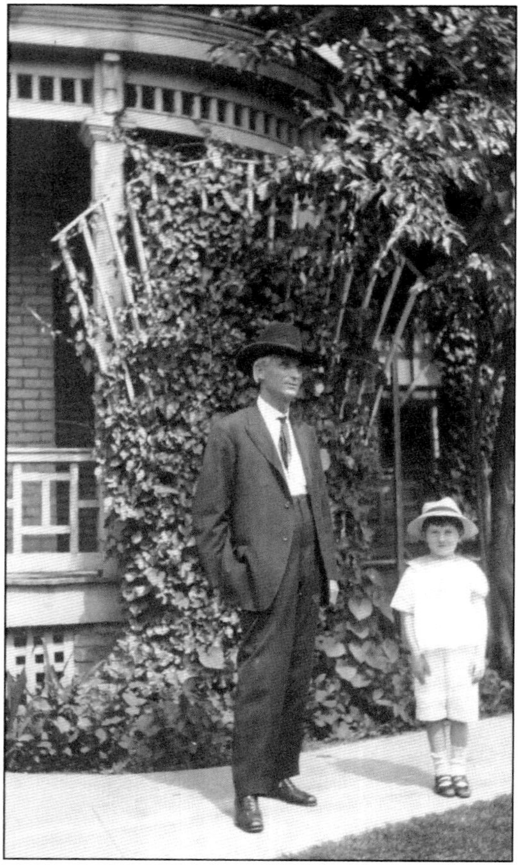

Sheriff J.W. Freeland and his son J.W. Freeland Jr. are seen here in front of the Hill County Jail in 1914. The elder Freeland, the superintendent of the county poor farm, was elected sheriff of Hill County in 1910 and served two terms. He was elected mayor of Hillsboro, and then, in 1928, sheriff again. In 1933, he tracked and arrested the notorious Raymond Hamilton, a member of the Barrow Gang, made famous by leaders Clyde Barrow and Bonnie Parker.

The Hill County Jail was designed by W.C. Dodson, who also designed the Hill County Courthouse. The Hill County Historical Commission states that the jail was built in 1893 by Lovell & Hood. The front part of the building served as living quarters for the sheriff's family, and the rear housed the cell blocks, the kitchen, and the office. Prisoners were kept here until 1983, when it became the Hill County Cell Block Museum.

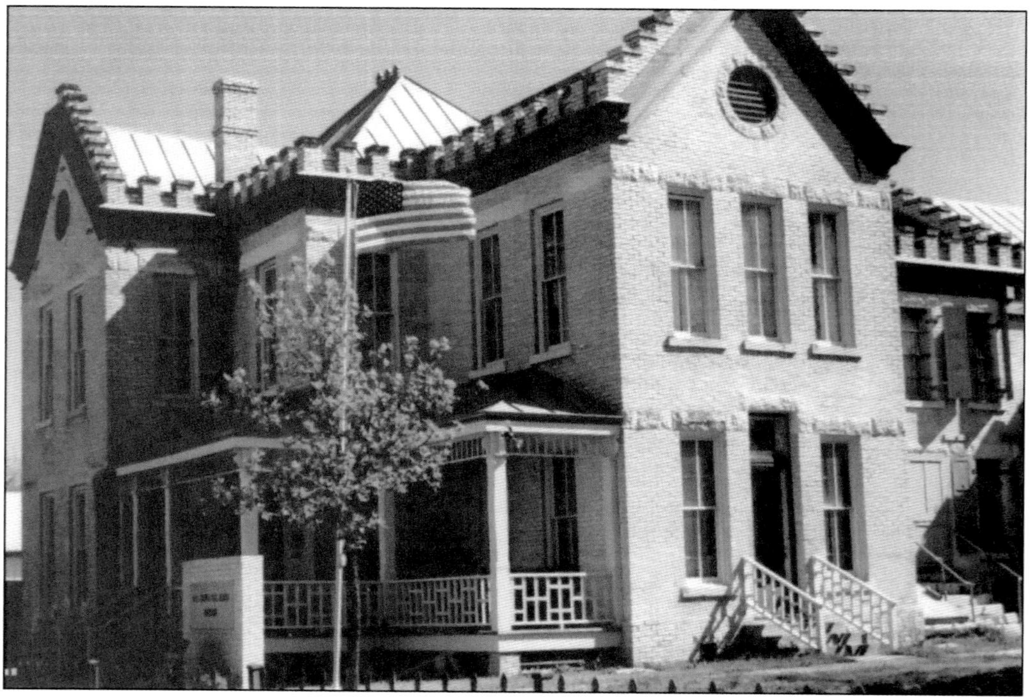

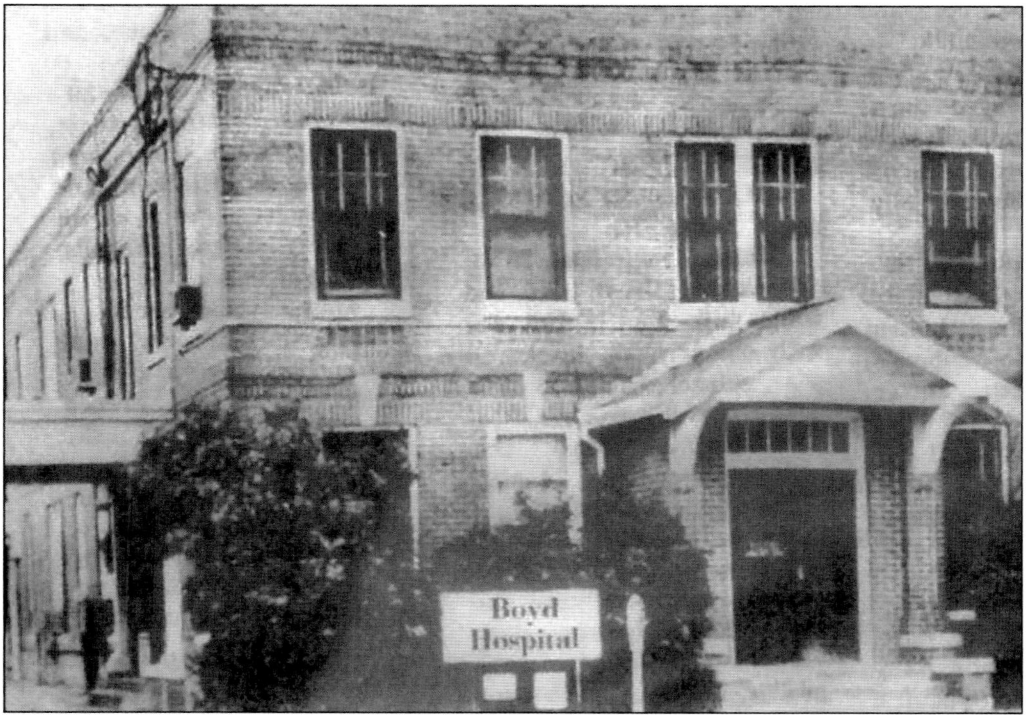

The 22-room Boyd Sanitarium was built in 1922 at 206 East Elm Street by Dr. J.E. Boyd. In 1925, it added 20 more rooms. It was given national approval by the American College of Surgeons, and Dr. Charles A. Garrett was the general surgeon. It was purchased in 1957 by Dr. Silas Grant and Dr. James Buie and renamed J.E. and Rosa Boyd Hospital. It was later renamed Grant-Buie Hospital.

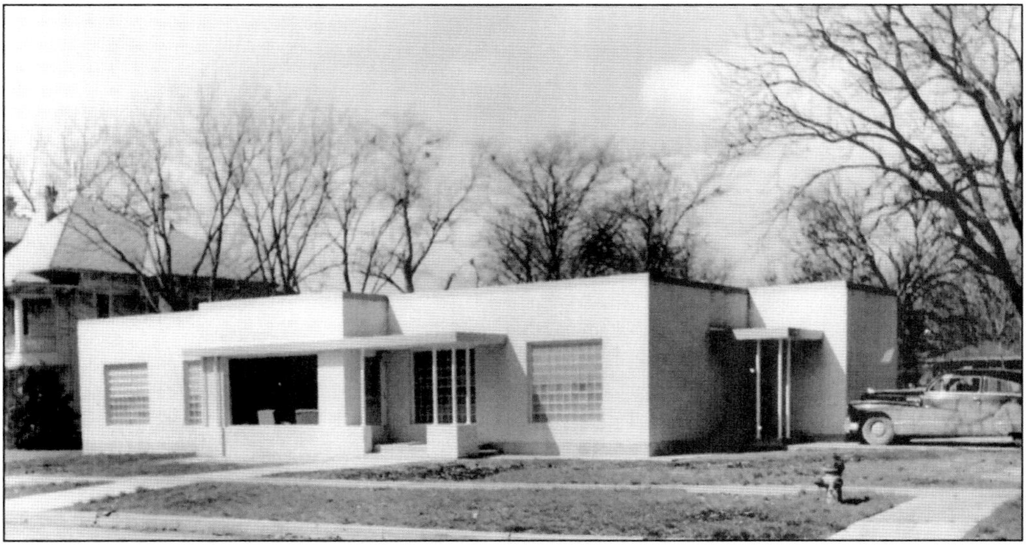
Hillsboro Clinic, at 213 Craig Street, was built by Dr. Ben Smith and his son, Dr. Nellins Smith, in 1948. They were soon joined by Dr. Charles Garrett, Dr. Thomas Rolan Barnett, and Dr. Richard Newton Beskow. The firm became the Hillsboro Clinic-Hospital in 1949 with the opening of the hospital wing. After the closing of the clinic, the property was deeded to the American Legion in 1996 and eventually transferred to the City of Hillsboro.

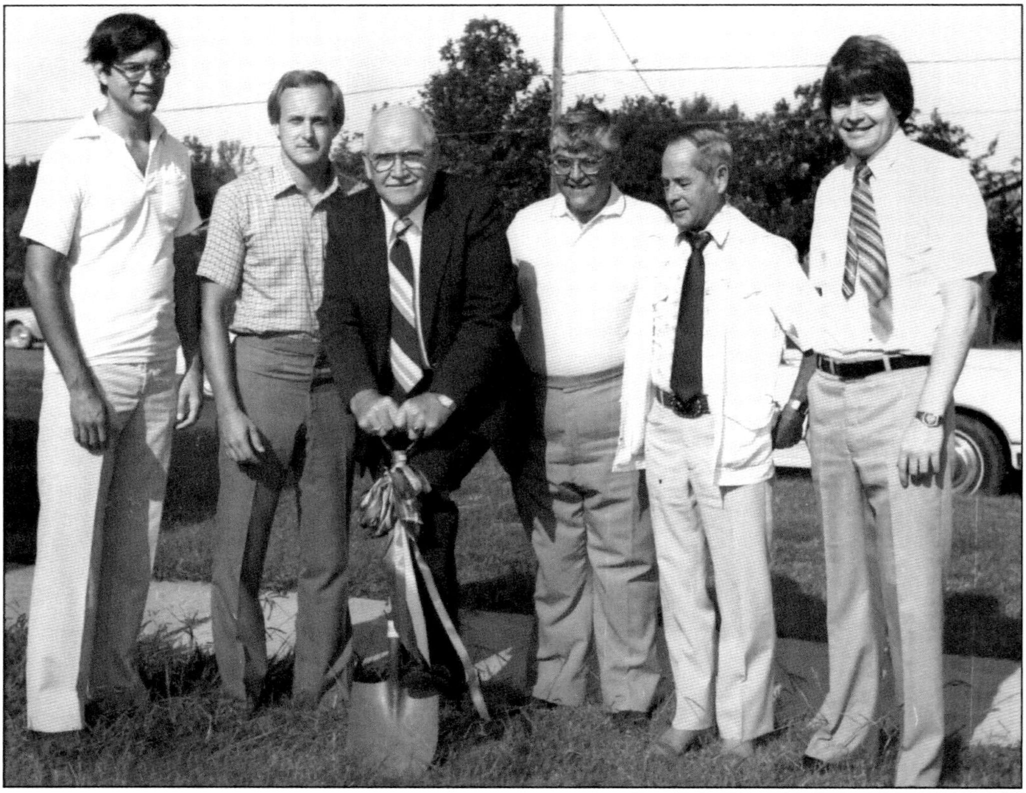

The ground-breaking for the new Grant Buie Hospital, at 101 Circle Drive, was held in 1981. The new facility opened in 1982. Seen here from left to right are Dr. David Skelton, Dr. Scott Hinzman, Dr. Morgan Buie, Dr. John "Skip" Johnson, Dr. John McCurley, and Dr. Larry Davis.

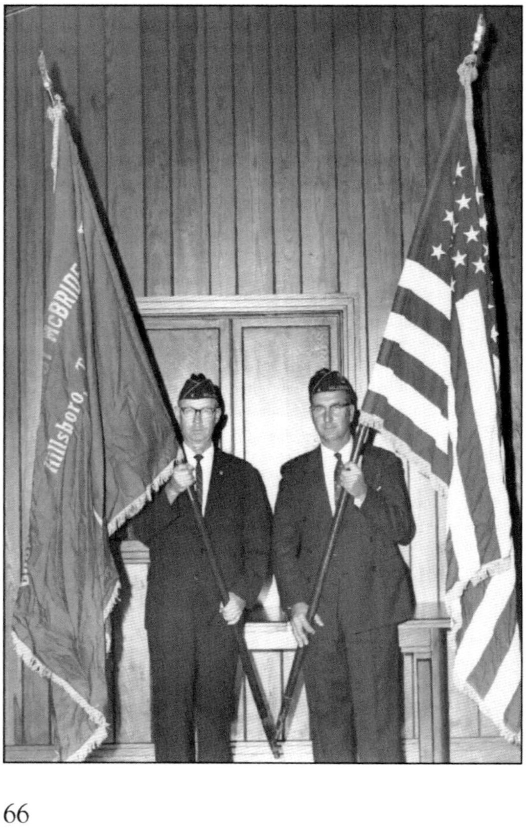

Dr. Jack Steel (left) assists in the presentation of the flags at the Robert Vaden–Ernest McBride American Legion Post No. 4. The post was given its permanent charter in 1921. The first post commander under temporary charter was W.E. Jackson.

Over 100 men volunteered for service in Company M, 3rd Texas Volunteer Infantry. The company was mustered out on February 22, 1899, but did not see service outside the United States. E.G. Shields was captain of the unit, which also included George Abbott, first lieutenant; Tom Adams, second lieutenant; William M. Browning, quartermaster sergeant; John Reagan, company sergeant; Jon Lovejoy, first line sergeant; and Ben Ballard Sr., Elmore Moore, Walter S. Scott, and Oscar Keene, corporals. (Texas Heritage Museum.)

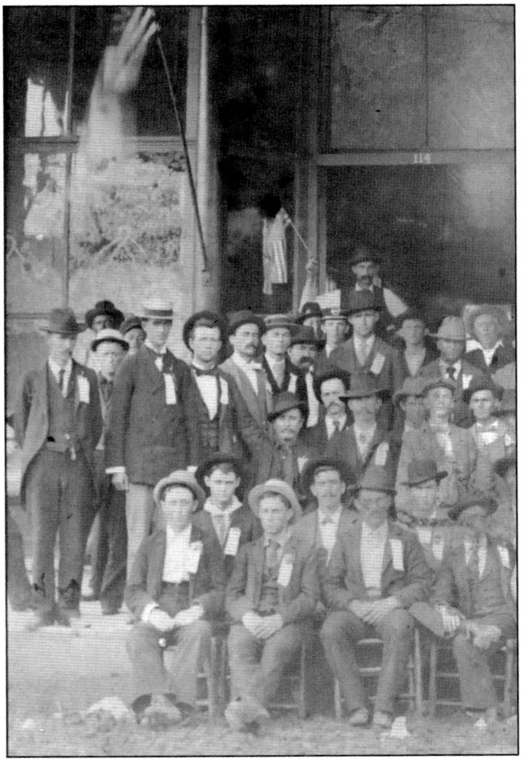

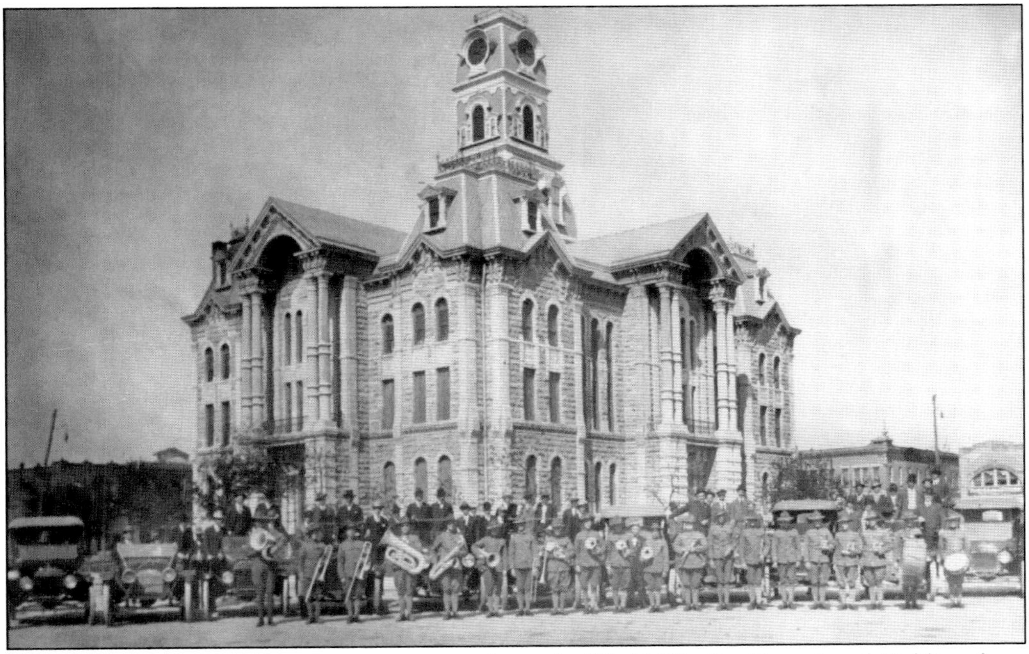

Seen here on the courthouse square are members of a World War I military band. Soldiers from Hillsboro who gave their life for America in World War I include James H. Atchley, Christodoulos Basiloplos, William H. Bennett, Jim William Burk, John E. Cacy, V. Clark, George W. Davis, James Davis, Tullie Florence, William V. Franklin, Lloyd Clarence Glover, Jefferson Jones, Frank Leszenzynski, Burdette McGrew, Charlie D. Smith, Roy Stirmon, and Robert Vaden.

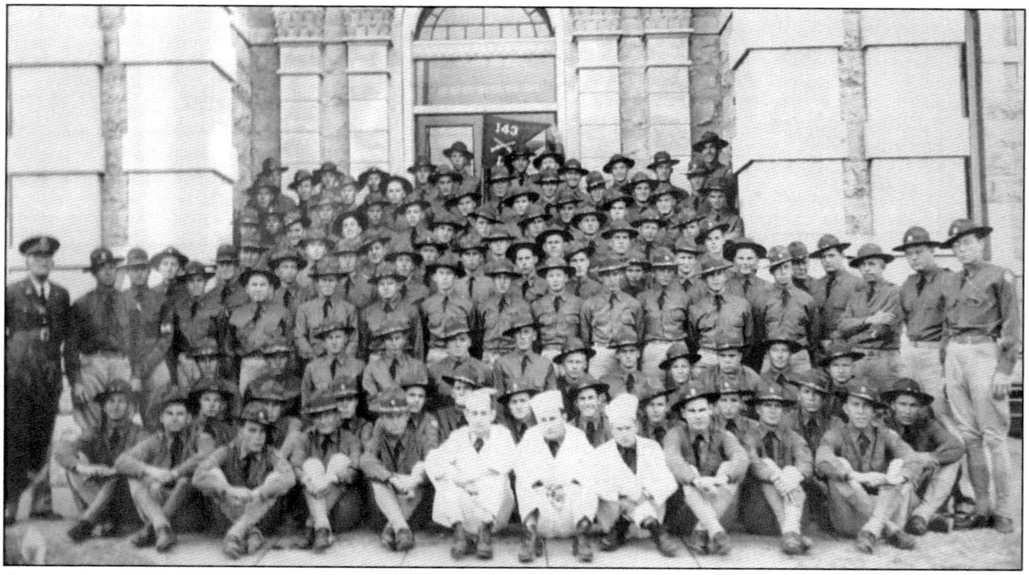

Succeeding Company M, the pre–World War I company that saw duty on the Mexican border and in France, was Company L, 143rd Infantry, Texas National Guard. The new unit was organized and mustered into service in 1921 with Capt. Horton B. Porter, who was instrumental in getting the 2nd Battalion Headquarters Company of the 143rd mustered to Hillsboro in 1930. (Cell Block Museum.)

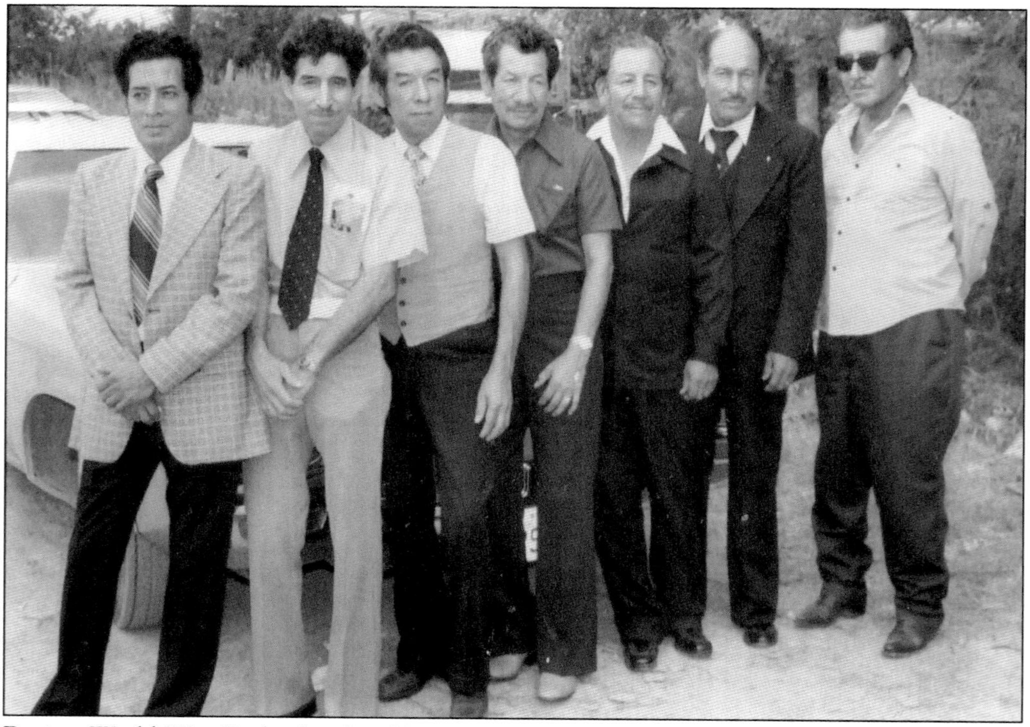

During World War II, the family of Lorenzo Ramirez, an MKT employee, sent seven sons to serve in the armed forces. The Ramirez brothers are seen here from left to right: Daniel, Steve, Joe, Joseph, Nick, Vicente, and Louis. Daughters Carmen and Josephine enlisted in the Marine Corps in 1957. (Texas Heritage Museum.)

Nelson Patterson Modrall was a Cumberland Presbyterian minister who located at Woodbury in Hill County by 1855 and purchased land from Rev. Thomas Newton McKee. Modrall was an early pastor of the Aquilla CP Church in Woodbury and helped organize the Aquilla (later Hillsboro) Masonic Lodge No. 196, chartered on January 22, 1857. Modrall wrote to an early Presbyterian publication, *Banner of Peace*, about the rich prairie lands surrounding the newly established town of Hillsboro. (Rose Mary Magrill.)

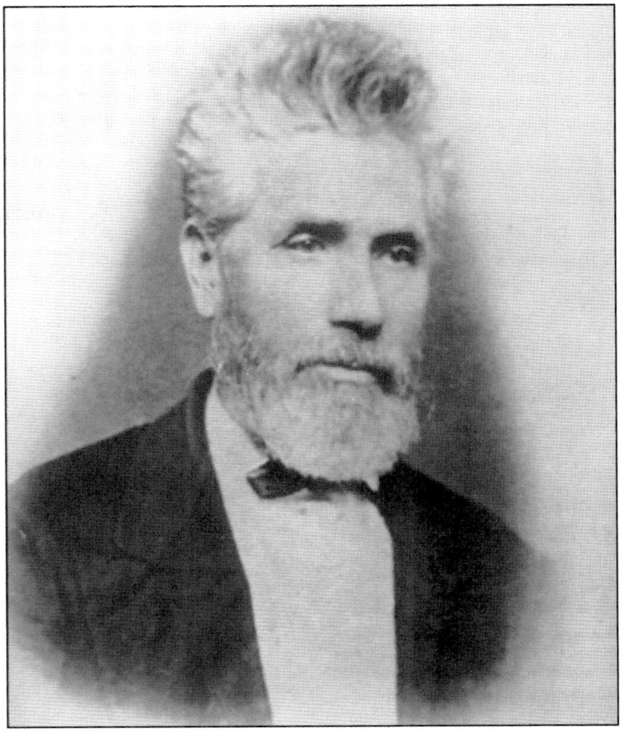

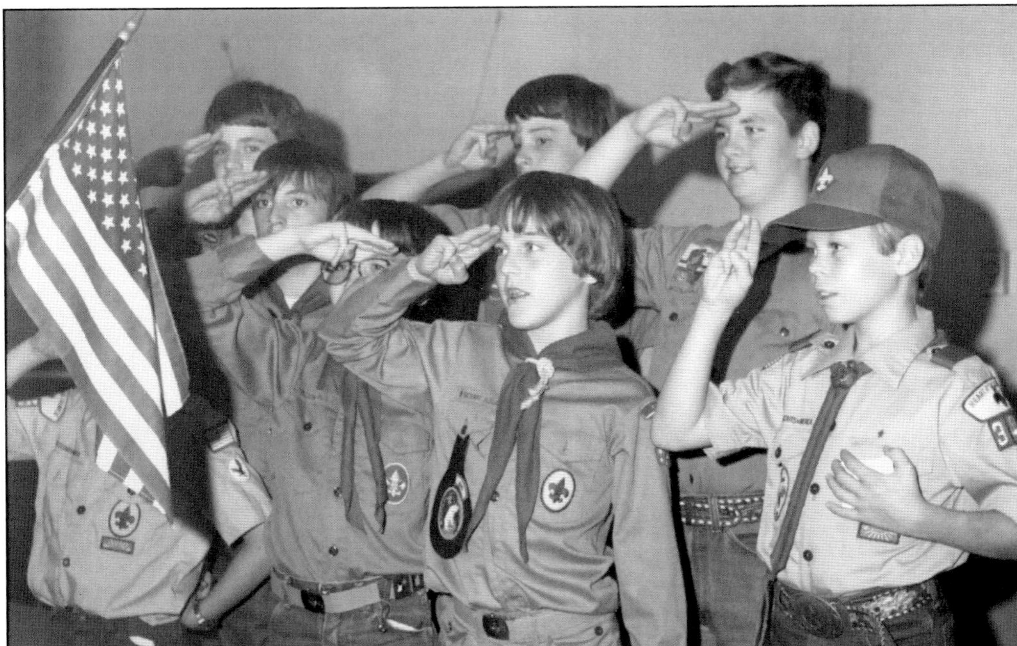

Troop 2, Boy Scouts of America, received its first charter from the national council in September 1922. Olin Culberson served as the first scoutmaster. The troop consisted of 30 regular scouts and three associate scouts, with meetings held in the county courtroom. Wilmer Sims was the first to attain the rank of Eagle Scout. Cecil Harris "Stubby" Stubblefield was a popular scoutmaster. Seen here are members of a 1984 troop.

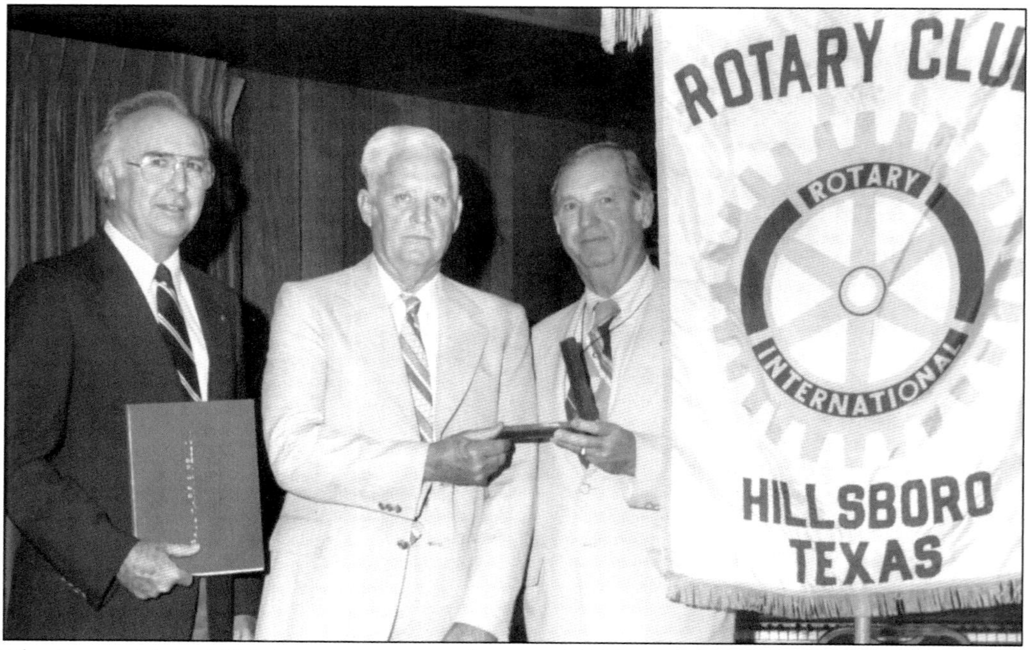

The Rotary Club of Hillsboro was organized in April 1921 in a meeting at the Wear Hotel. The first project was to develop Abbott's Grove as a city park. In 1935, the first award of Rotary Boy and Girl went to Hillsboro High School graduates Billy Patterson and Jane Ellis. Here, G. Ray Sawyer (left) receives the Paul Harris Fellowship Award from a Rotary official in 1984.

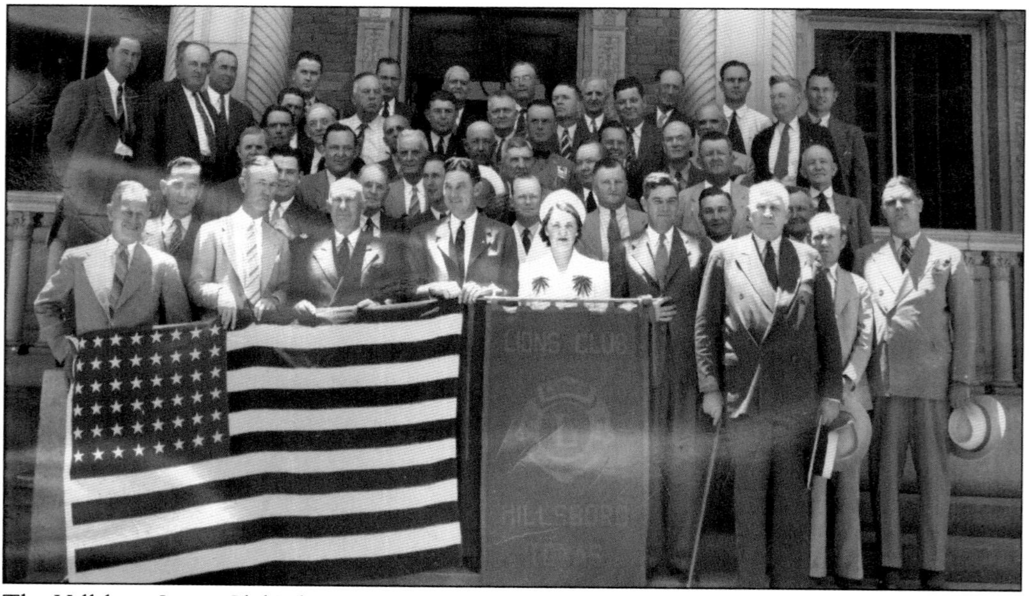

The Hillsboro Lions Club's first meeting was held on the south side of the square at 62 West Elm Street in the White Swan Café (Martin-Showers-Smith-McDonald) in November 1921. The club sponsored a Boy Scout troop and secured the paving of streets in front of the schools. This photograph shows Lions Club members on the steps of the Hillsboro post office during World War II. Frances Robertson Jackson was the pianist and the "club sweetheart." (Cell Block Museum.)

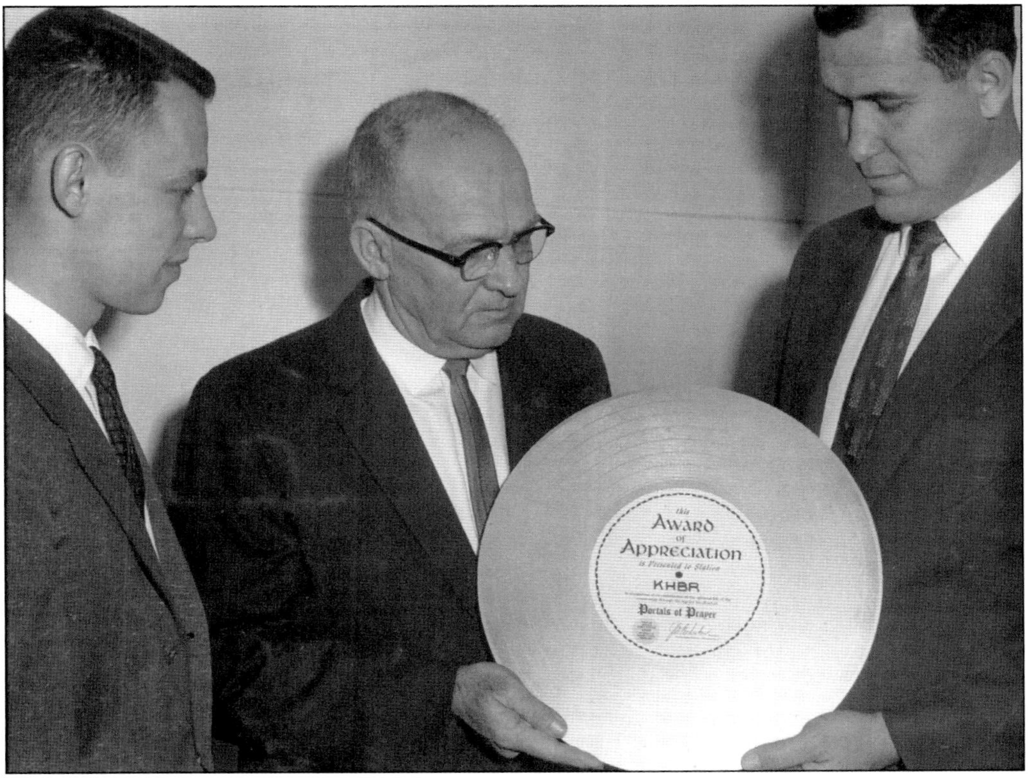

KHBR Radio (1560 AM) began broadcasting in 1947 and was purchased by Nelson Galle in 1950. The original studio was located near the Pruitt gin off old Highway 77/81 before a fire destroyed it in 1954. It first moved downtown, and then to its present home on Country Club Drive in 1962. Here, Henry Markwardt (left) and Christ Lutheran Church pastor Herbert Borchelt present Galle with an Award of Appreciation in 1959. (Christ Lutheran Church.)

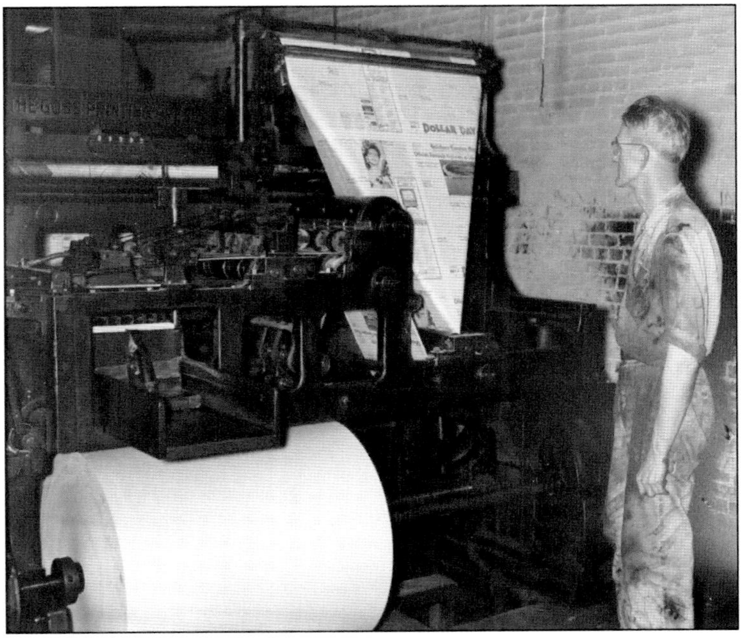

Lois Reagan prepares to print copies of the *Hillsboro Evening Mirror* in the mid-1950s on the Goss International flatbed press that served the newspaper for decades. In 1959, the name was changed to the *Hillsboro Daily Mirror* after being purchased by the Great Bend (Kansas) Tribune Company from Dallas financier M.M. Donosky. The *Mirror* became a daily newspaper in 1896 and ceased publication in 1972. (Jack Loftis.)

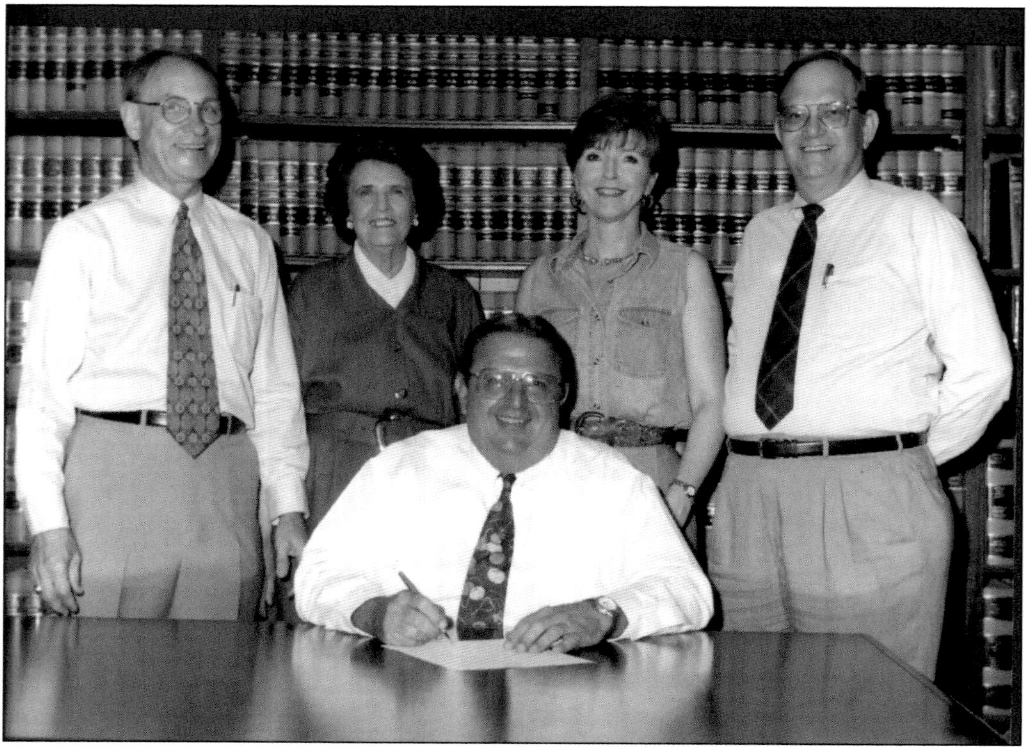

The Hillsboro Heritage League was chartered on April 27, 1976. The application for the original charter was submitted by Bitsy Gannon, Barbara Smith, and Virginia Ringer. The league pledged to preserve and restore the heritage, perpetuate the customs, and enrich the community life of Hillsboro. Above, Hillsboro mayor Henry Moore signs a proclamation for Preservation Month in 1995. The officers, standing from left to right, are Gene Smith, vice president; Virginia Ringer, treasurer; Janice Summerhill, secretary; and Will Lowrance, president. The Junior Heritage League (below) had its first organizational meeting on April 6, 1981, and went on to become the Junior Historian Chapter at Hillsboro Junior High School. Youth who were interested in learning about and preserving the history of the area were invited to join.

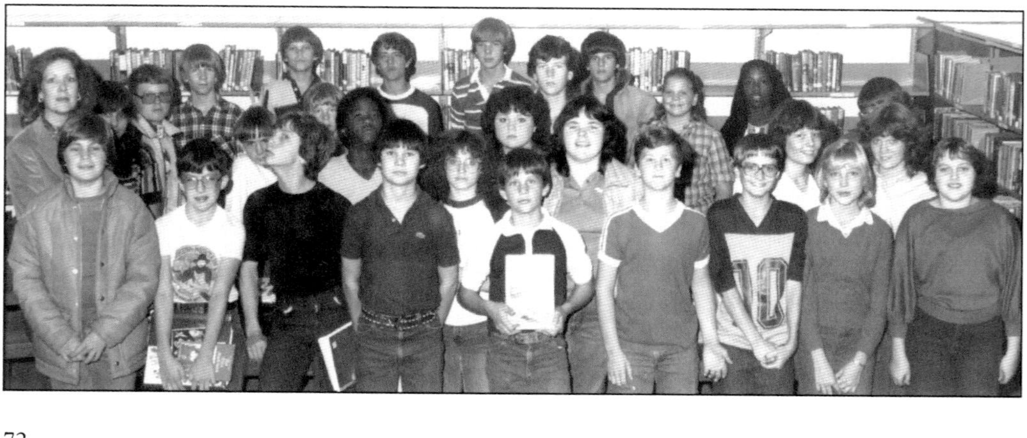

Six

Home and Hearth

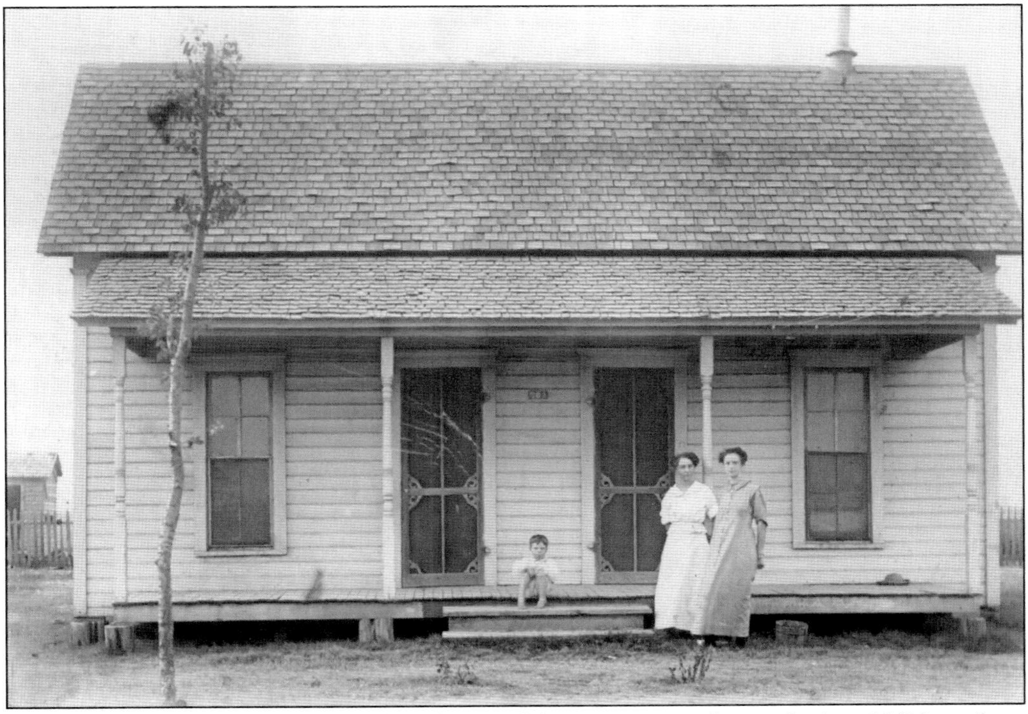

This type of architecture was typical for the wood-frame, one-story houses built in Hillsboro from the late 1870s to the early 1890s. The coming of the MKT Railroad and the expanding cotton industry stimulated the growth of the town and brought prosperity to its citizens. An era of brick construction began in the fall of 1881.

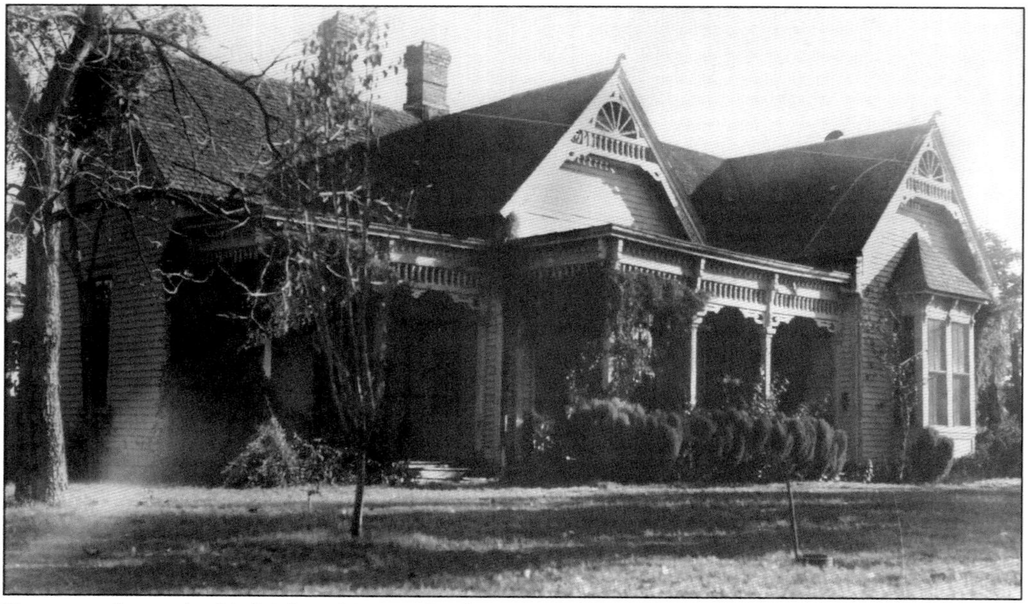

Known today as the Turk-Maier House, this home, at 227 East Franklin Street, was built of cypress in the Victorian style in 1890 for Judge Benjamin Dudley Tarlton. Exterior modifications in the 1920s transformed the home to the Prairie style of architecture. The home was the residence of T.P. Turk, part owner of a mercantile establishment. His oldest daughter, Pearl, lived in the house and married C.W. Maier, the mayor of Hillsboro from 1931 to 1935.

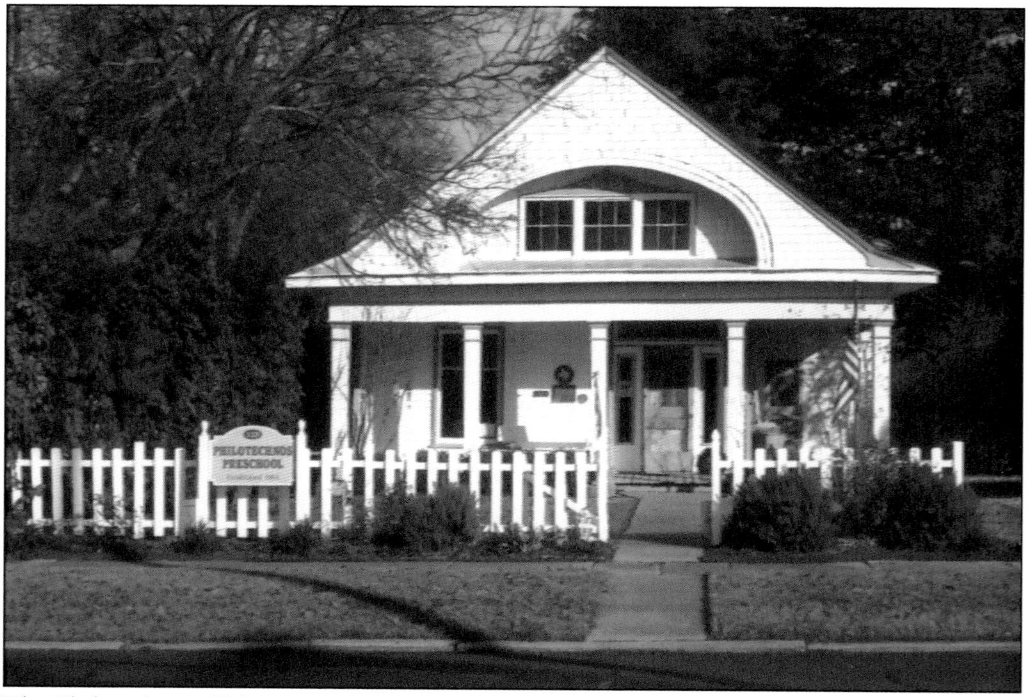

The Philotechnos Club, a group of young mothers, organized in 1950 in the home of Margaret Martin. The Philotechnos Preschool was a product of this organization, and classes were held in this historic home at 133 Corsicana Street, originally built by Judge Jo Abbott for his son James Abbott and his wife, Nancy, in 1896.

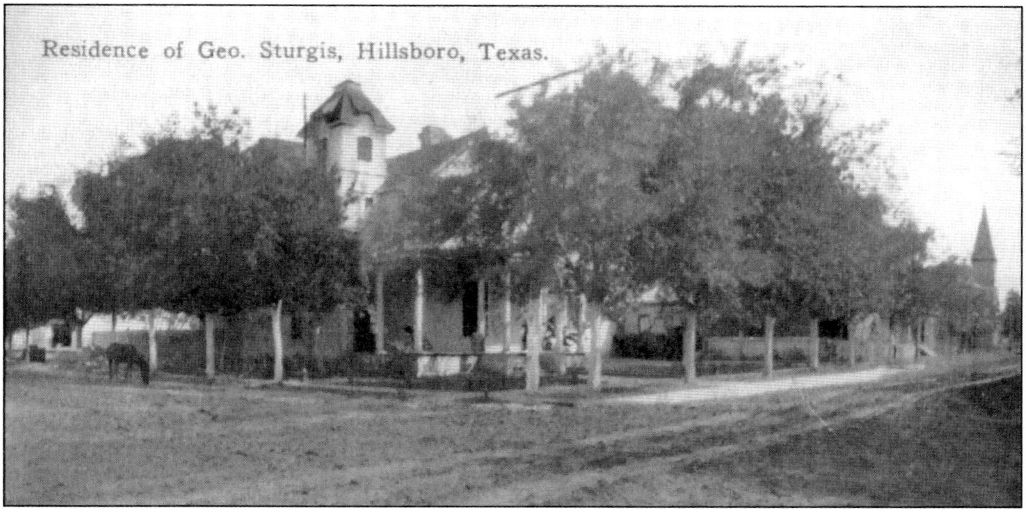

George Sturgis, the president of Sturgis National Bank, built this Queen Anne–style home at 114 Craig Street. The home is seen here in 1893, shaded by tall trees and with a horse grazing on the left. Visible to the right is the spire of Central Christian Church, at the southeast corner of Craig and Pleasant Streets. Before his death in 1887, George and his wife, Julia Vineyard Sturgis, had moved to a new home at 405 Corsicana Street.

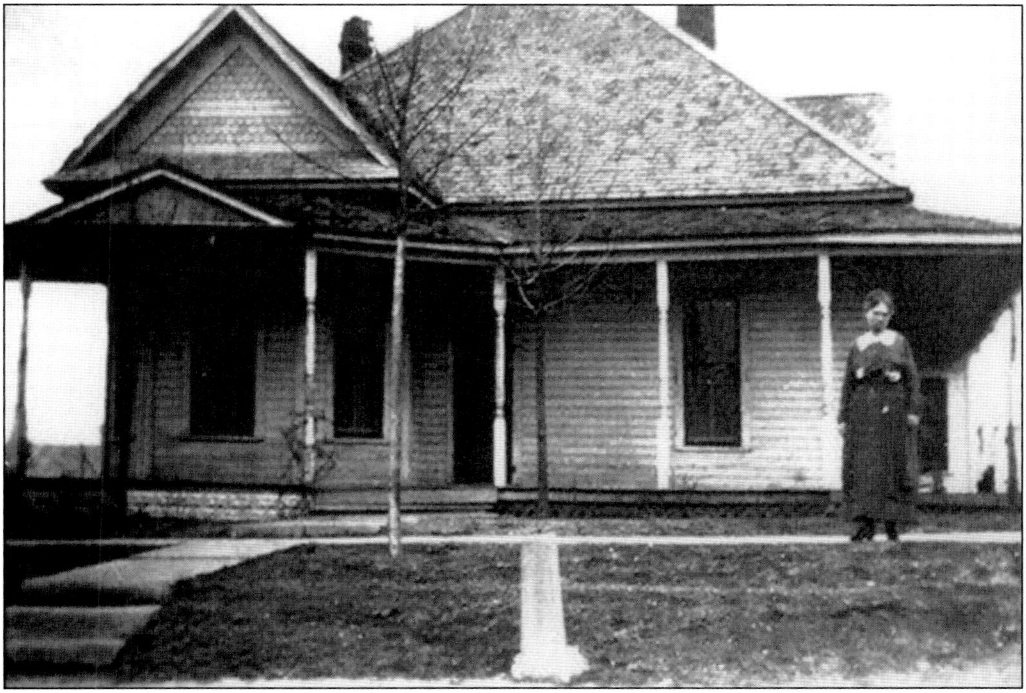

One of the oldest houses still standing in Hillsboro, this wood-frame, late Victorian–style home with a wraparound porch was built by William L. Booth, an attorney who settled in Hillsboro in 1854. His daughter Lucinda, seen here in front of the home, lived in the house, at 206 North Waco Street, until it was purchased by Fred Long, the Hill County sheriff, for his family in 1918. Sheriff Long's daughter Minnie Beall Long lived there until 1989.

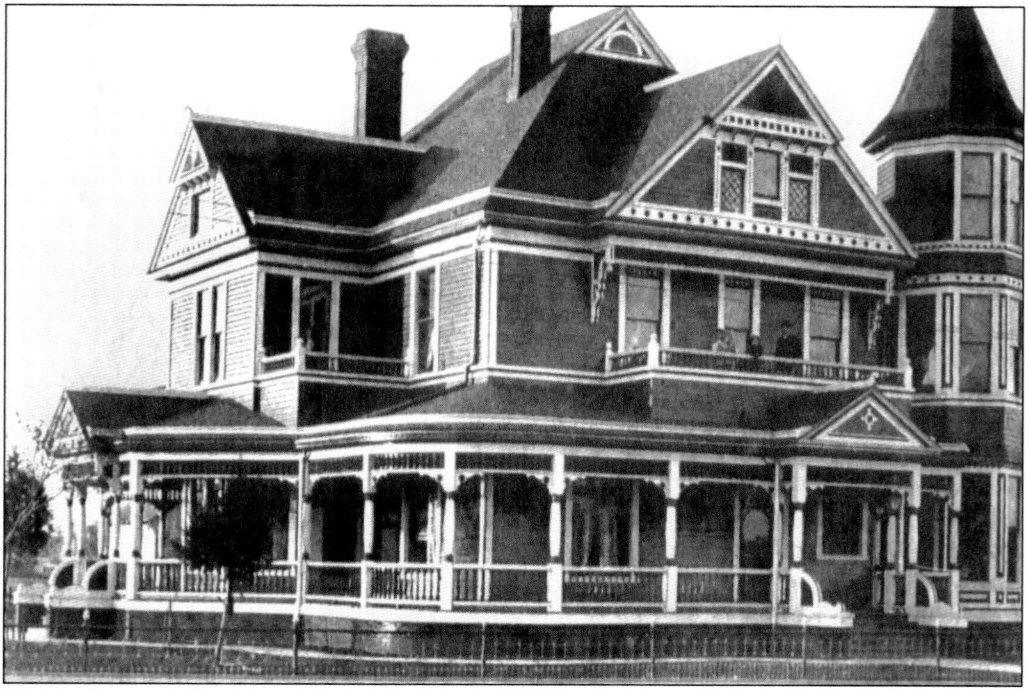

This architecturally commanding home, at 130 Corsicana Street, was built in 1898 by Edward S. Davis, a civic leader, cotton producer, and banker. Davis was active in Farmers National Bank and was a licensed engineer. Fine Victorian ornamentation decorates the tiles, floors, and windows of his house. Note the people standing on the second-floor balcony. The Davis family lived in the home until 1960, according to the Hill County Historical Commission.

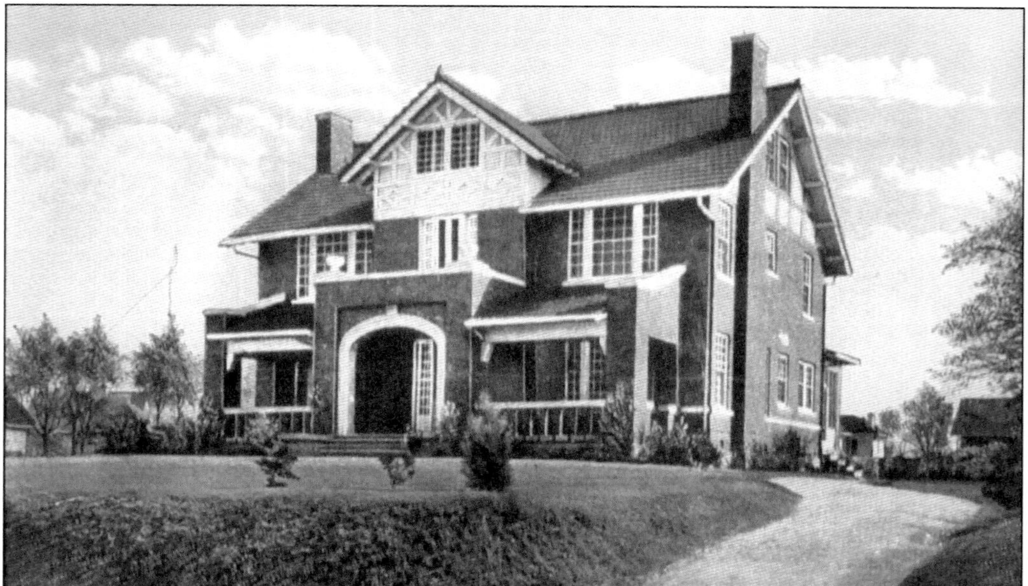

This stately home was constructed in 1913 for Hillsboro banker William M. Williams and his wife, Mary, at 414 Corsicana Street. Its architectural style has sometimes been described as eclectic, but it is essentially a Prairie-style home with Mediterranean influences, as seen with the French tile roof. The Tudor style is also prominent in the half-timber decorative accents of the gables.

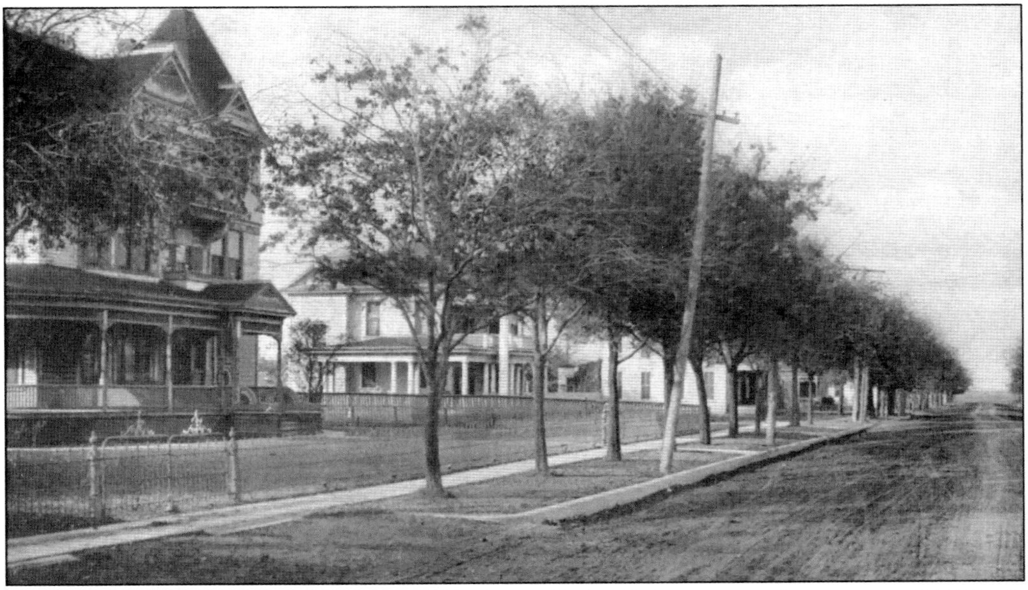

The Victorian home on the left was built by Greene Duke Tarlton, a noted attorney, at 211 North Pleasant Street. The home was one of the finest in town, with hand-carved mantels, stained-glass windows, a "speaking tube" between the kitchen and a third-floor bedroom, and a dumbwaiter. A cistern on the back porch supplied cool water year-round. Outbuildings included a stable and a coach house, according to the Hill County Historical Commission.

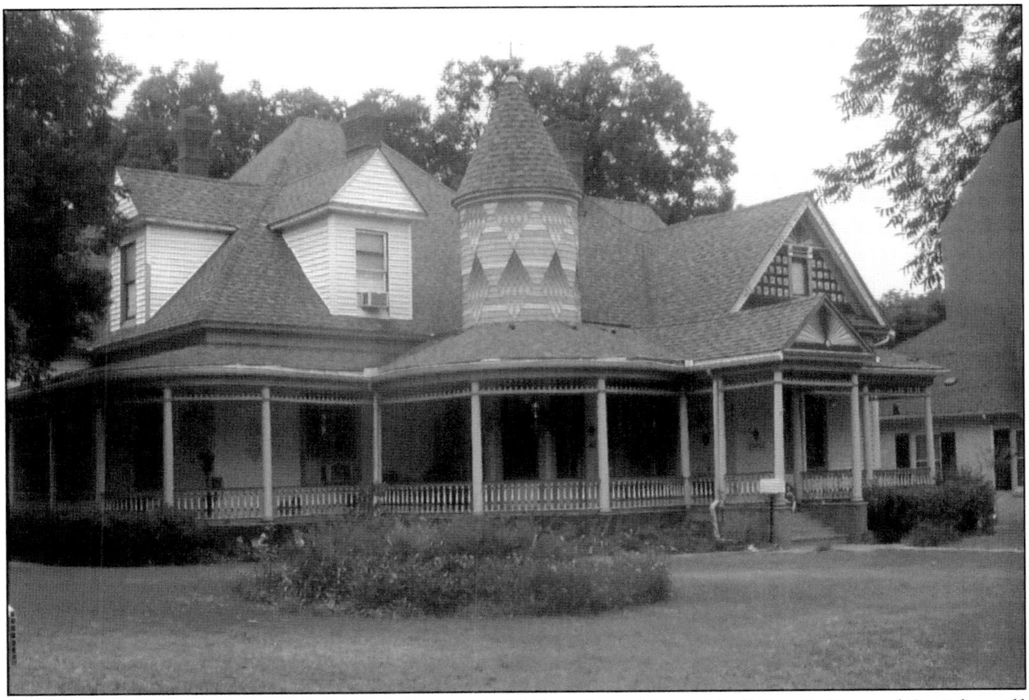

The 1896 Victorian home of Andrew Lewis "A.L" Smith and his wife, Minnie Stroud Smith, still stands at 444 Craig Street. Smith was the president of Citizens National Bank and Hillsboro Cotton Mills and was co-owner of Smith & Tomlinson Hardware at the time of his death in 1930.

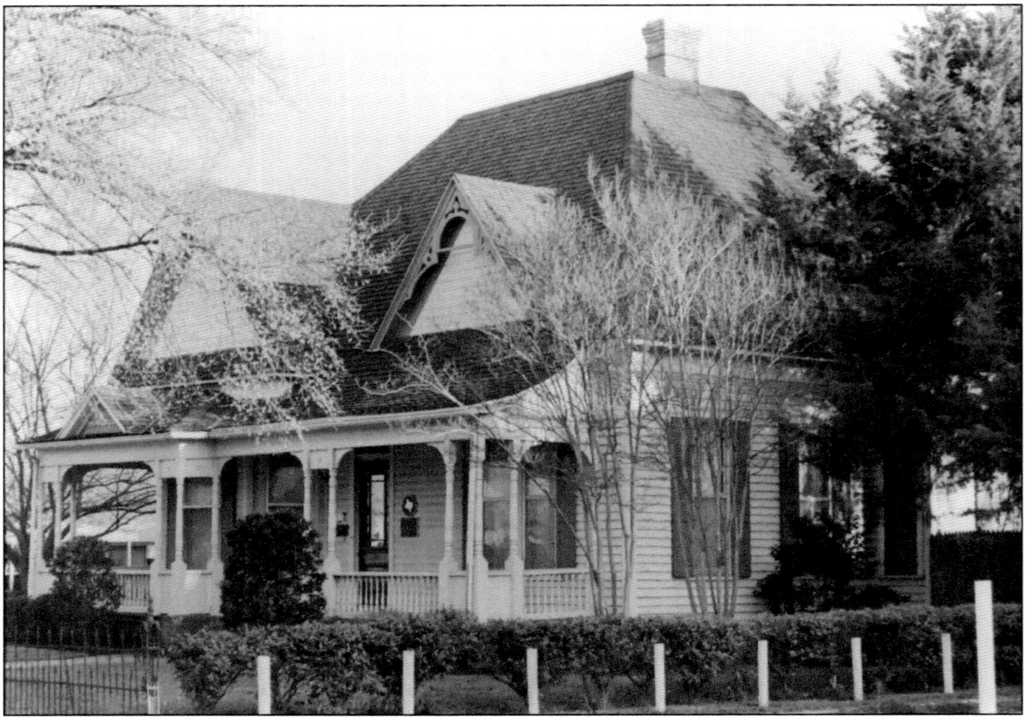

In an era of growth after the railroad came to Hill County, contractor John Self Robinson built this residence around 1882 for R.S. Lumpkin and his wife, Mary, at 418 East Franklin Street, according to the Hill County Historical Commission. The style of the house reflects the success of Lumpkin as an early saddle and harness maker. The home is a Queen Anne–style cottage surrounded by an iron fence.

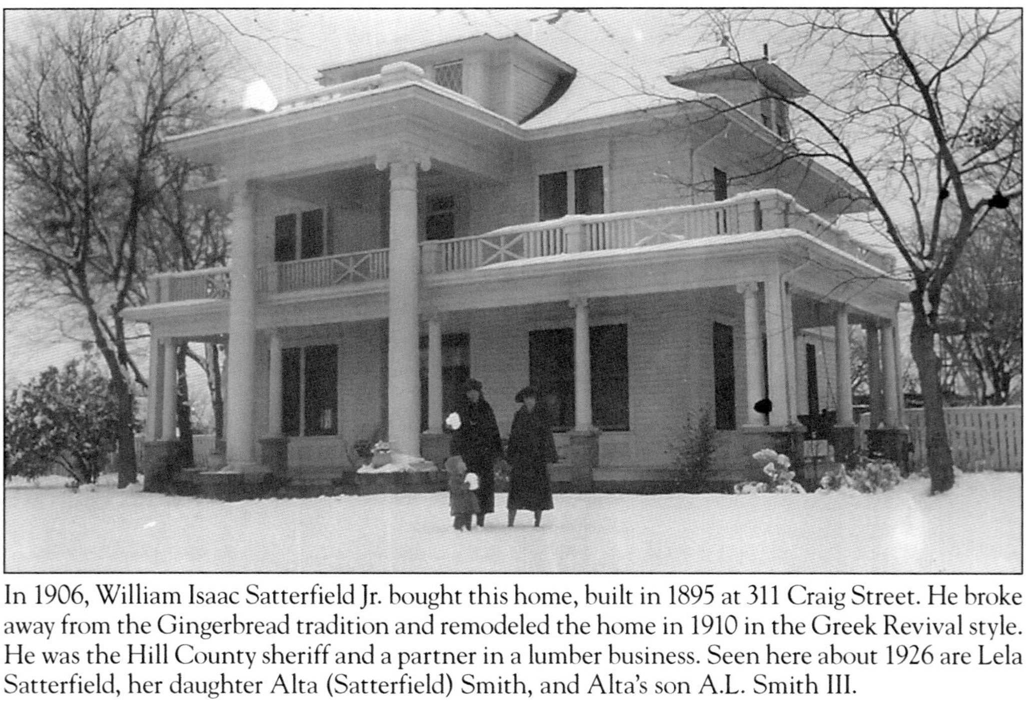

In 1906, William Isaac Satterfield Jr. bought this home, built in 1895 at 311 Craig Street. He broke away from the Gingerbread tradition and remodeled the home in 1910 in the Greek Revival style. He was the Hill County sheriff and a partner in a lumber business. Seen here about 1926 are Lela Satterfield, her daughter Alta (Satterfield) Smith, and Alta's son A.L. Smith III.

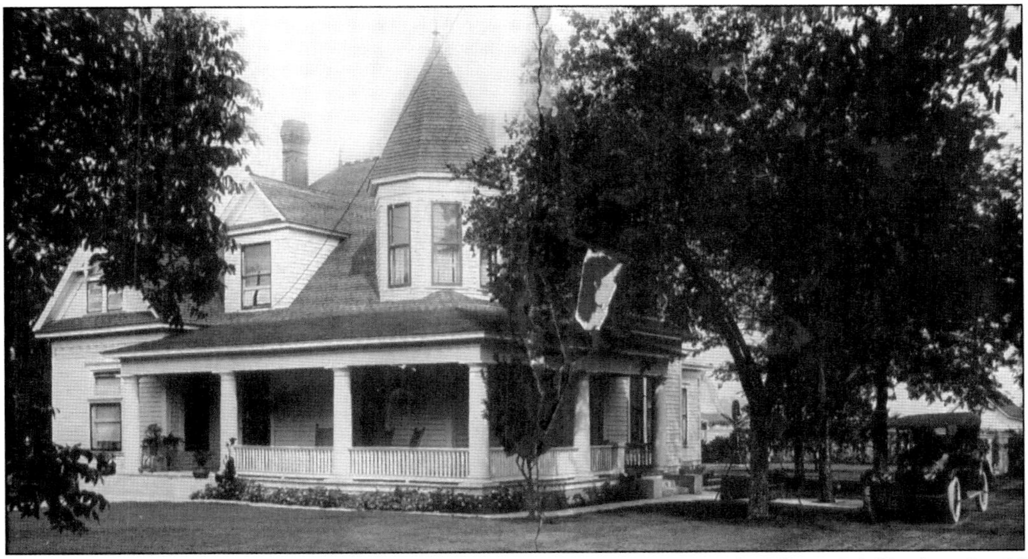

Hillsboro attorney Robert T. Jones and his wife, Mary, commissioned William M. Keith to build this Victorian Queen Anne residence in 1896 at 109 Corsicana Street. In 1917, it was purchased by Louis and Rebecca Brin. Born in Poland of Jewish descent, Louis Brin established L. Brin & Son Dry Goods Store and became a civic leader. Members of the Brin family owned the home until 1980, according to the Hill County Historical Commission.

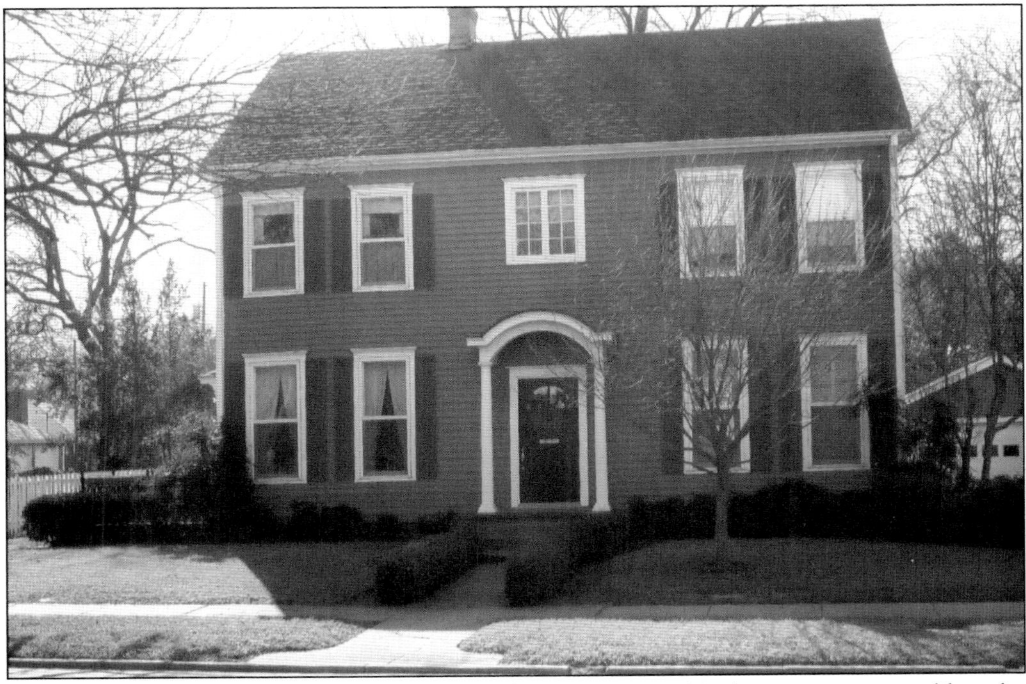

The original home at 130 Craig Street was built in 1892. In 1898, the property was sold to the present owner's great-grandparents, Rev. William H. and Allene Miller LeFevre. They established the LeFevre Insurance Agency in 1896. After her husband's death in 1900, Mrs. LeFevre became one of Hillsboro's earliest businesswomen. The house was substantially rebuilt in 1930–1931.

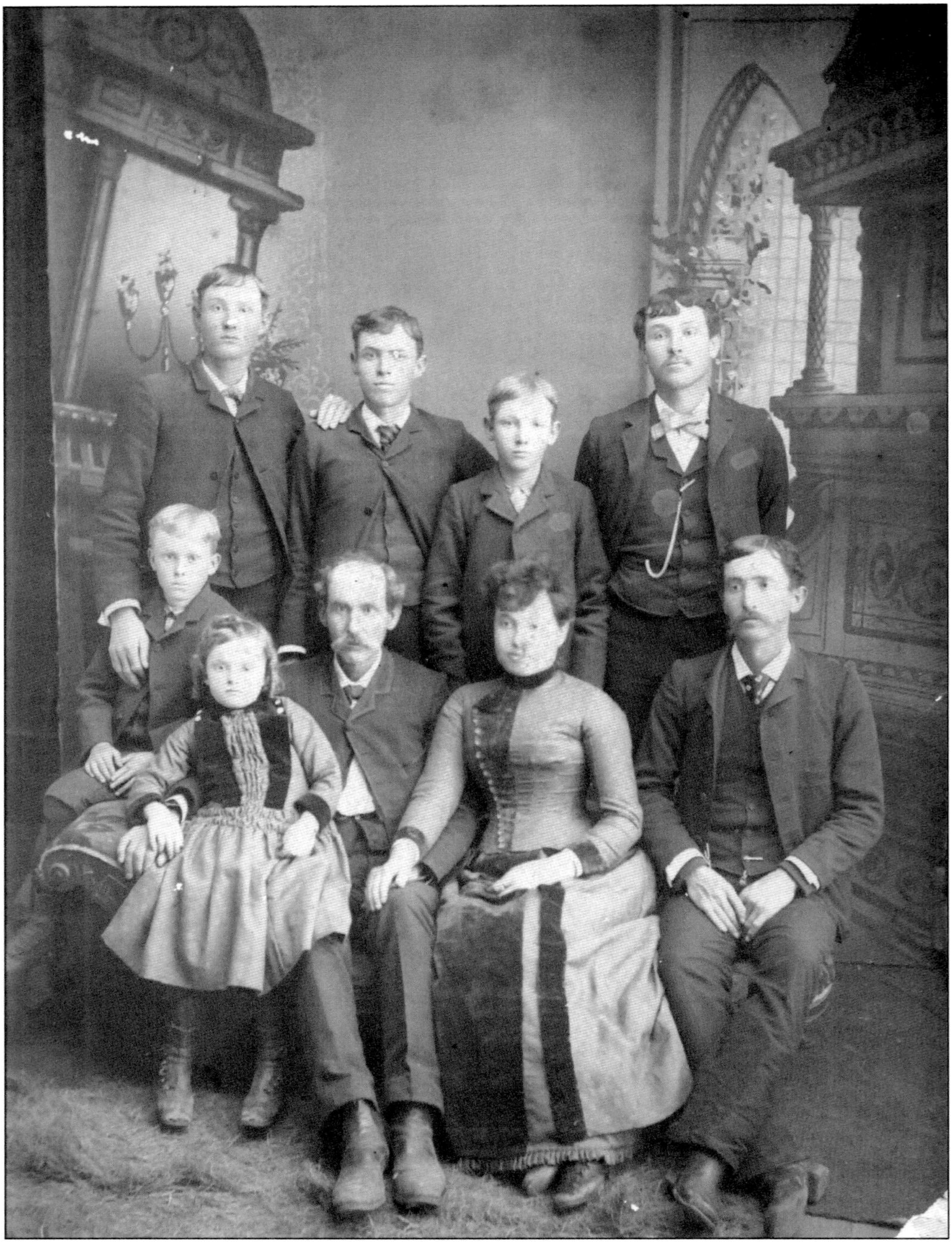

James Franklin "Frank" and Amanda Cato Marshall moved to Hill County after 1880. Their eight children, seven of whom are seen here with their parents, were Anna, Ford, Gilbert, Maggie, George, Smith, Clair, and Morris Franklin. Ford Marshall was the father of Glenn and Louie Marshall, the founders of Marshall and Marshall Funeral Home. Gilbert Marshall was the father of J. Robert Marshall, an early partner in the business who then established Marshall Insurance Company. Smith Marshall was a longtime Hill County law enforcement officer, and M. Frank Marshall Sr. was the father of M. Frank Marshall Jr., a partner in Marshall & Simmons Real Estate.

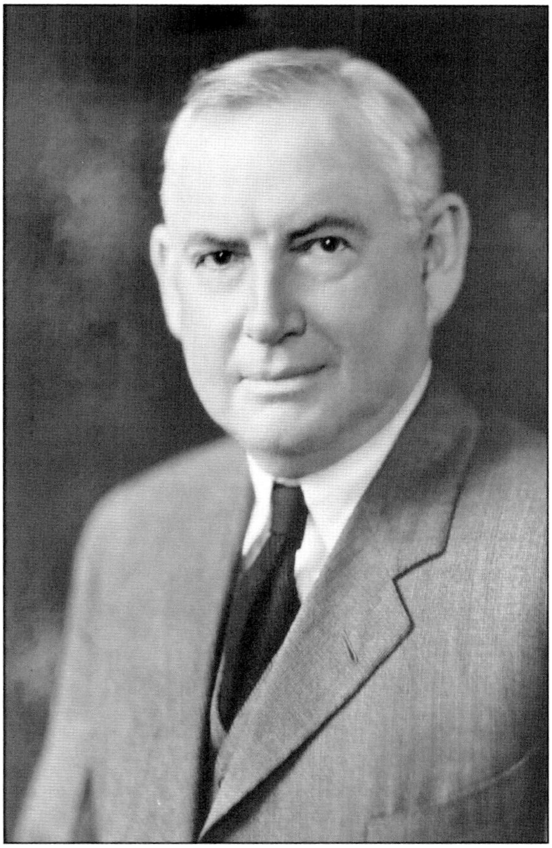

On April 14, 1920, after giving a round of speeches in support of the League of Nations, former president William Howard Taft spent the night in the residence of Edward Woodall (right), a former mayor and the secretary-treasurer of the Colonial Trust Company. Located at 412 East Franklin Street, the house (below) was built for the Woodalls around 1911. It includes influences from the eclectic, Prairie, and Classical Revival styles.

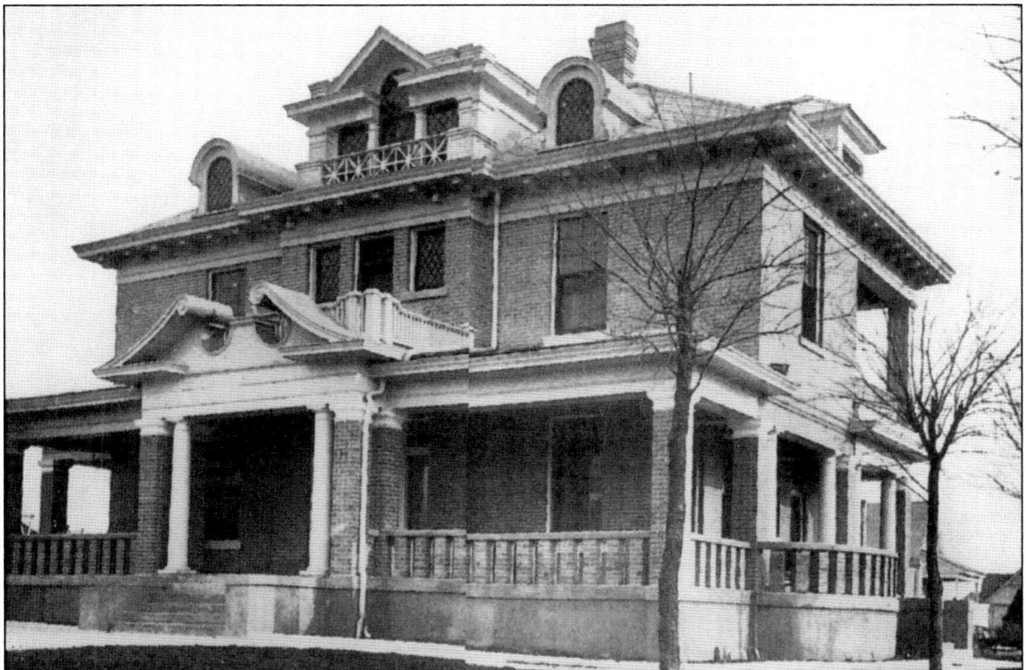

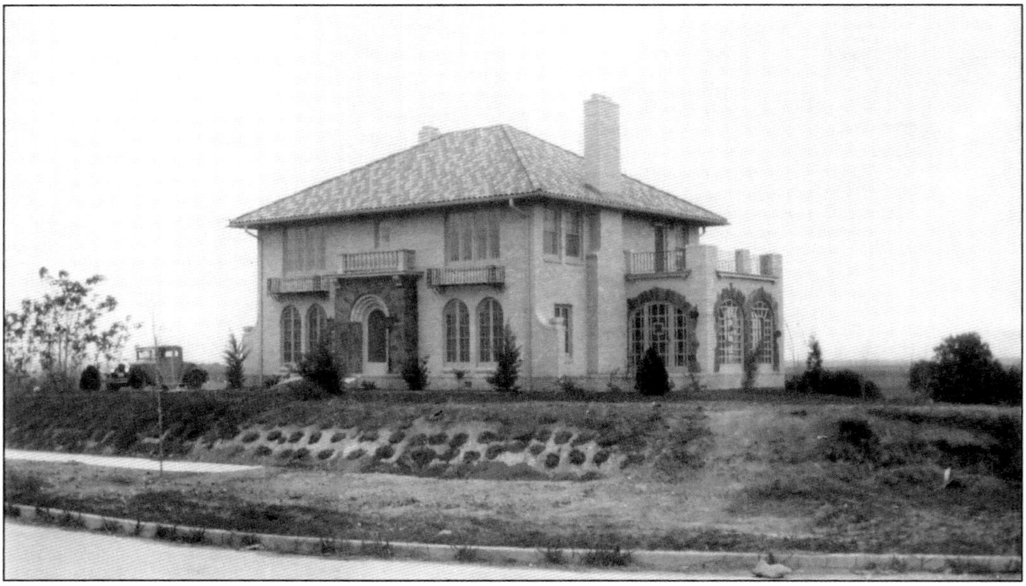

The home of Andrew Lewis "A.L." Smith Jr. and his wife, Alta Satterfield Smith, was built in the Mediterranean Revival style. Construction was completed on the house, at 415 Corsicana Street, in 1929. Smith was president of the Hillsboro Cotton Mill and Citizens National Bank.

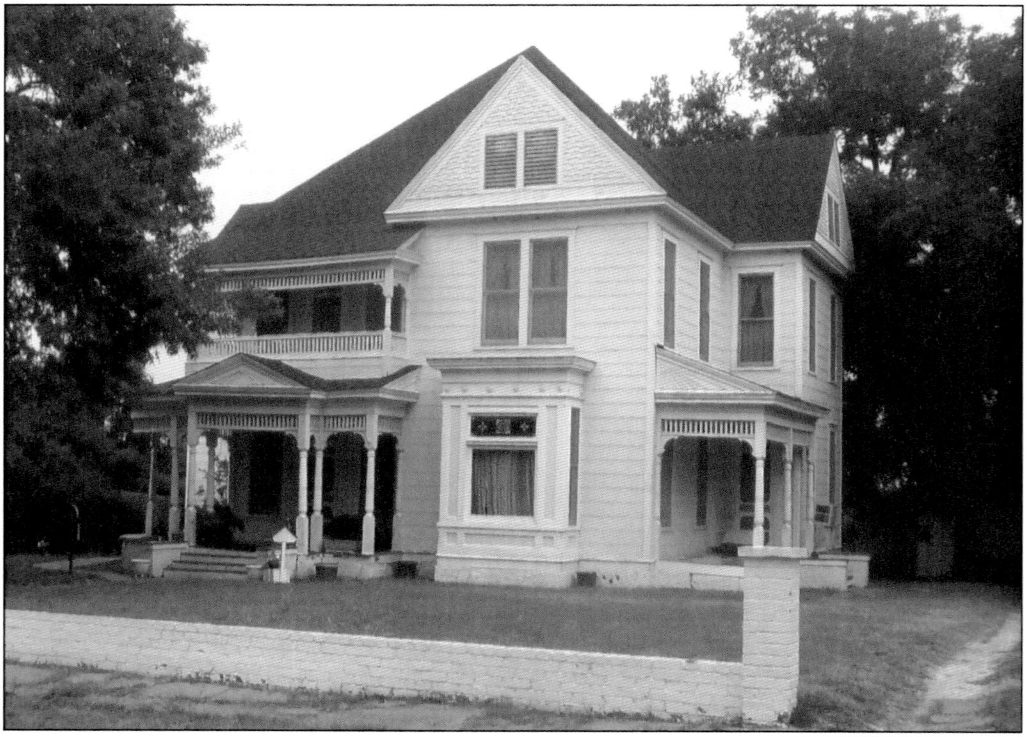

This Victorian style home with a "flying wing" staircase was erected in 1896 at 205 Corsicana Street by A.P. McKinnon, a prominent local attorney. He served as the Hill County attorney in 1878 and 1879. As recorded by the Hill County Historical Commission, the house sold in 1903 to Samuel Houston Anderson, a local banker, who lived there for 35 years. Nelson Phillips, chief justice of the Texas Supreme Court, roomed there soon after it was built.

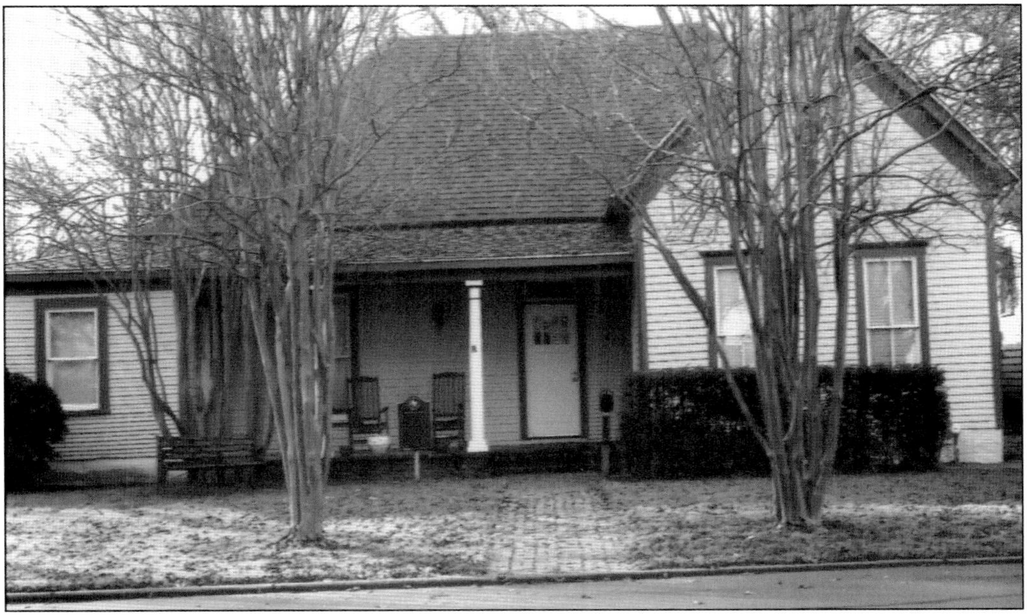

The original section of this house, which consisted of two rooms and a detached kitchen, was built before 1870. Later additions were made during the ownership of Dr. William Thomas Sims, who purchased the property in 1906. Dr. Sims, a dentist, was also a leader in church and civic activities. In later years, Leroy and Lalia Womack owned the residence, at 104 Corsicana Street, as recorded by the Hill County Historical Commission.

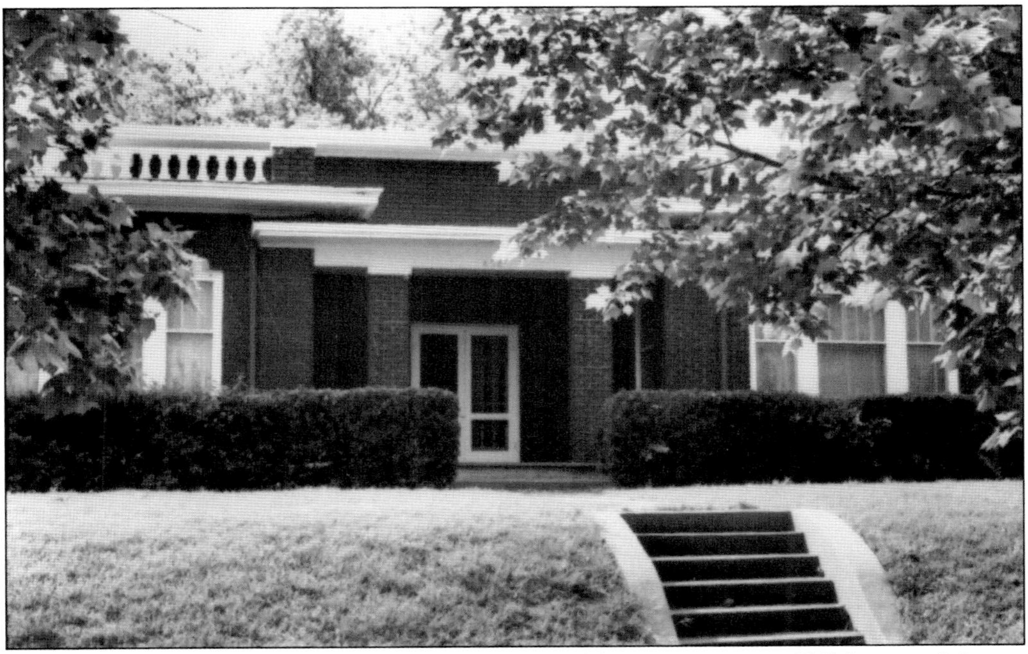

The 1920s brick home at 424 Corsicana Street is one of the most unique in Hillsboro, with low or flat rooflines, wide eaves, and a basement. Dr. Edwin Vaughan, a prominent Hillsboro physician, and his wife, Ada, who taught piano from the home for years, lived there until Ada's death in 1969. Ada Vaughan was an antique collector, a member of the Sesame Club, and was active in the work of the First Methodist Church.

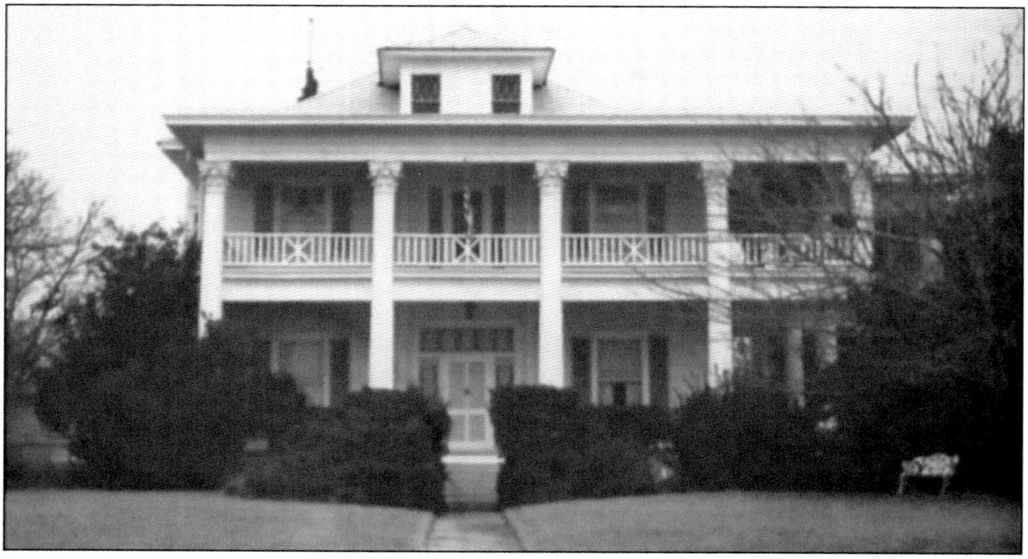

Purchased in 1889 from W.H. Abernathy, this home, at 313 Craig Street, was remodeled from the Gingerbread style into this Classical Revival–style home by Wesley Hardin Ellington in 1910. His family lived in a tent in the backyard until the work was complete. Ellington, along with George Murphy, opened the Mississippi Store on East Elm Street in 1891. Will and Louisa Bond purchased the home in 1949.

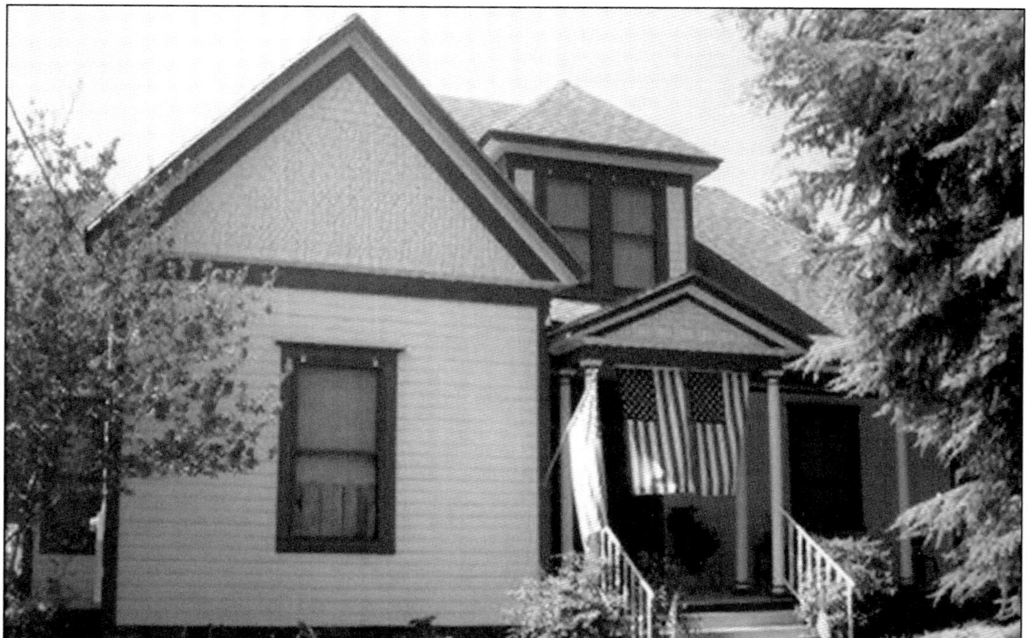

In 1881, George L. Porter married Roxie Brooks, the daughter of early Hill County official Cincinnatus Ney Brooks. The Porters were community leaders. In 1901, they hired Roxie's brother O.D. Brooks to construct this Queen Anne–style house at 400 Corsicana Street, which features a wraparound porch, Tuscan columns, decorative shingling, and a massed plan with a hipped roof and cross gables. Will and Betty Lowrance restored the home in 1985, and the property was designated a Recorded Texas Historic Landmark in 2004.

Greek immigrants Gus and Angelica Andrews are seen here with their daughter Catherine. Along with Gus's brother Jim and his family, they owned and operated the famed Andrews Café, at 103 South Waco Street, from 1916 to 1969. They served famous people like Pres. Lyndon B. Johnson, Vice Pres. John Nance Garner, W. Lee O'Daniel, John Wayne, Roy Rogers and Dale Evans, Elvis Presley, Mae West, Hank Williams, and others on Irish-linen tablecloths made by Angelica. (Catherine Andrews.)

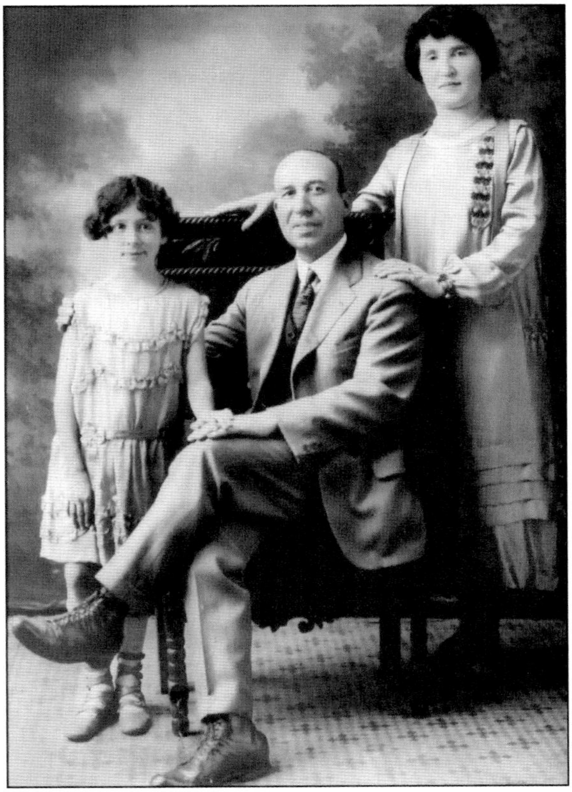

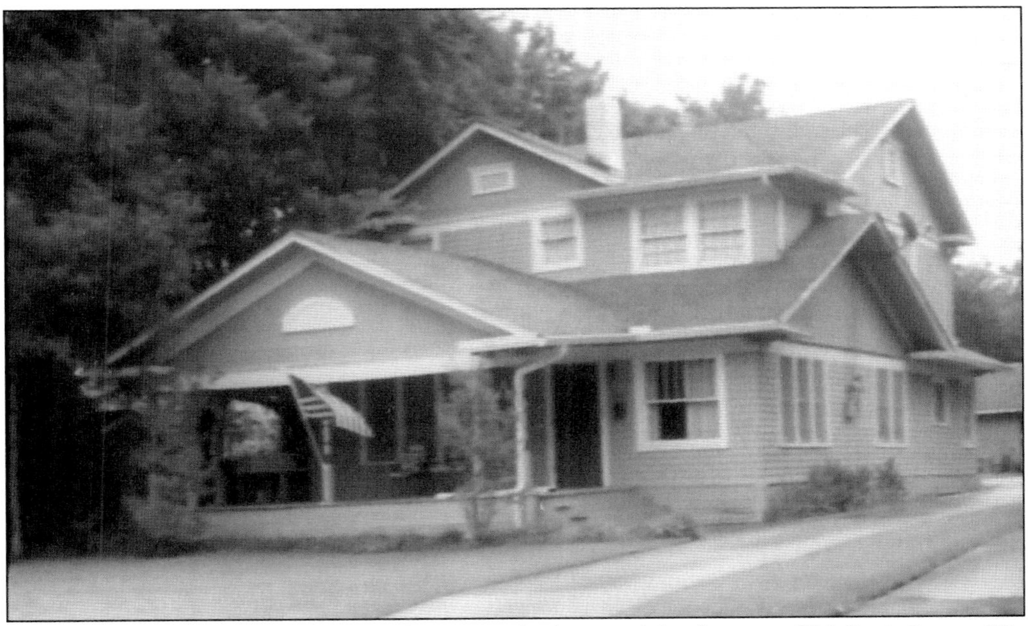

Lt. Gov. Bob Bullock was born in a downstairs bedroom of this home at 504 Craig Street. His parents, Thomas and Ruth Bullock, moved to Hillsboro in 1919 when Thomas became an engineer and water superintendent for the City of Hillsboro. Thomas was responsible for major projects such as the city storm water system, the First Methodist Church rebuilding project, Doughty Hall, the Hill County Fairgrounds, and other landmarks.

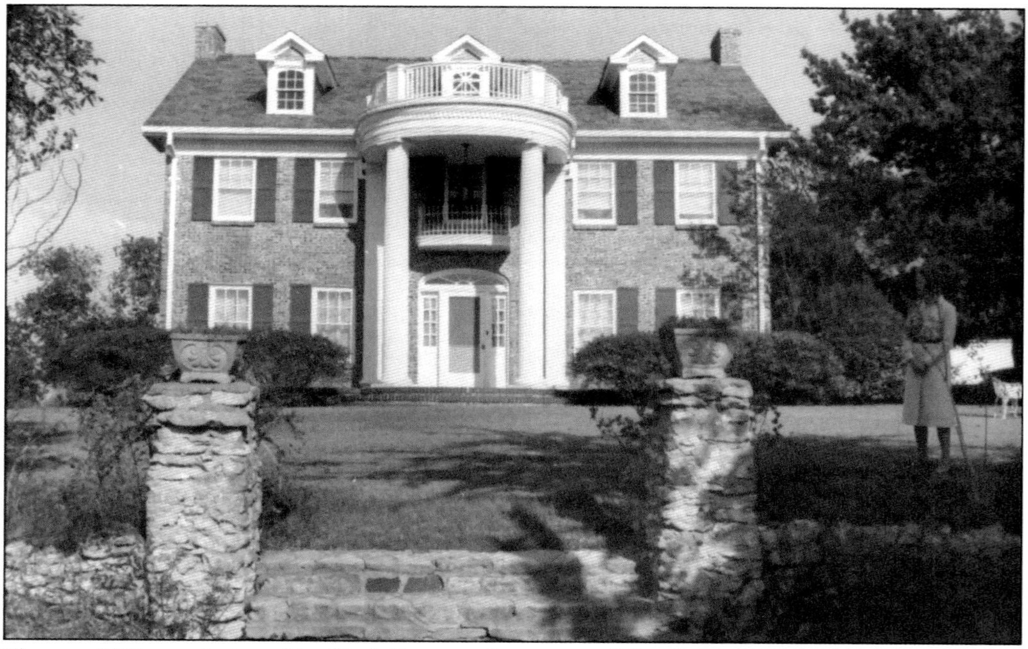

Pleasant Hill was designed by Fred Grimes, the owner of the famous Grimes Garage, as stated in *Heritage of Hill County*. The Grimes family home's exterior is made of Bridgeport Standard common brick, with a gray slate roof, white woodwork, dark green shutters, and a spacious red-tile front porch with imposing white Doric columns in the Georgian Revival style. The house is built on acreage that was on the eastern outskirts of Hillsboro in 1926.

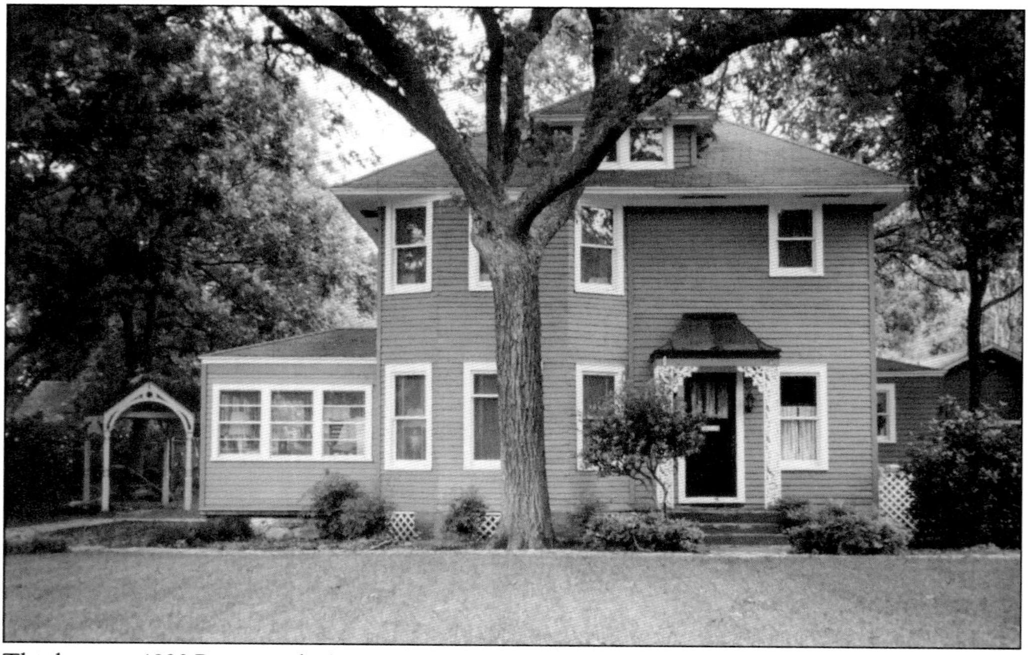

This home, a 1920 Prairie-style American Foursquare mail-order house, is located at 1112 Park Drive. The home was selected from a Harris Brothers catalog, shipped by rail from Chicago, and erected by Robert Kirkpatrick. Judge Frank McDonald recounted seeing the kit unloaded from the train and loaded onto a wagon pulled by two mules to the building site. (Robert and Carole Moore.)

Seven

Centers of Learning

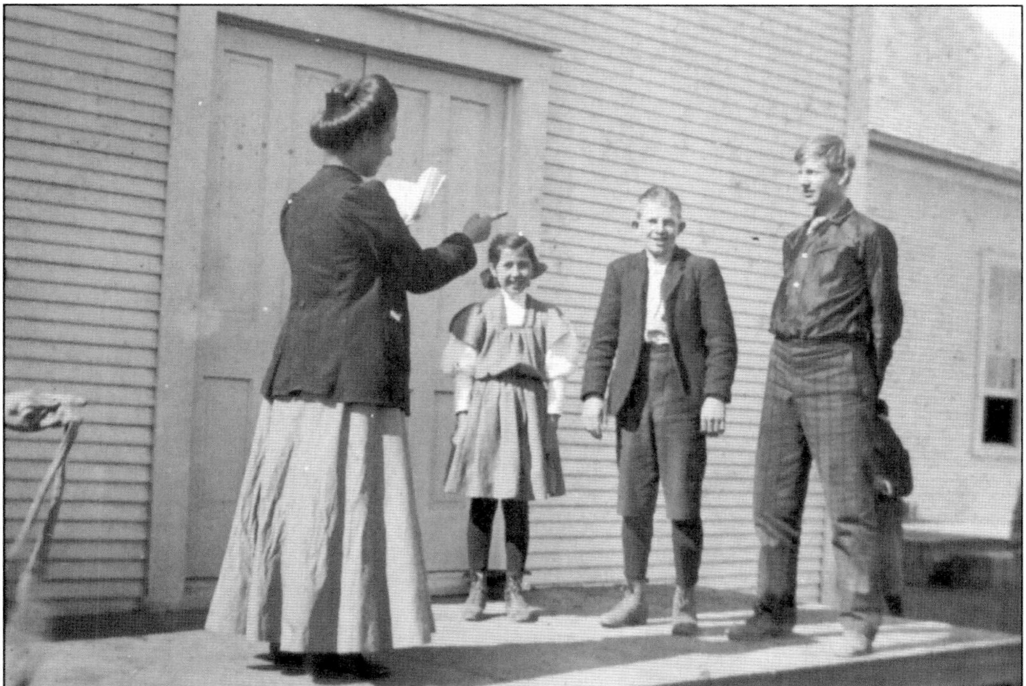

The first schoolhouse owned by Hill County was erected in Hillsboro at a cost of $20 in the fall of 1853 and served residents until 1860. Built of elm poles, it was located on a lot east of the public square, between East Elm and East Franklin Streets and fronting Church Street.

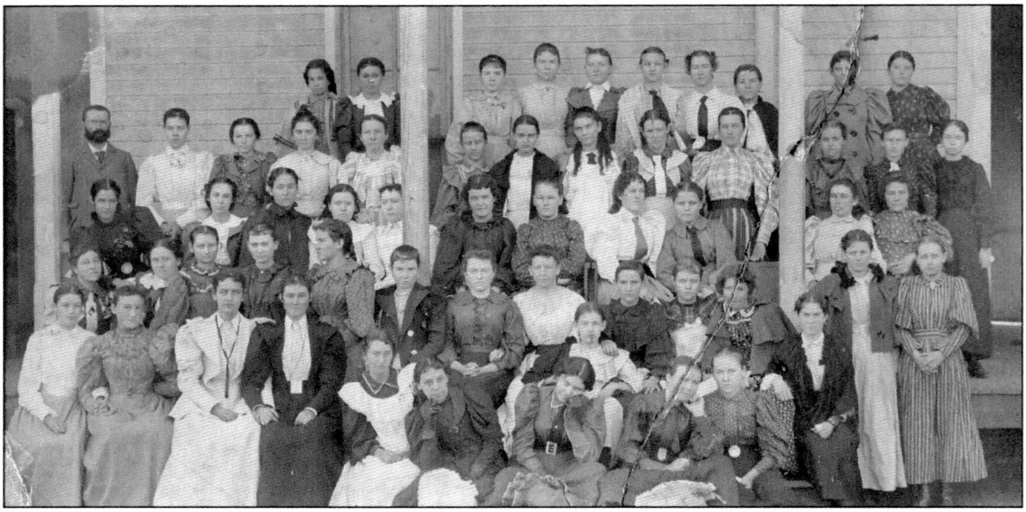

Rev. W.A. Patterson, the pastor of Hillsboro's Cumberland Presbyterian Church, established Patterson's Institute at 304–308 Corsicana Street in 1885. The school provided a dormitory for girls and a classroom building for primary school and college prep students. The faculty included Prof. Joseph Didiot, a native of France. The Pattersons left Hillsboro in 1900, and J.M. Carlisle, the former state superintendent of public instruction, bought the school and operated it for a year until it closed. Seen here is a class of young ladies at Patterson's Institute around 1895.

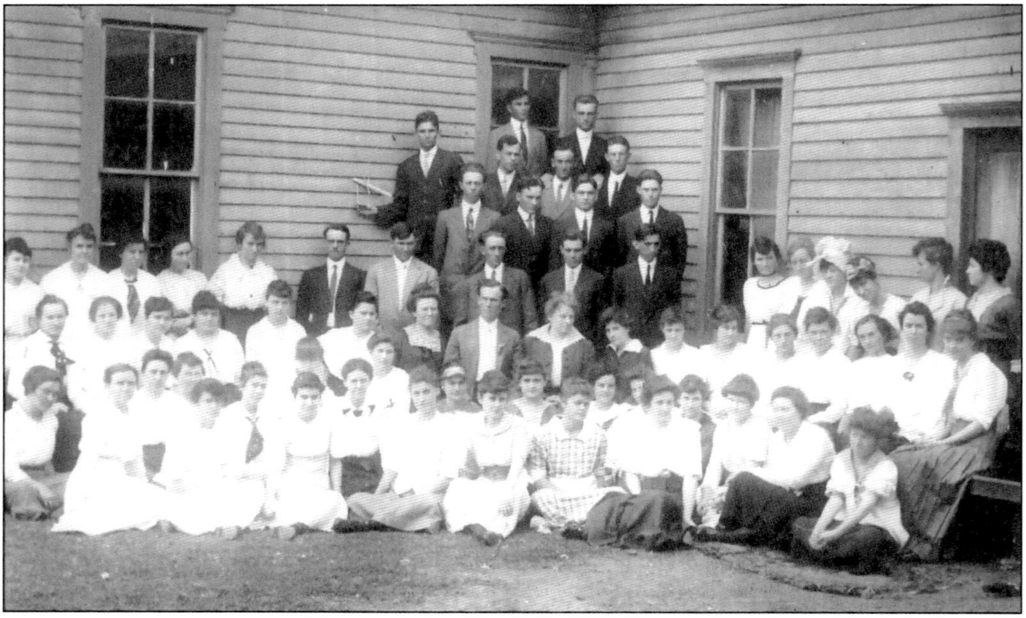

William and Martha Culberson operated Culberson Select School to prepare young men and women to take the state exams to become teachers. They moved the school to Hillsboro in 1893 from Woodbury, locating it on the corner of Walnut and New Streets, where they also had their home. This photograph is from about 1914. (Cell Block Museum.)

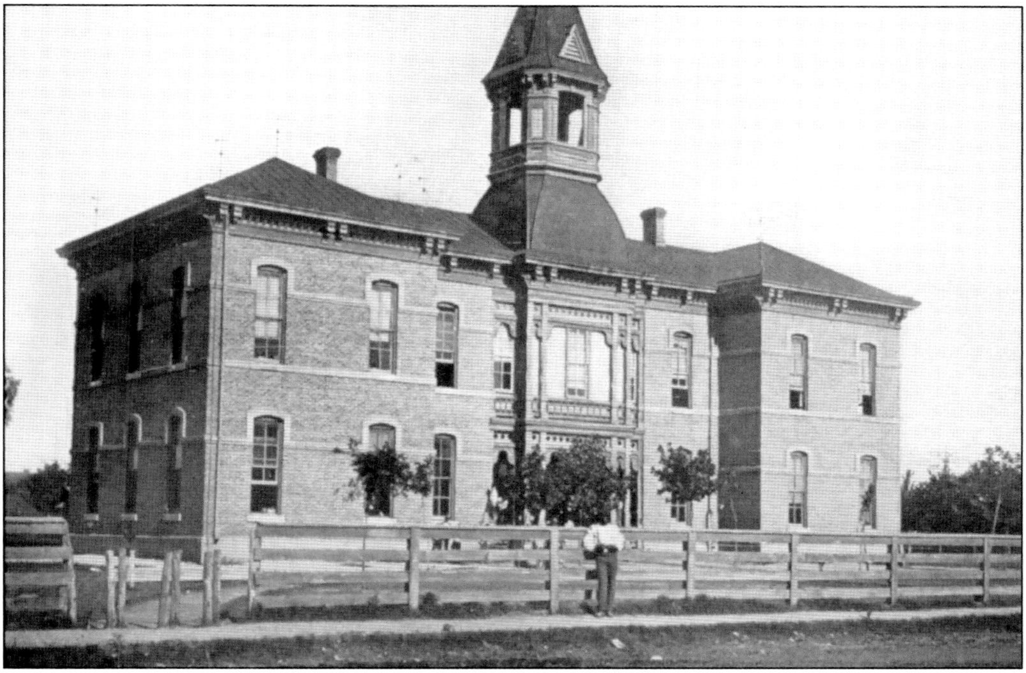

The city council, led by mayor E.B. Stroud in 1885, issued bonds to build a city hall that could also be used for public school purposes. In 1886, the brick building above was constructed on a lot at Franklin and Church Streets. Judge Jo Abbott was the master of ceremonies at the laying of the cornerstone, which drew 2,000 spectators. Named Central High School, the new building served Hillsboro students until 1906, when Hillsboro High School (below) was built at 310 East Walnut Street. The 1906 Hillsboro High School building burned in April 1922, and the new Junior College/High School building was erected on the footprint of the original building and opened for classes in September 1923.

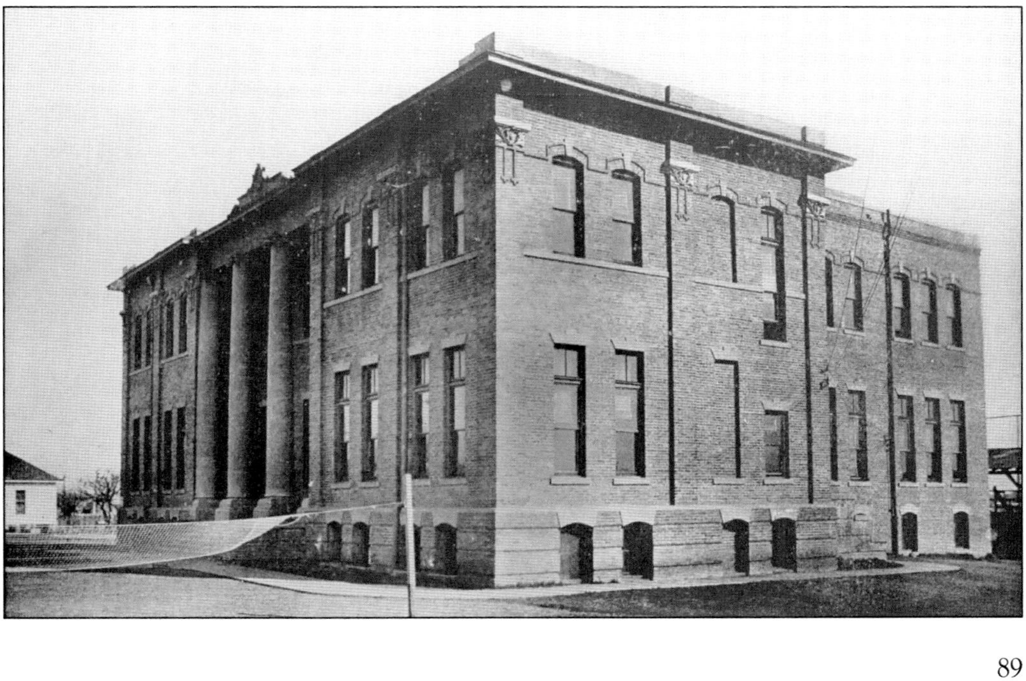

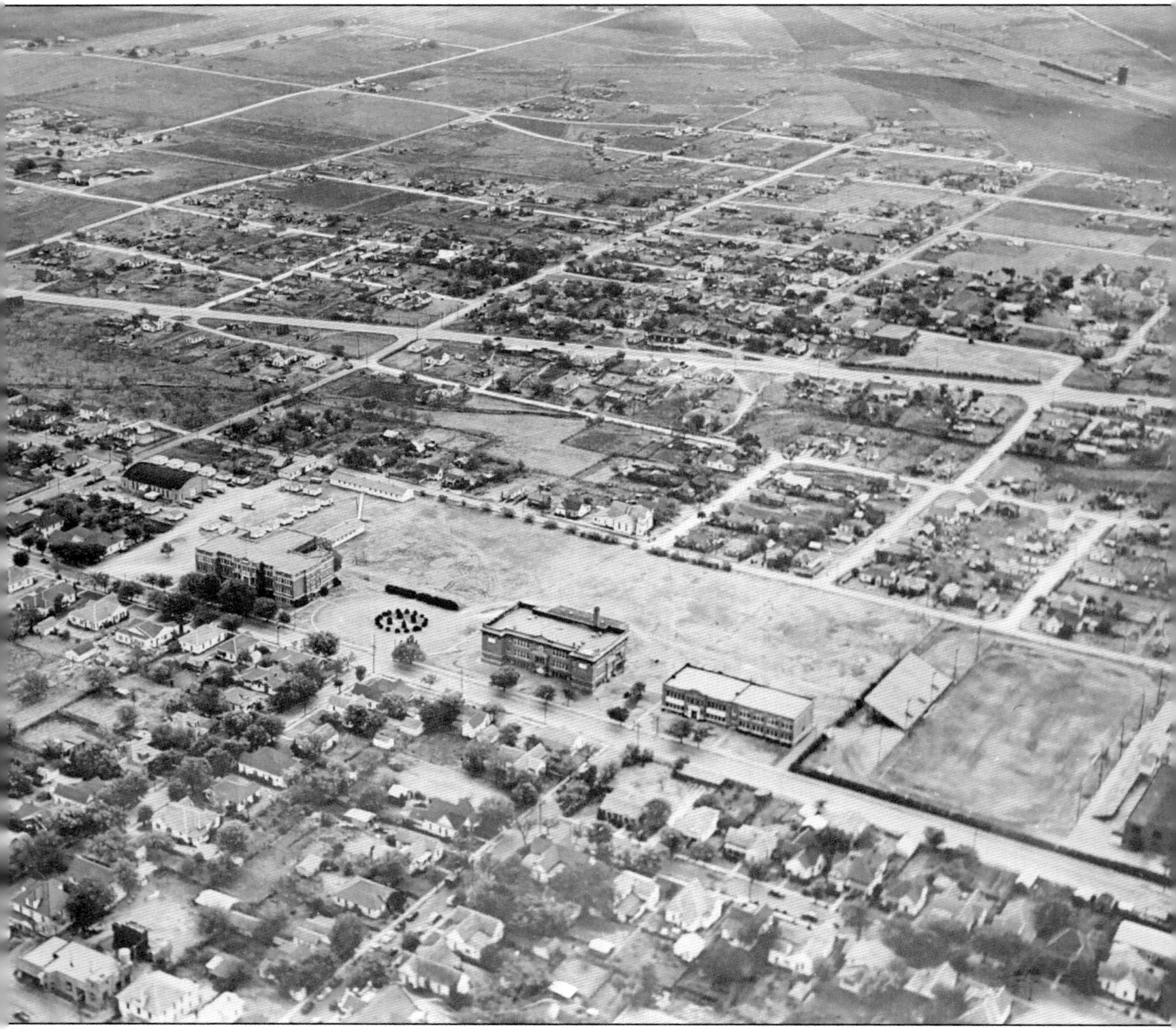

The Hillsboro public schools, seen in this 1945 aerial view, have occupied the area of Walnut Street between Church and Abbott Streets for over 100 years. The first lot purchased for the schools was at 310 East Walnut Street, and in 1906, the first Hillsboro High School was constructed on that site. The building burned in April 1922, and the new Hillsboro Junior College/High School was erected on the same site, opening in September 1923. Bowman Field, the first athletic field, was located south of the high school and was replaced by Frazier Field, which was used until the new high school was constructed in 1964. To the west of the Junior College/High School was Hillsboro Grammar School, constructed in 1914. In the 1920s, Travis Elementary was erected to the west of the Grammar School, soon followed by Frazier Field. In 1929, Doughty Hall was constructed on the southeast corner of East Walnut and Church Streets, and served as a gymnasium, field house for Frazier Field, and a community auditorium.

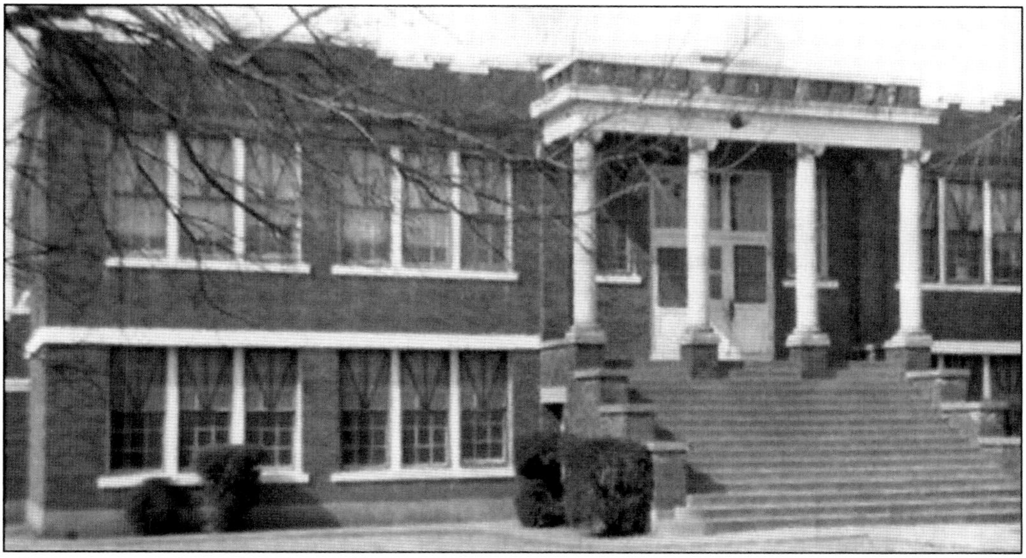

The coming of the railroad to Hillsboro in 1881 saw a rise in population and the construction of Harris School, a frame building on the west side. The first building was used until a bond issue passed in 1917 resulted in the construction of a two-story brick building (above). This building faced Duncan Street, as did the first Harris School. This building was replaced in 1949 by a new facility that faced Line Street. Local contractor Robert Kirkbridge was the builder. Below, faculty members at Harris Elementary School pose for a photograph in the schoolyard in March 1953. From left to right, they are principal Wayne Dandridge, Dorothy Pauling Warden, Fannie Curtis Smith, Alta Clack Lowrance, Gwendolyn Lewis Sullins, and Louise Adams Leslie.

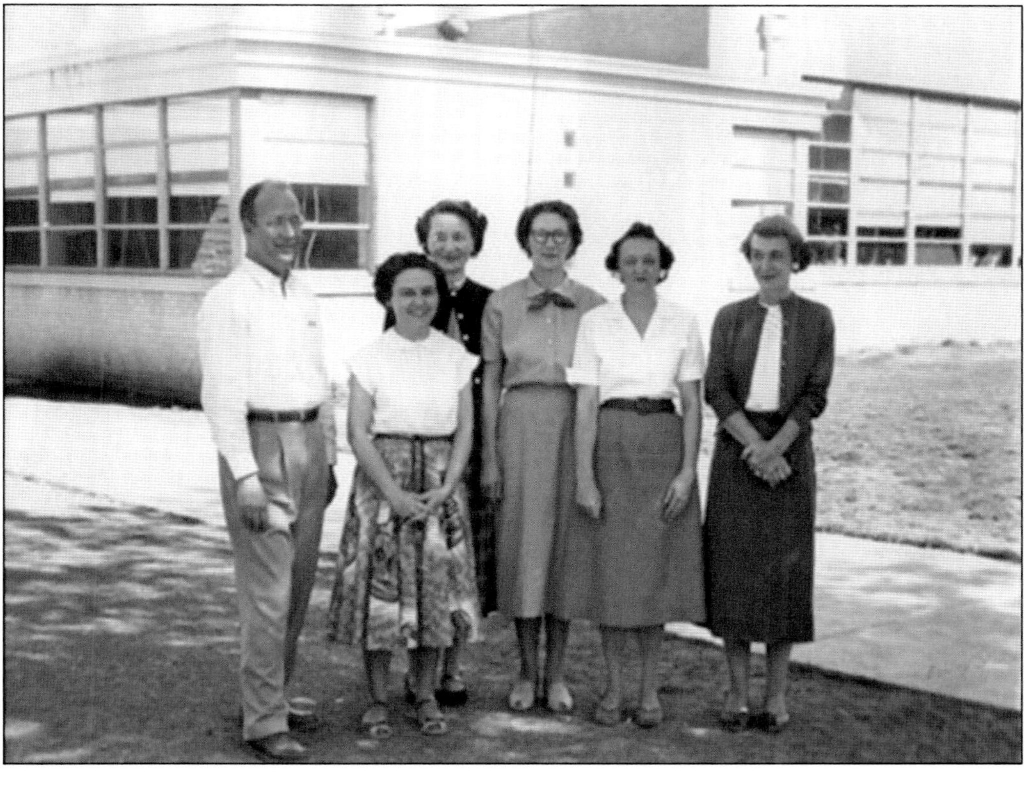

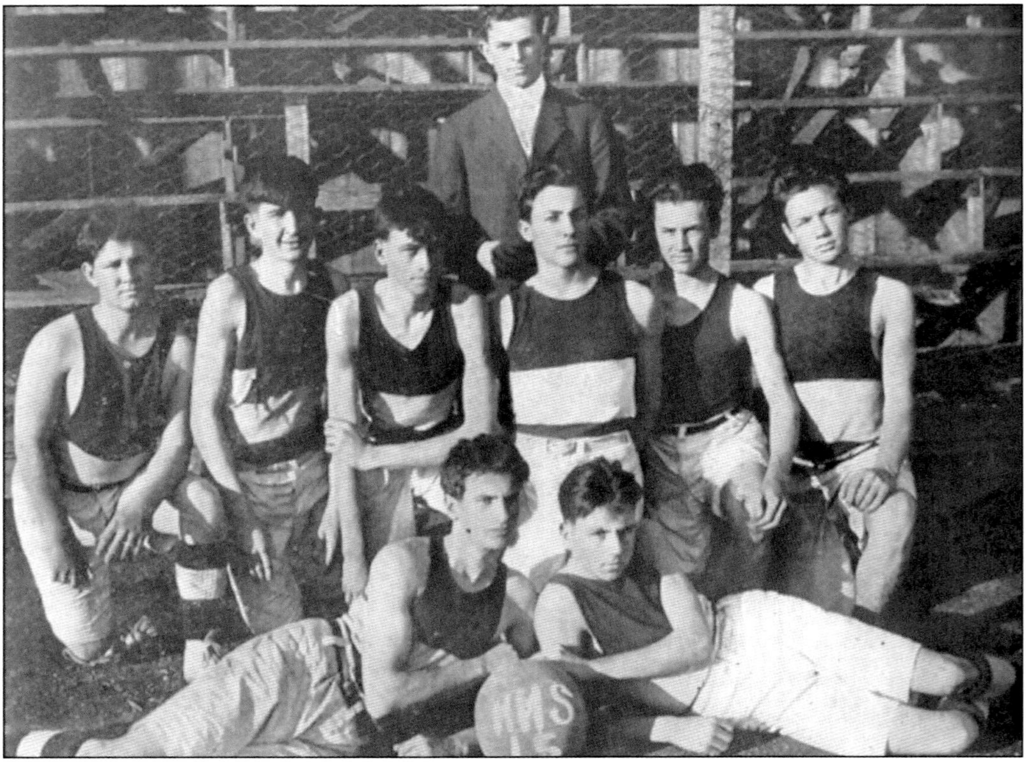

The 1914–1915 Hillsboro High School boys' basketball team (above) and girls' basketball team (below) played outside on clay courts, as the first gymnasium in Hill County was not built until 1929, when Doughty Hall was constructed at the southeast corner of Walnut and Church Streets. Thomas A. Bullock, the father of Lt. Gov. Bob Bullock, was the Hillsboro city engineer. He designed and oversaw construction of Doughty Hall, which was built to serve as a school gymnasium and city auditorium. The handsome facility was named for Hillsboro Junior College president and superintendent Walter F. Doughty, the former state superintendent of public instruction.

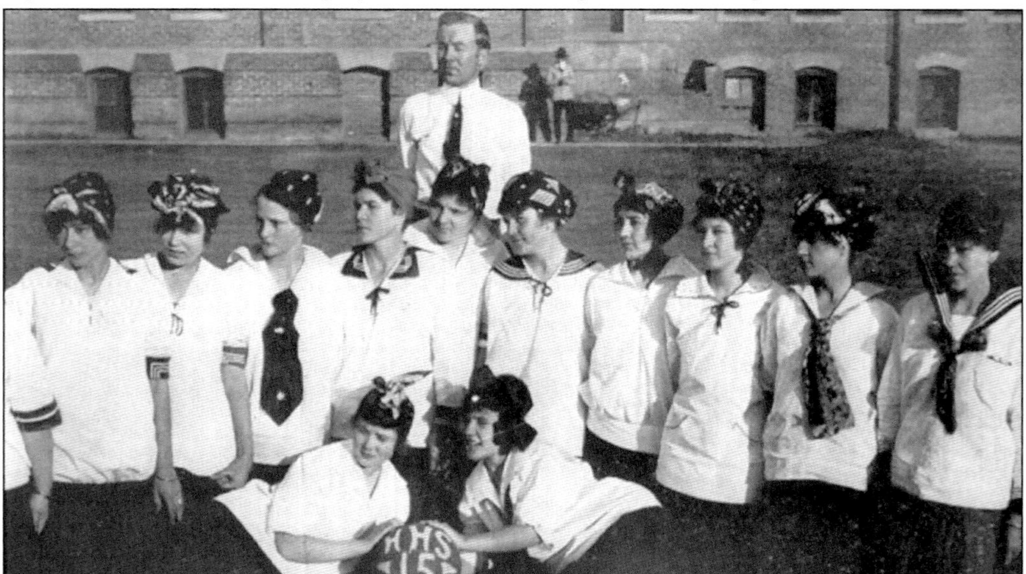

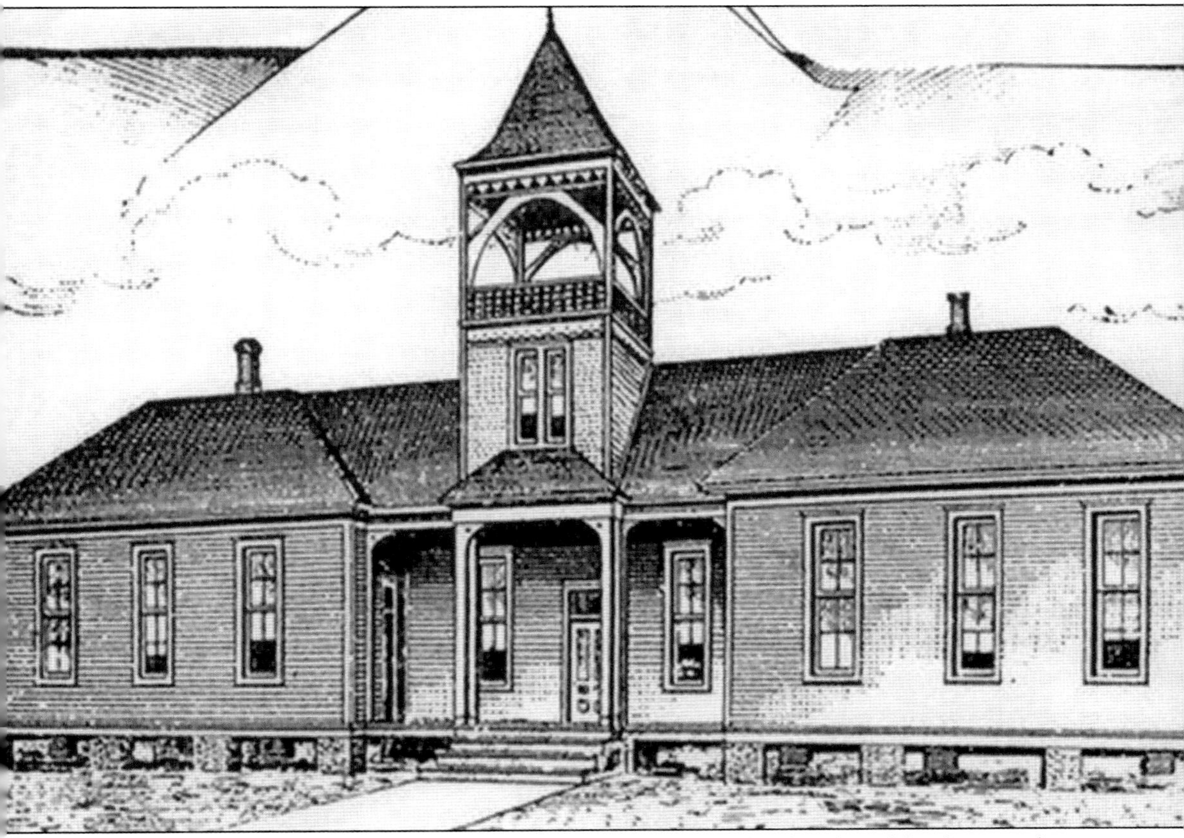

The Peabody School was named for George Peabody, a banker who distributed funds to southern states following the Civil War to educate African American students. Hillsboro voters in 1885 passed a bond issue for school construction that included a school for African-American students. This frame building was constructed after the 1885 bond passed, and served students in the Freetown area of Hillsboro until it burned in 1919. A bond issue for $18,000 was passed to erect in 1919 a two-story brick building on Peabody Street at Pine and Brown Streets. A new Peabody School on Francis Street opened in 1950 and was built with the same bond issue that constructed a new school on the Harris campus. T.H. Love, J.W. Sanford, and T.W. Moseley were remembered as strong, effective administrators throughout Peabody's history. The final graduating class for Peabody High School was in 1966, and the Francis Street building burned in 2005.

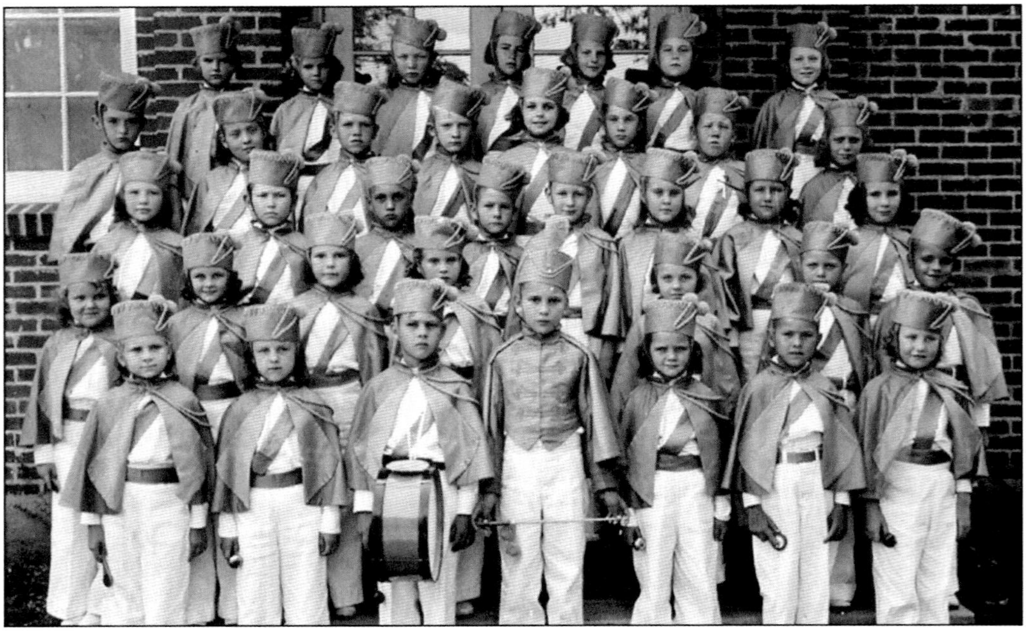

Rhythm bands were popular in elementary schools soon after 1900. Members wore uniforms and instruments included woodblocks, tambourines, triangles, sand blocks, rhythm sticks, cymbals, and maracas. The bands would play at special events on the Hillsboro school campus. Future lieutenant governor Bob Bullock is seen here, third from the left in the first row, performing with the Franklin Elementary School rhythm band. (Bob Bullock Collection.)

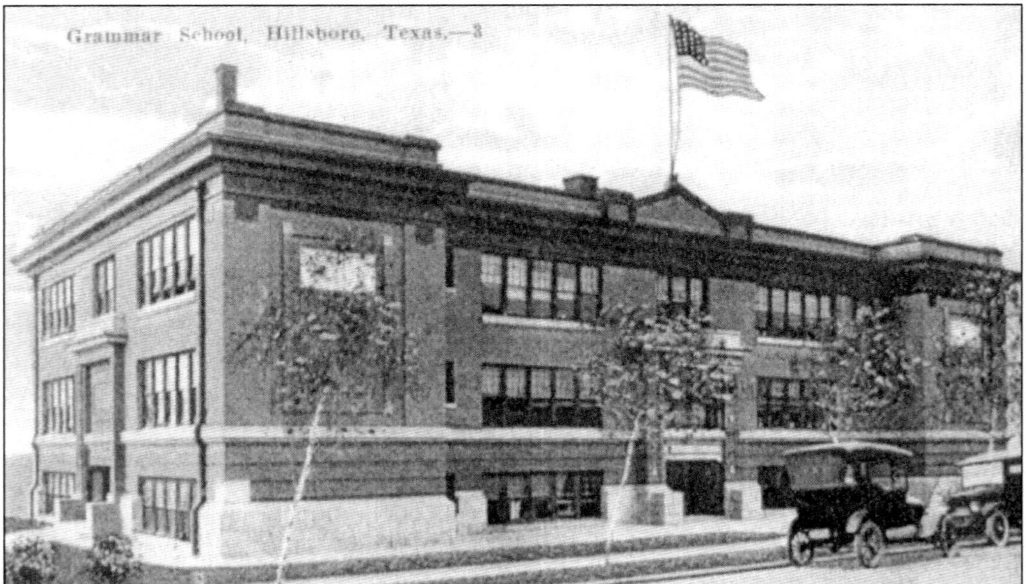

Hillsboro Grammar School was built in 1913–1914 at 224 East Walnut Street, west of St. Helen's Catholic Church and the 1906 Hillsboro High School at 310 East Walnut Street. Through the years, the building was known as the Grammar School, Hillsboro High School, Hillsboro Junior High School, Central Elementary School, and Travis Elementary School. "Pop" Christian was the engineer in charge of the coal boiler used for heating. An addition to the south side in 1920 provided a cafeteria and agricultural education classrooms.

Bowman Field was the first athletic field on the Walnut Street campus. Named after school board member and early leader of the Texas Good Roads Association Oliver W. Bowman, it was replaced in 1929 by Frazier Field, named after Albion Monroe Frazier, a school board member and advocate for the passage of the junior college bond. Frazier Field was demolished in 1964 to make way for the new high school, which is now occupied by Hillsboro Junior High School.

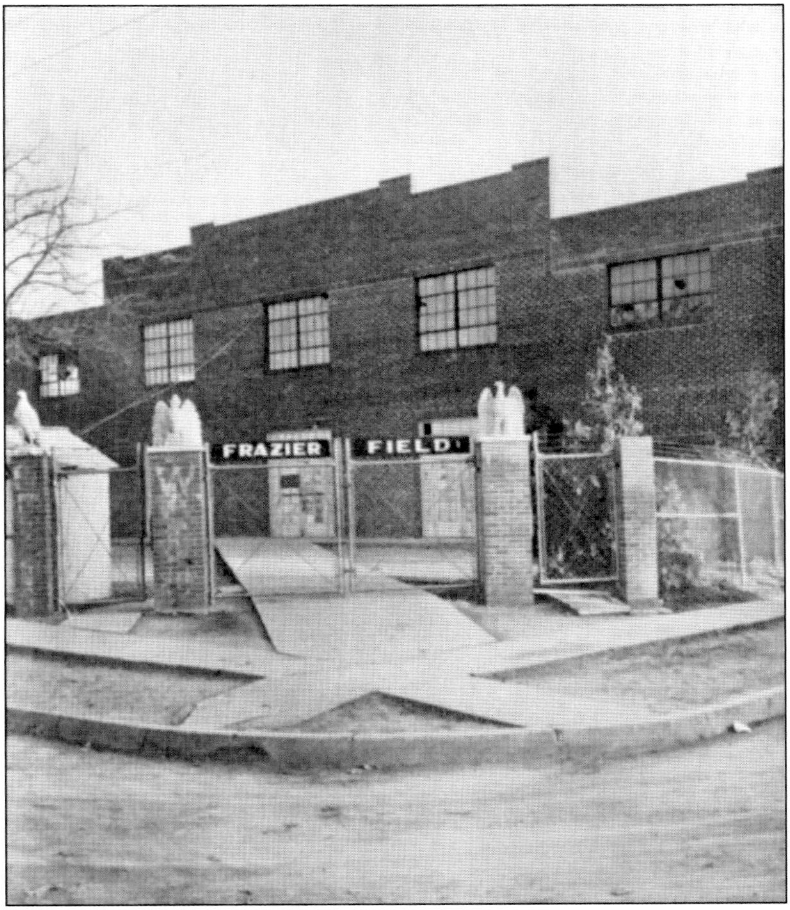

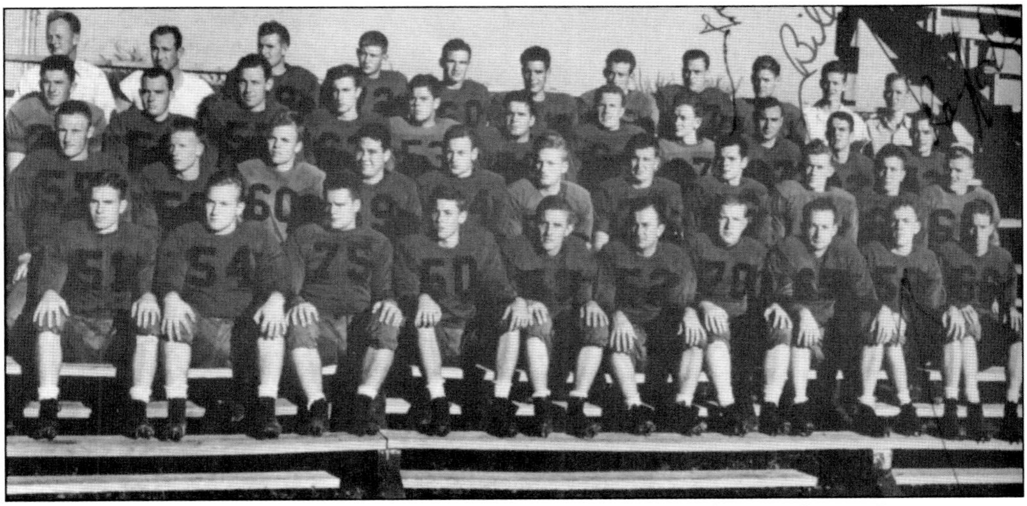

The 1947 Hillsboro Junior College Indians football team won eight straight conference games to win the Northern Zone championship and then defeated Uvalde, the Southern Zone champion, for the Texas Junior College Athletic Conference championship. The team received and accepted a bid to the first annual Junior Sugar Bowl in Monroe, Louisiana, in December. (Bob Bullock Collection.)

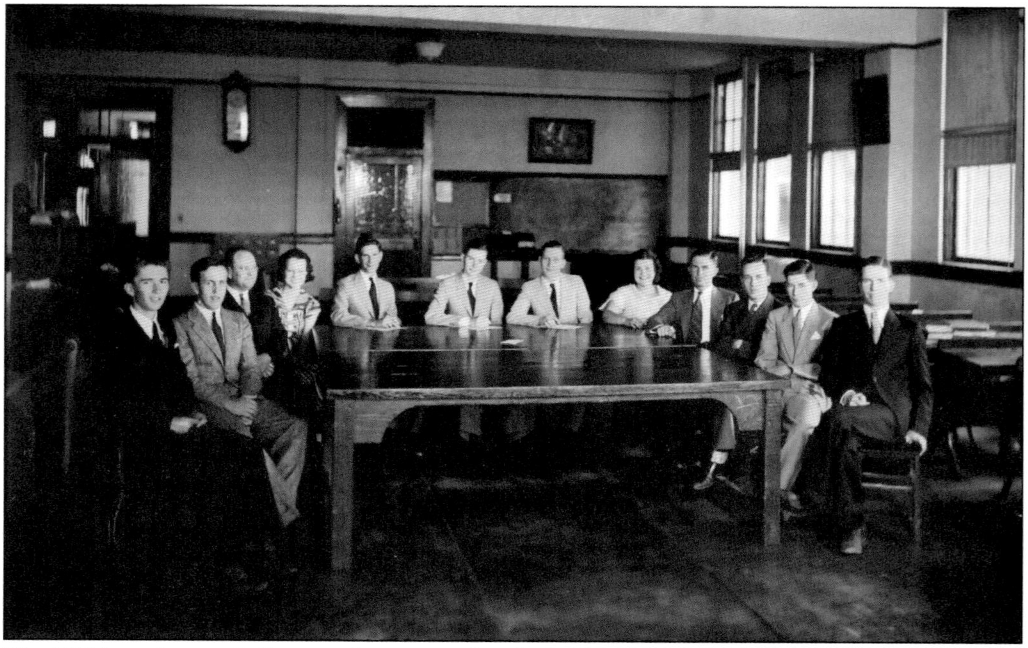

The Hillsboro Junior College student council gathered for this meeting in the spring of 1934. The members are, from left to right, Mart Cole, Sidney Bond, faculty advisor W.I. Hill, Louise Cook, Crawford C. Martin, president Francis G. McDonald, secretary John Graham Turk, Coralyn Whitten, Leighton Jones, Renshaw Innis, Dudley Peterson, and James Robertson.

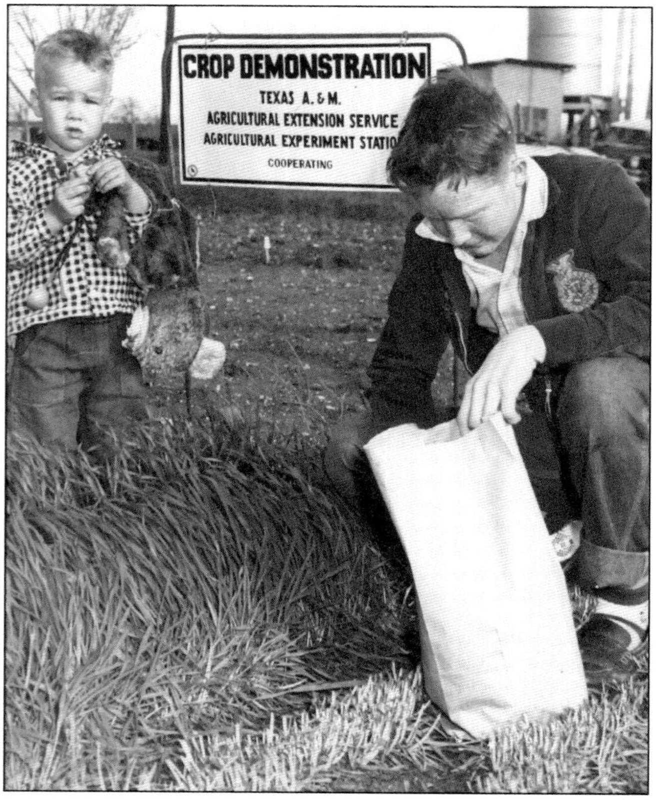

Vocational Agriculture was established in Hillsboro schools in 1918 for the purpose of training boys between the ages of 14 and 21 for the business of farming. The Hillsboro Vocational Agriculture judging teams have always been highly respected in the state. Here, younger brother Barry Tufts looks on as Bobby Tufts of the Hillsboro High School Future Farmers of America works on a soils project. (Usa Lee Tufts.)

John G. Read was a partner in the Simmons-Read Company. He was elected president of the Hillsboro school board in 1917 and served for 16 years. Read proposed that a junior college be added to the high school. A bond issue was passed in 1921 establishing one of the first junior colleges in Texas. Classes began in the fall of 1923, and accreditation by the state department of education followed.

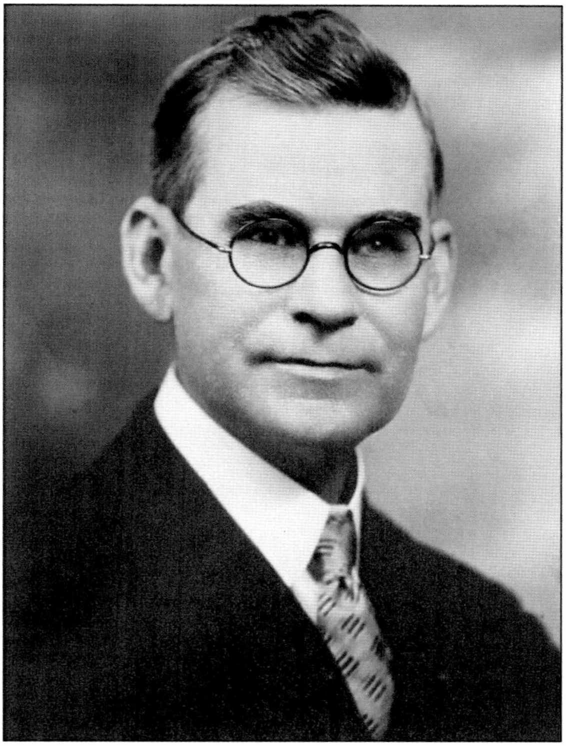

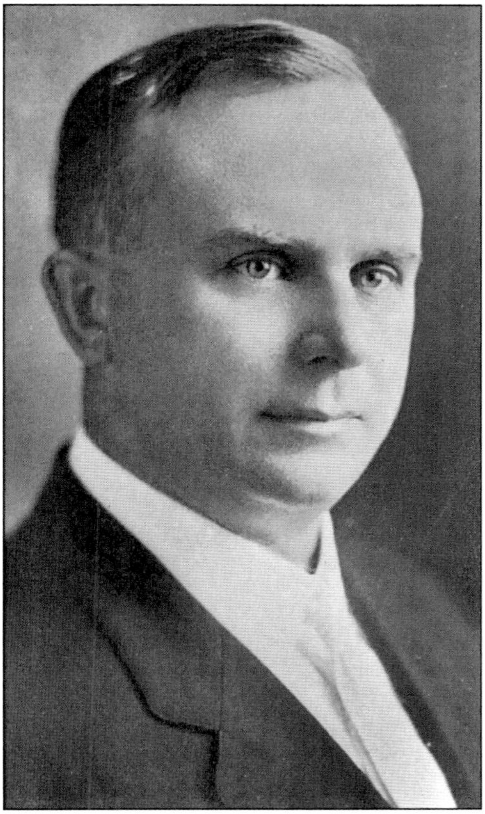

Walter F. Doughty, the former state superintendent of public instruction, followed W.T. Lofland as Hillsboro School superintendent from 1924 to 1931. Doughty implemented a progressive plan of school organization. Under his tenure, Frazier Field, Doughty Hall, and Travis Elementary School were built. By 1929, the college offered pre-professional courses in law, medicine, engineering, and business administration, serving almost 200 students.

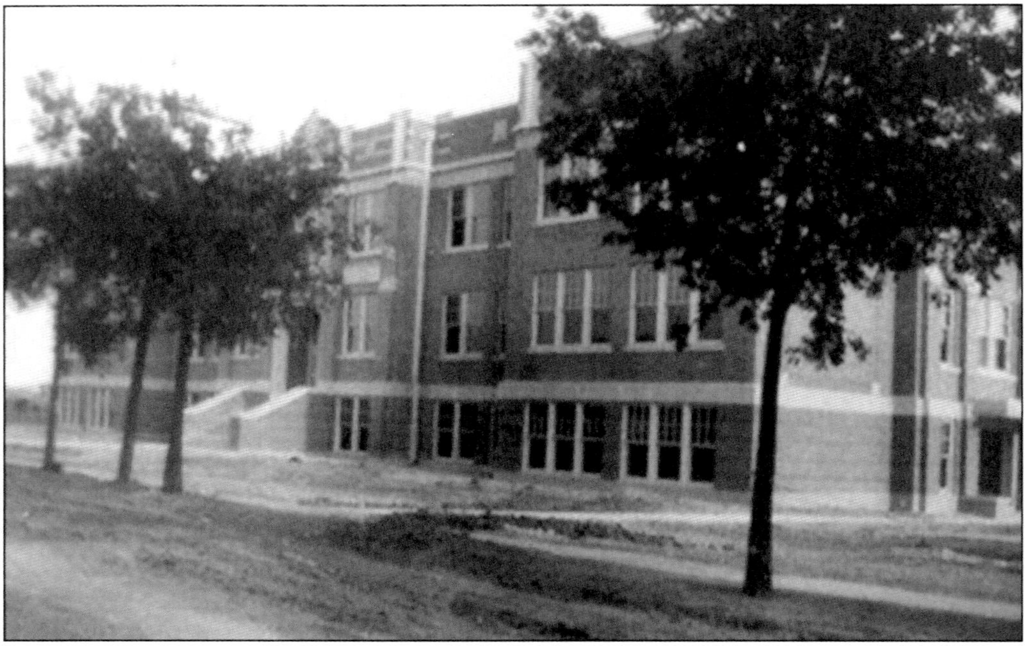

The Hillsboro High School–Junior College building (above) was built in 1923. The bond issue to create a junior college passed in 1921, assisted by publicity provided by J.C. Butts, the editor of the *Hillsboro Evening Mirror*. The bonds were sold by 1922, and construction was set to begin when Hillsboro High School burned down. The new building housed both the high school and the two-year college. College classes continued until voters closed the college in 1950. Hill Junior College (now Hill College, below) reopened in 1962 with Dr. W. Lamar Fly as president and has expanded to include a large campus in Cleburne and several additional campuses in the surrounding area. The main campus remains in Hillsboro and has dormitories, sports teams, and a military history museum complex begun by retired Air Force colonel Harold B. Simpson, according to *Hill College: An Illustrated History*.

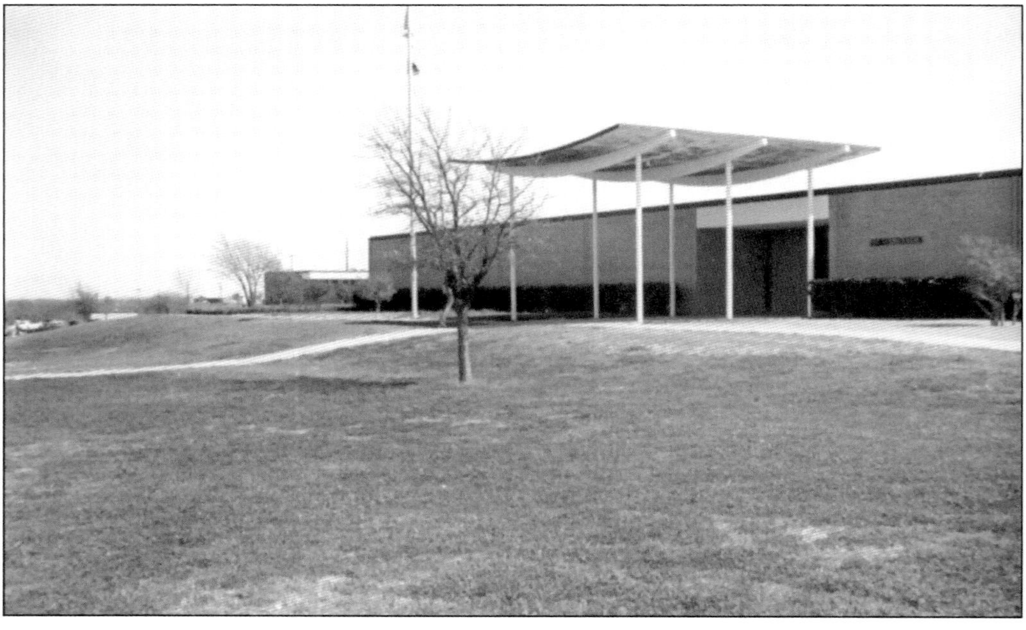

Eight

Social and Cultural Pursuits

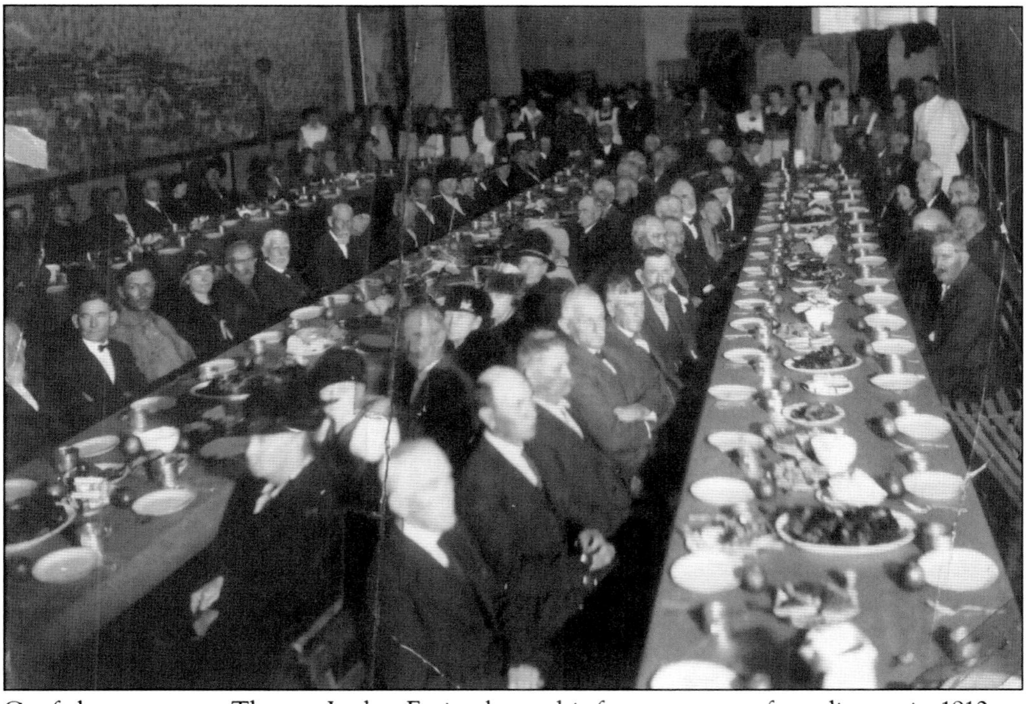

Confederate veteran Thomas Luther Epting began his famous possum feast dinners in 1910, as stated in *Heritage of Hill County*, Volume II. The dinners were an annual social event until 1927. Epting's son Adam provided the possums and Hillsboro merchants donated sweet potatoes. Local cafés like Andrews Café and the White Swan roasted the possums and yams. Ladies brought sweets, vegetables, and extras. The annual event was hosted on the courthouse lawn or in the courthouse and other public buildings.

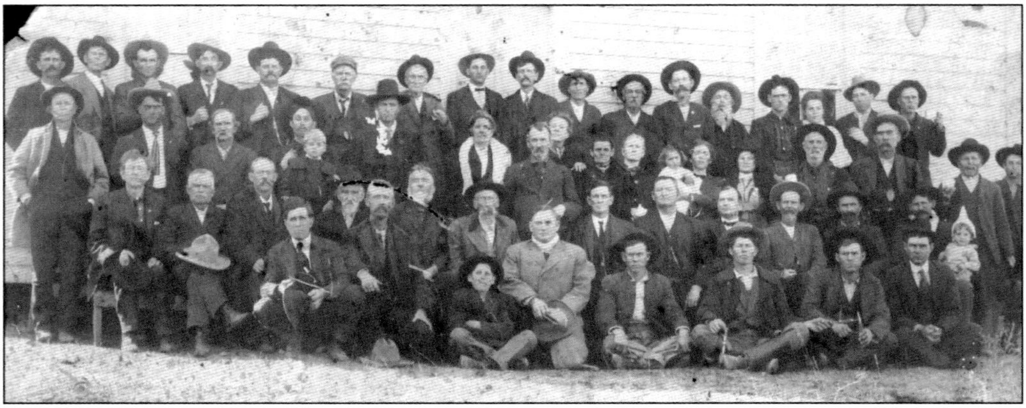

In August 1898, upon the initiation of D.C. Wornel, an informal group calling itself Old Settlers of Hill County (above) met in the courthouse and formally organized the Hill County Old Settlers Association. The association elected T.B. Smith as president, Dr. J.M. Griffin as vice president, and D.C. Wornel as secretary-treasurer. The association worked with Hill County Camp No. 166 of the Sons of Confederate Veterans to establish the Hill County Reunion Grounds on land purchased in 1901. Prior to the purchase of the Reunion Grounds, annual Confederate and Old Settlers Reunions were held in Abbott's Grove, now Hillsboro City Park. Below, Ellen Varnell (far right), her children, and neighbors pose for a photograph at the Hill County Reunion Grounds. She was the wife of Powhattan Varnell, one of the first settlers in the area. (Both, Cell Block Museum.)

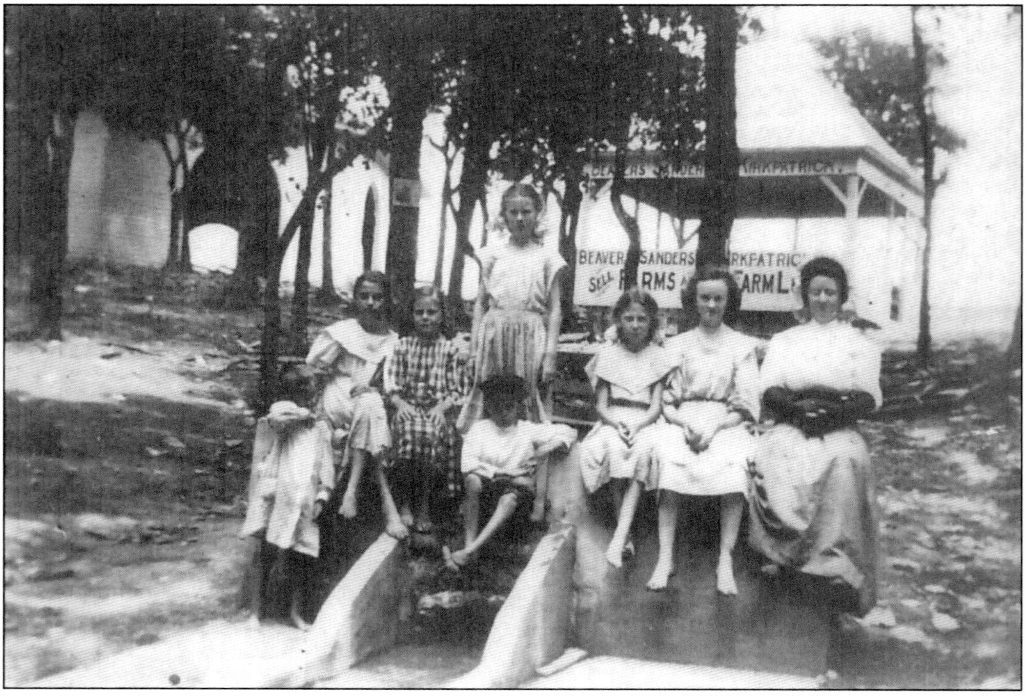

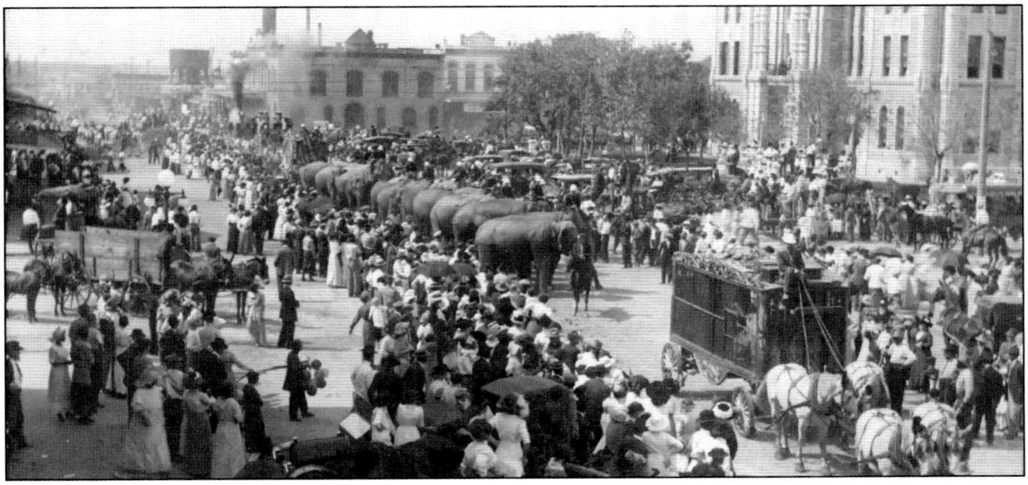

On October 10, 1913, onlookers gathered on the south side of the courthouse square to watch what was considered the ultimate in entertainment: the Ringling Bros. Circus parade, which marched east on Elm Street. At the height of the circus era, circus animals and acts were brought into town on as many as 84 railcars.

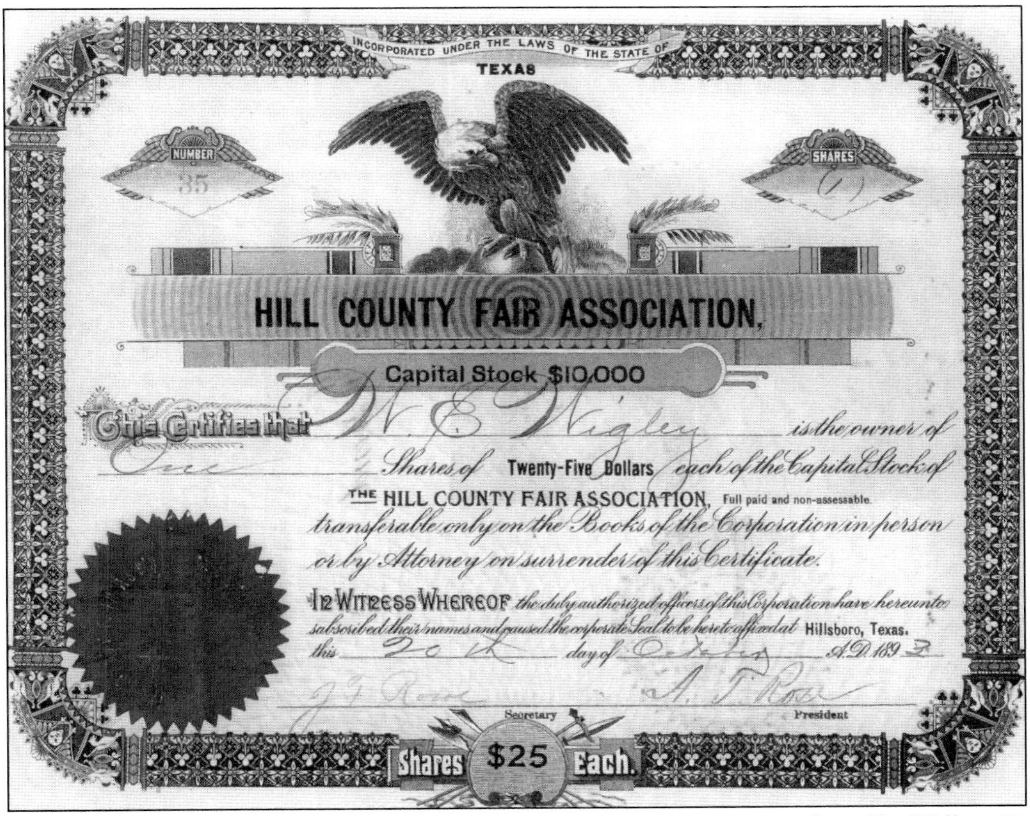

INCORPORATED UNDER THE LAWS OF THE STATE OF TEXAS

NUMBER 35 — SHARES (1)

HILL COUNTY FAIR ASSOCIATION.

Capital Stock $10,000

This Certifies that W. E. Wigley is the owner of One Shares of Twenty-Five Dollars each of the Capital Stock of THE HILL COUNTY FAIR ASSOCIATION, Full paid and non-assessable. transferable only on the Books of the Corporation in person or by Attorney on surrender of this Certificate.

In Witness Whereof the duly authorized officers of this Corporation have hereunto subscribed their names and caused the corporate Seal to be hereto affixed at Hillsboro, Texas. this 20th day of October A.D. 1893

J. F. Rowe, Secretary — A. T. Rose, President

Shares $25 Each.

This $25 share of capital stock in the Hill County Fair Association was purchased by William E. Wigley, a hardware merchant, on October 20, 1893. It was signed by J.F. Rowe, secretary, and A.T. Rose, president. The fair has a long history. It was first located on the northern edge of Hillsboro, adjacent to Katy Lake, before moving to its present southern location, adjacent to the Hillsboro High School football stadium.

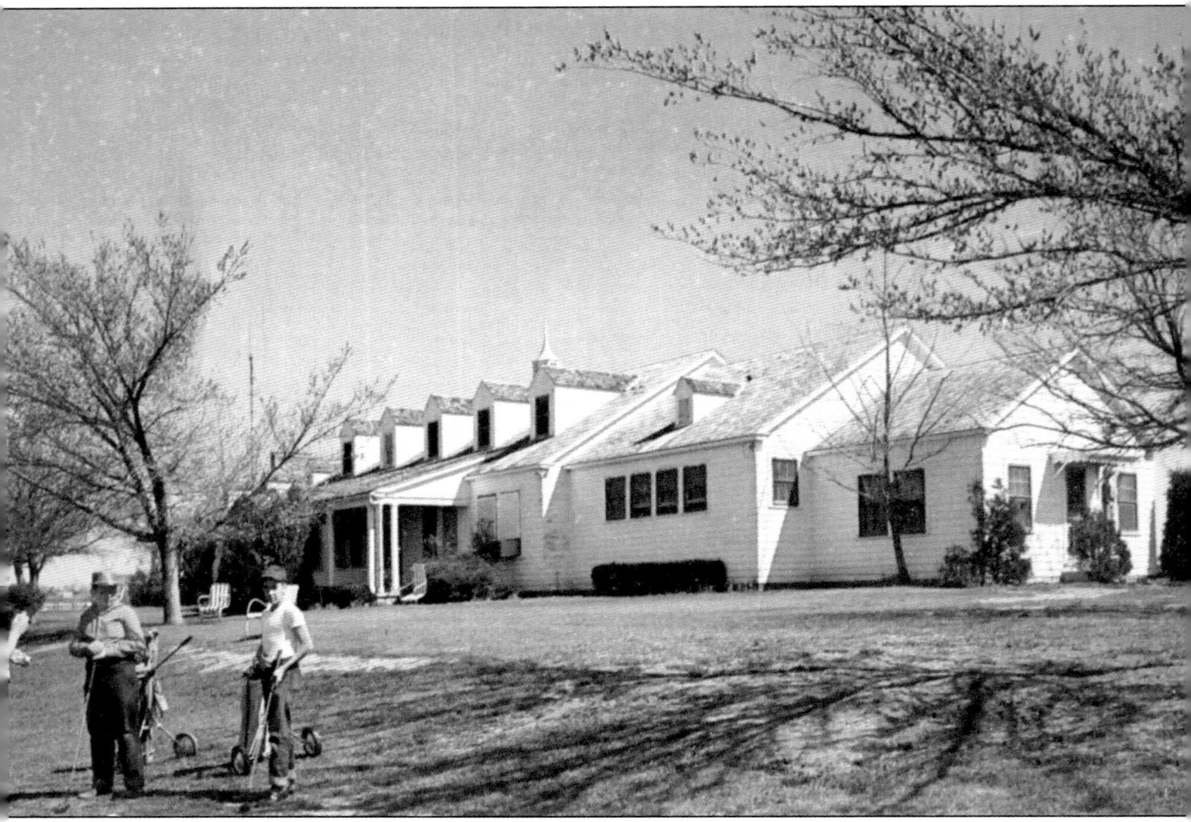

Hillsboro Country Club is a popular place for a swim on a hot Texas day or a round of golf in the cool of the evening. The golf course was built around 1938 by the Works Project Administration on land owned by Hill County. The clubhouse was built at the same time on land owned by the Hillsboro Country Club, a private organization. In the late 1940s, Hill County deeded the course to the country club. The course has always been open to the public. Seen here about to tee off from the first hole in the late 1950s are, from left to right, Melvin Hoffman, Henry Moore, and Kyle Cowan.

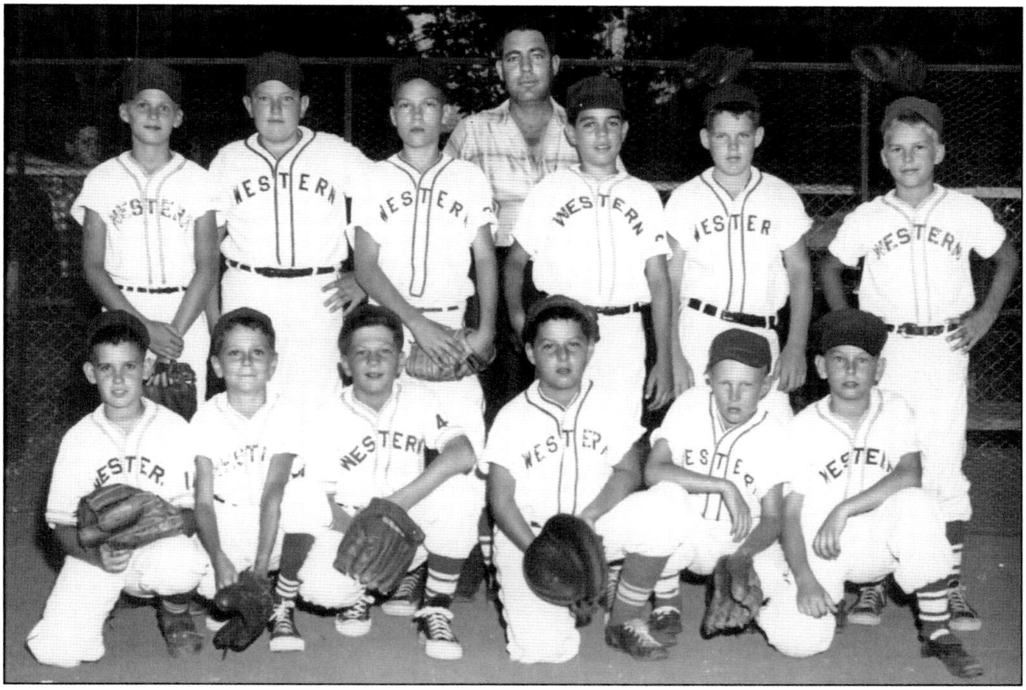

This Western Auto Little League team played locally around 1958. The team included, from left to right, (first row) Mike Fleming, Johnny Nelson, Ricky Bailey, Jimmy Malone, Freddie Popp, and Lynn Gray; (second row) Larry McCullough, Harold McClung, Tommy Bessire, coach Pete Yocham, M.C. Yocham, Larry Nelson, and Warren Tune. (Lynn Gray.)

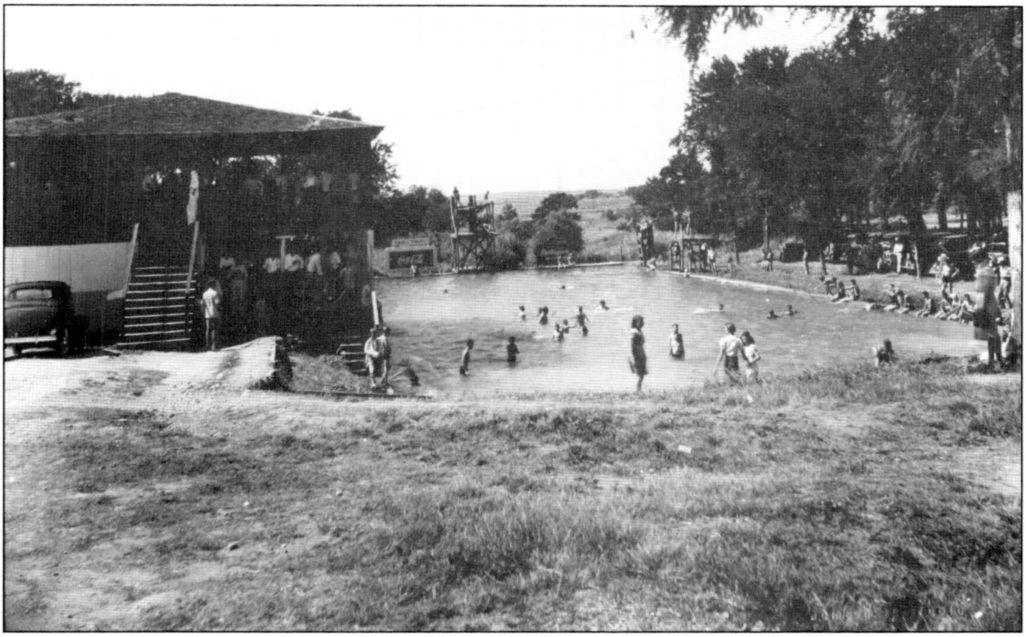

Mountain Springs Resort was built in the late 1920s and was a popular spot from the 1930s to the 1950s. It was originally a spring-fed concrete pool with a tree-shaded picnic ground. An open-air, roofed dance floor was then added on top of the wooden bathhouse. There was a stop on the interurban nearby, making it a convenient trip for Hillsboro residents and soldiers on weekends.

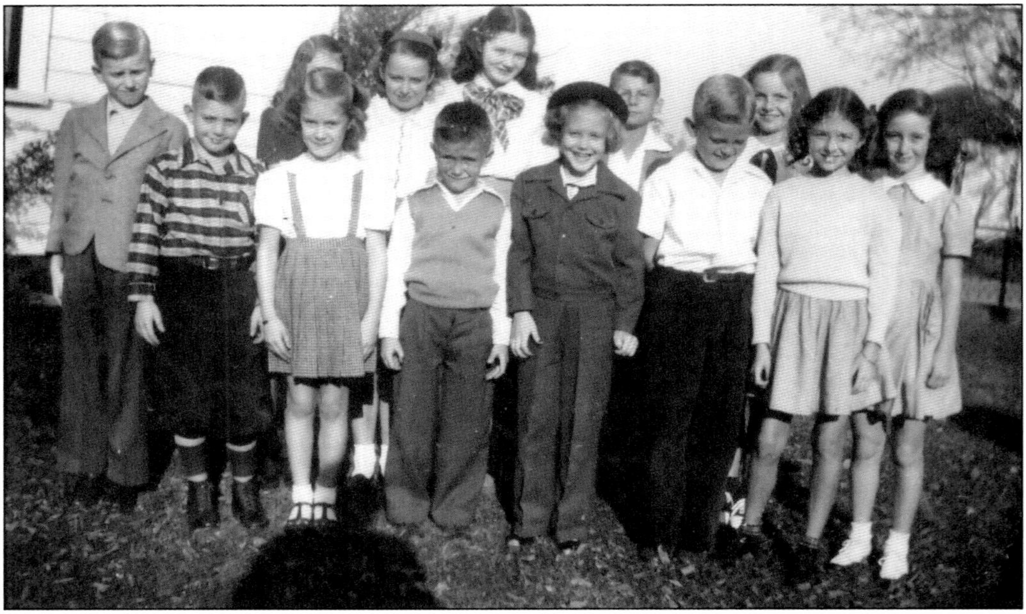

Vena McCarty Lowrey was a popular piano teacher in Hillsboro in the 1960s. Above, Lowrey's students pose for a photograph in 1947 at her home at 308 South Houston Street. Below, young pianists were presented on stage after a piano recital in the basement of the First Methodist Church around 1956. Participants included, in no particular order, Linda Kay Allen, Connell Andrews, Pat Atkins, Melinda Brooks, Carol Cunningham, Dana New, Jacque Sue Raymer, Buddy Russell, Jean Roberts, Jimmie Waller, Ann Dudley, and Sherry Martin.

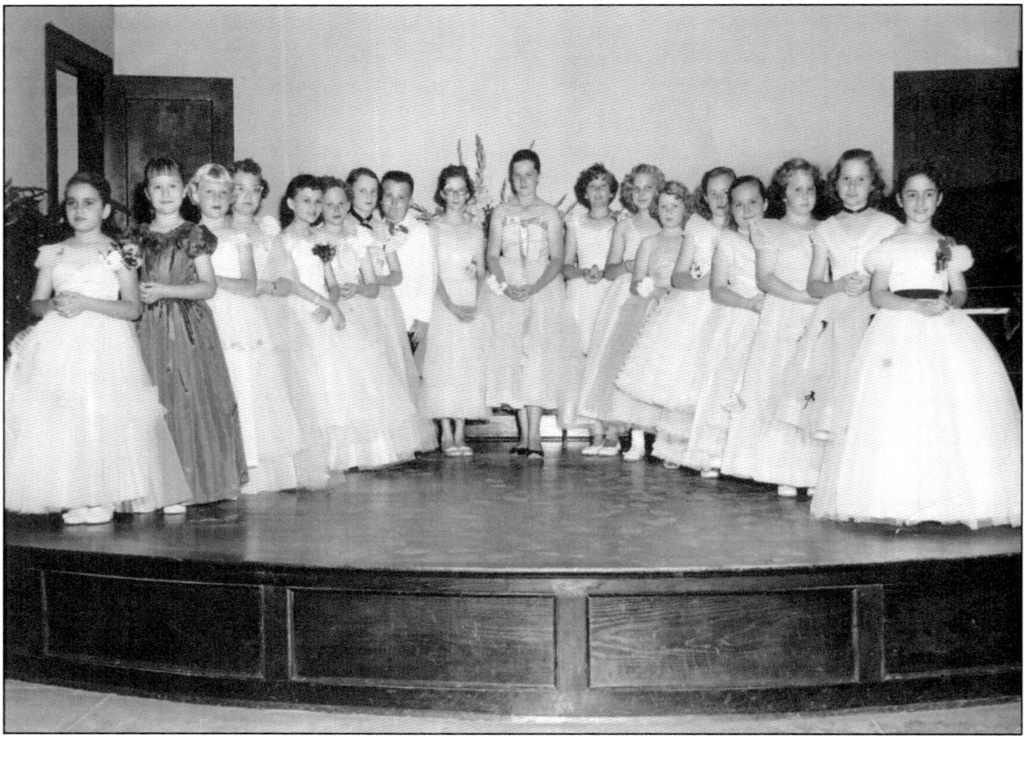

These entrants in a theatrical production during a Bond's Alley arts and crafts fair surely brought smiles to the audience. They are, from left to right, Sandra Sulak, Ali Dent, Sunny Garrett, and Lisa Herring.

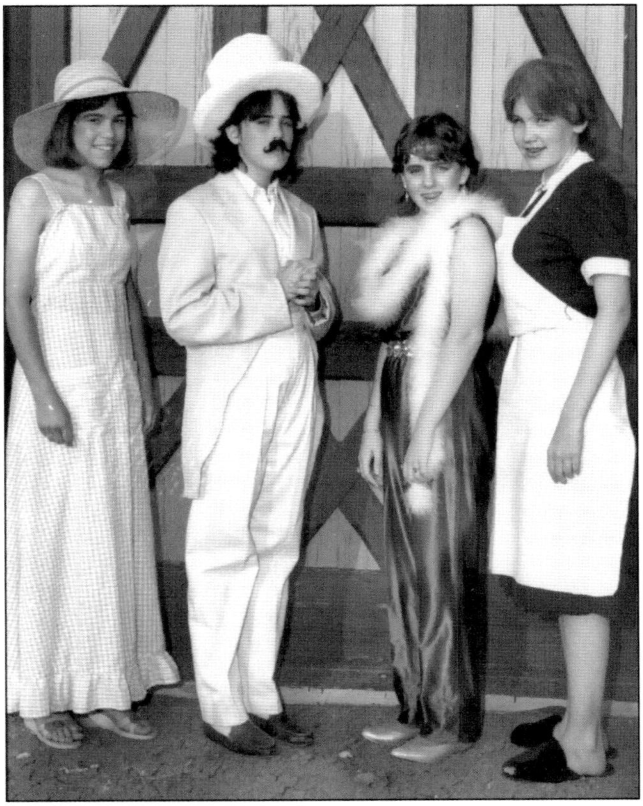

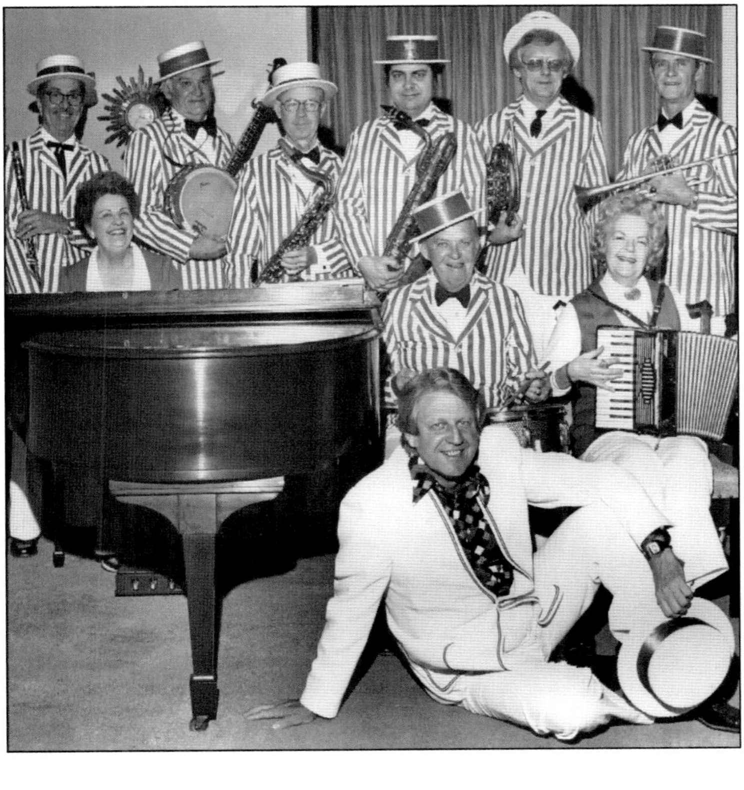

The Hillsboro Tooters Jazz Band was a community group of business and professional people. The Tooters played annually at the Bond's Alley Arts & Crafts Show, at the Corsicana Street Fourth of July parade, at concerts at the State Fair of Texas, at the Hemisphere Plaza in San Antonio, at the Lions International Convention in Dallas, and at a reception at Fort Hood for Gen. William Westmoreland.

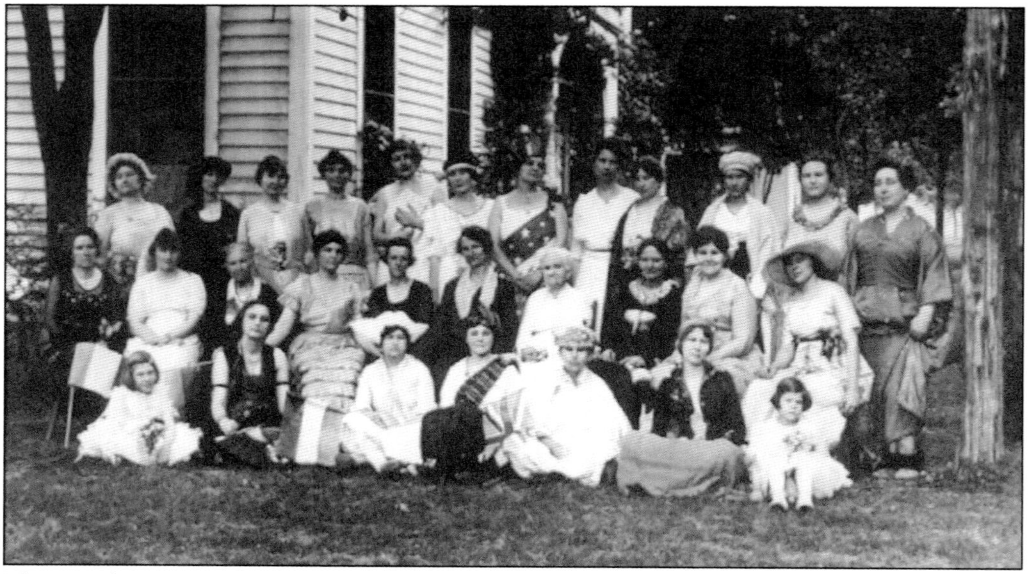

The Monday Review Club was organized in 1895 in the home of Mary Phillips at 606 East Franklin Street, with Alice Smith elected president. Active in improving the community, the club donated playground equipment for the city park and formed the first Girl Scout troop in Hillsboro. This photograph of the 25th anniversary of the organization of the club was featured in the June 3, 1921, *Dallas Morning News*.

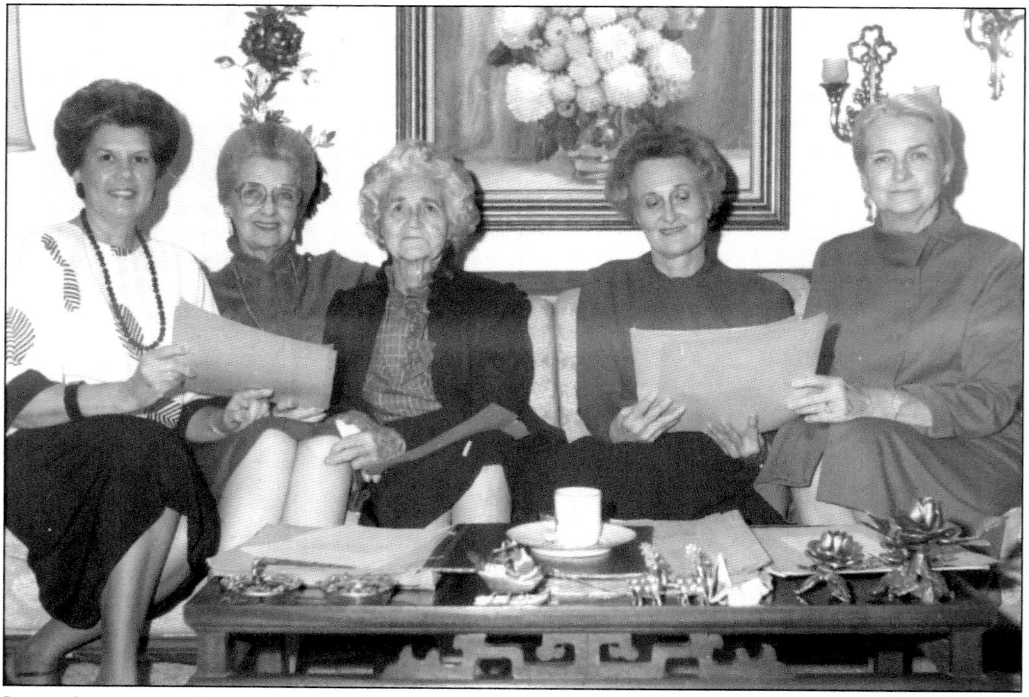

In 1913, a group of ladies met in the home of Judge Greene Duke Tarlton, at 211 North Pleasant Street, to organize the Les Causeuses, a social and service club. Members included Eunice Orr, Daisy Martin, Lillian Simmons, Nell Shipley, and Emma Turk. The club was federated in 1932. This photograph shows, from left to right, Lib Lavender, Millo Marcum, Dixie Giles Mash, Margaret Mash Martin, and Margaret Buie.

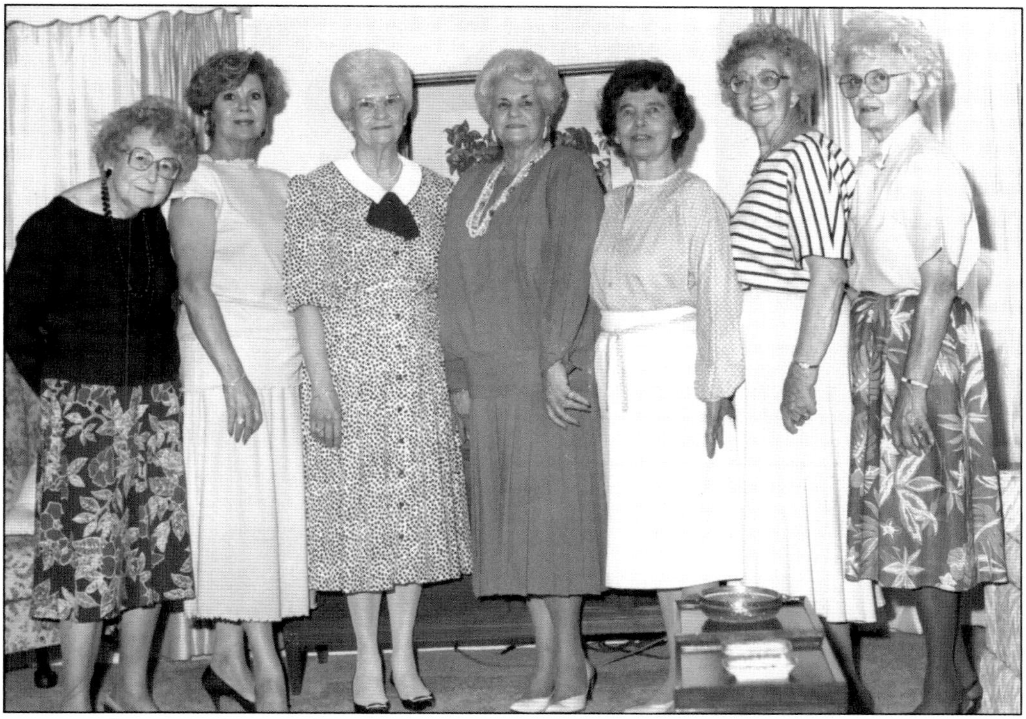

In November 1947, the Monday Review Club voted to organize a garden club, and the Hillsboro Garden Club began with 75 members. Seen here from left to right are the 1984 Hillsboro Garden Club officers: Ora Mae Scott, Betty Birdwell, Betsy Skarecky, Nona Donaho, Raye Buice, Fran Haigh, and Jerry Benham.

The Sesame Club was organized in 1893 as a women's study club in the home of Jennie Bragg at 403 East Franklin. In 1894, the club was active in establishing a public library, promoting a successful school bond election, forming the first cemetery association, and campaigning for other civic improvements. This photograph shows club members at a Christmas gathering.

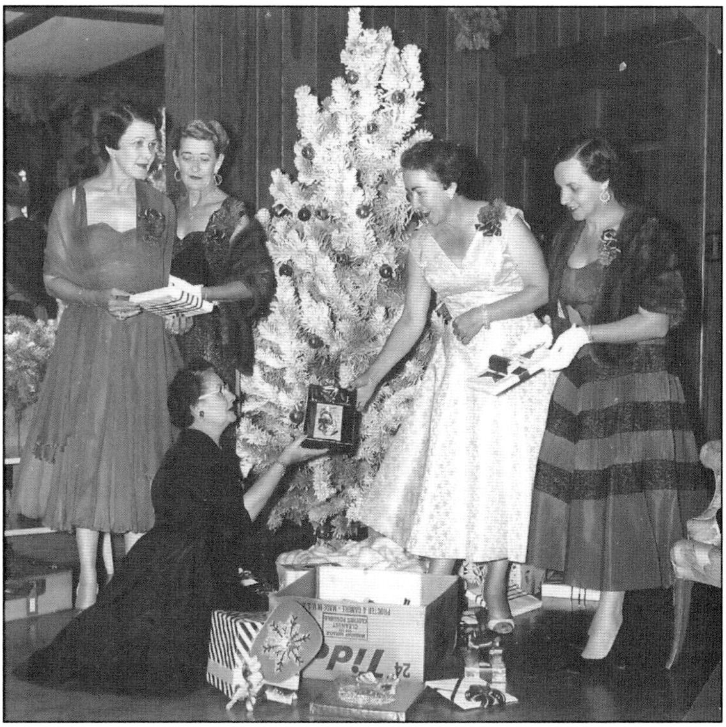

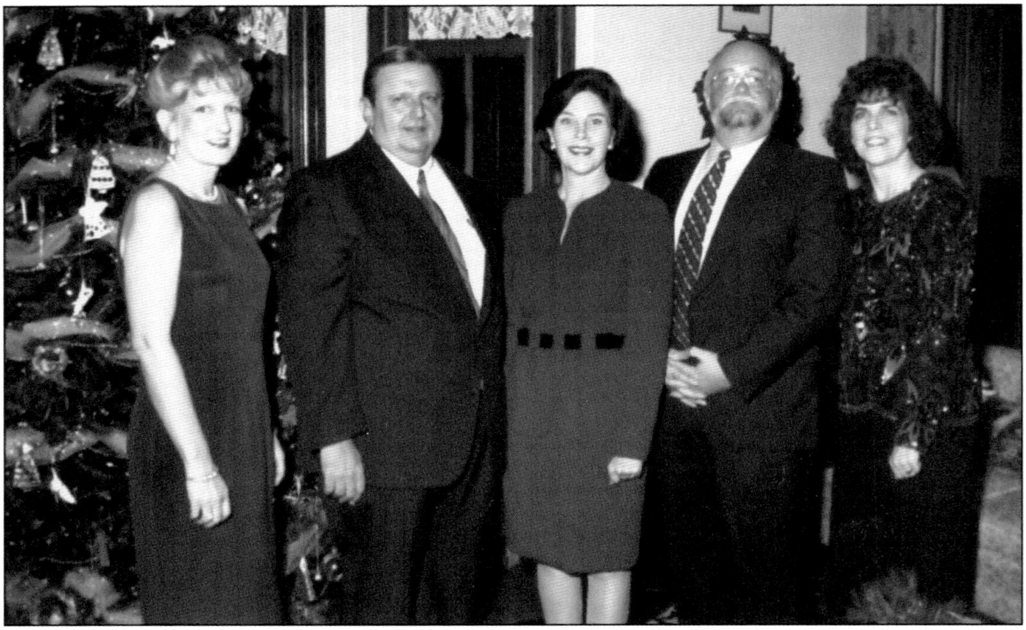

Texas First Lady Laura Bush made a visit to the Hillsboro City Library in December 1996. Seen here from left to right are Susan Mann, Hillsboro City Library director; Henry Moore, Hillsboro mayor; Bush; Robert Martin, director and librarian of the Texas State Library and Archives; and Betty Lowrance, Hillsboro City Library board president.

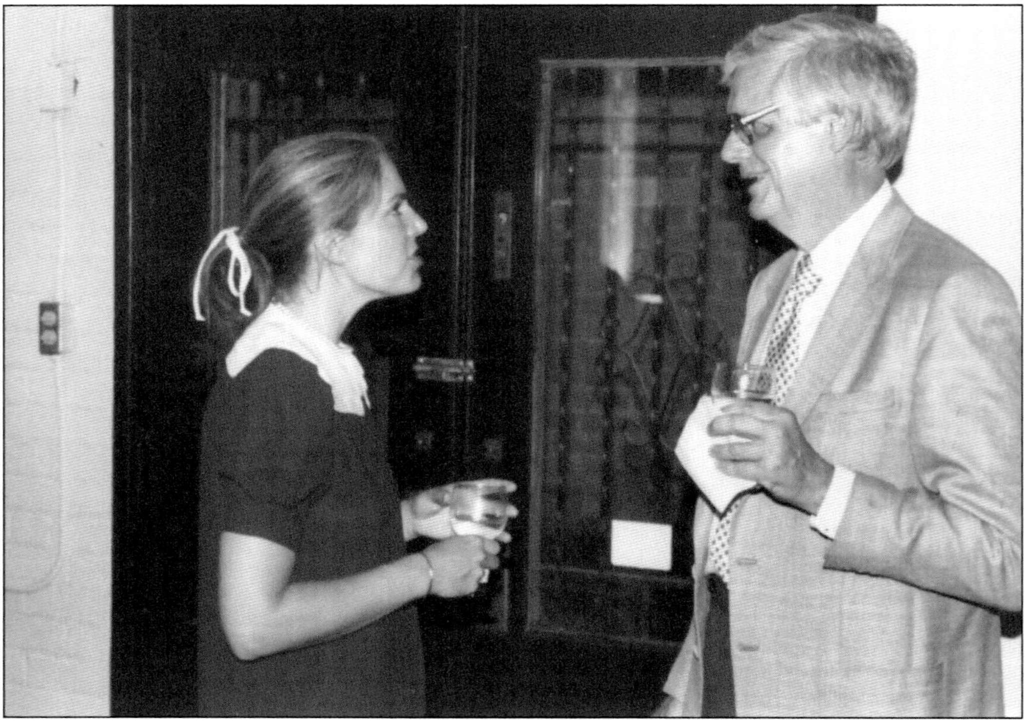

Paula Peters, the first director of the Hillsboro Main Street Program, shares a conversation with Dr. Dick Cason at a reception at the Hillsboro City Library. The Hillsboro Main Street Program began in 1981 as one of the original five Texas Main Street programs.

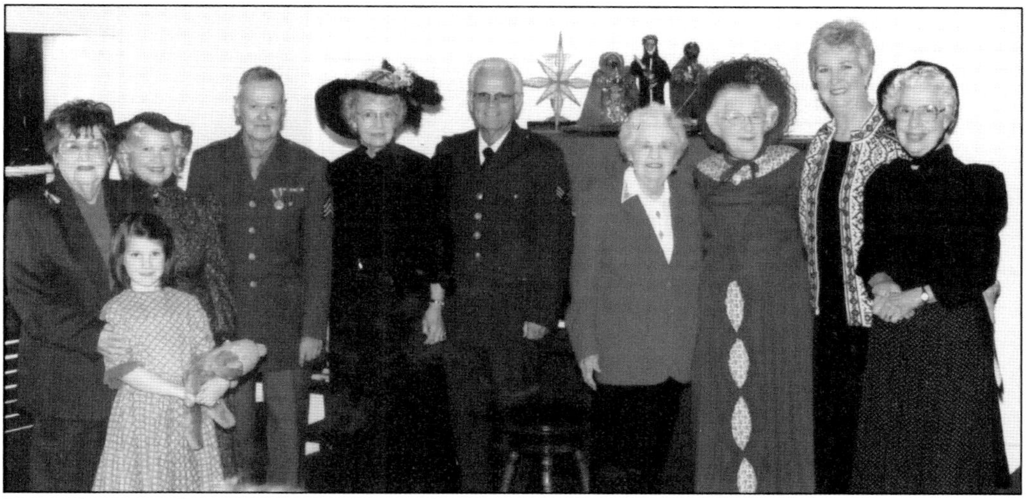

Dressed in period costumes, members of the Hill County Genealogical Society attend a Christmas open house at the Cell Block Museum. They are, from left to right, Edna Orr, young Emma Orr, June Carmichall, Richard Greenhill, Marie Lloyd, Neuman Lloyd, Frances Robertson Jackson Davis, Marilyn Topping, Florence Logan, and Joyce Hollingsworth.

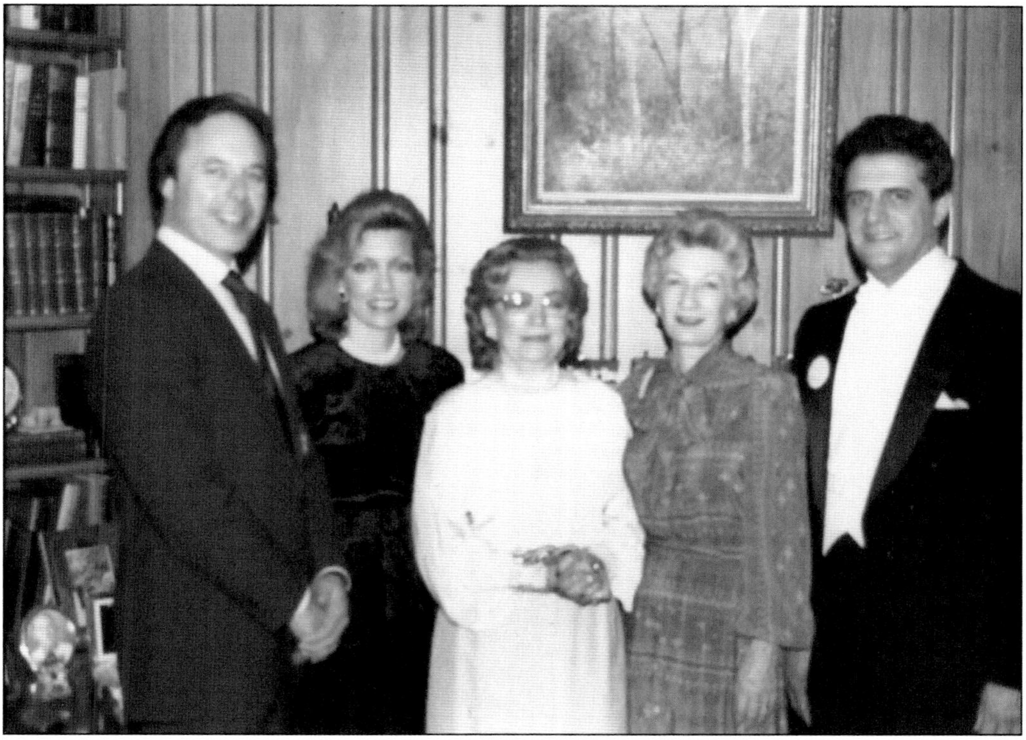

The Hillsboro Heritage League hosted the Fort Worth Chamber Orchestra for an annual performance for residents of Hillsboro and Hill County. Youth performances provided an introduction to the symphony and classical music. Seen here at a post-performance party are Jim Showers; his wife, Jan; Margaret Anne Smith; Dorothy Rhea; and John Giordano, the orchestra conductor. Jim and Jan Showers hosted the party in their palatial home at 1120 Park Drive, originally built in 1939 by Will and Thenia Morrow.

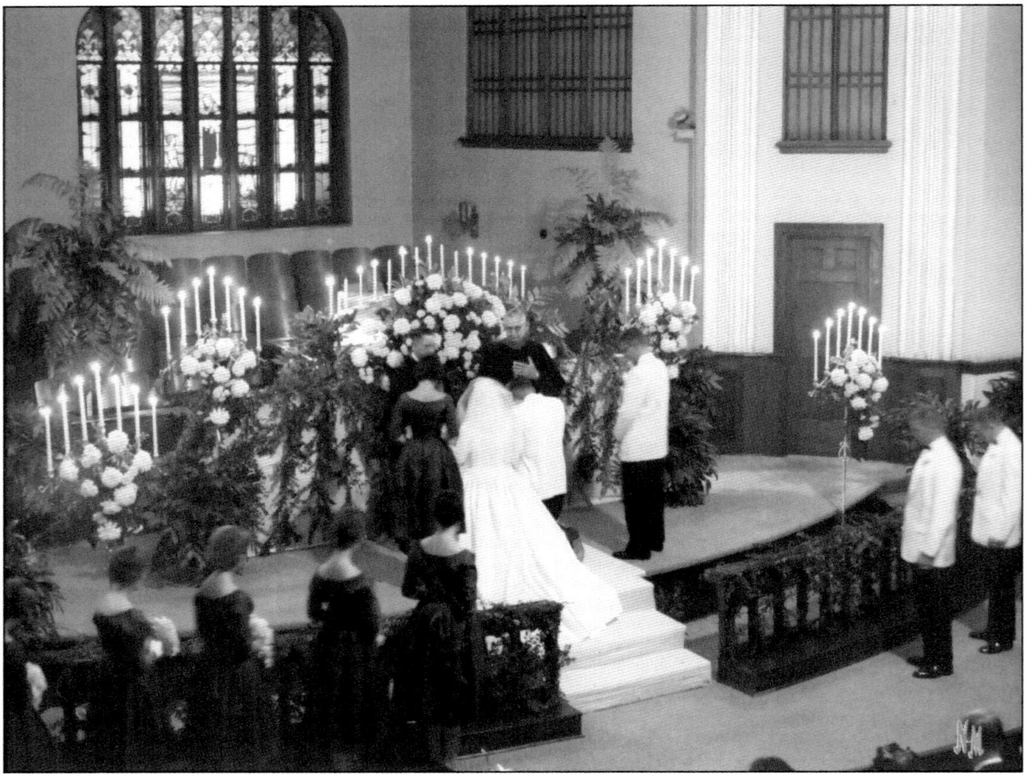

Linda Weatherby, the daughter of Ab and Mary Frances Weatherby, and Jack Teague, the son of US congressman Olin Teague and his wife, Freddie, were married in the First Methodist Church on August 30, 1960. Afterwards, a wedding reception was held at the Hillsboro Country Club. (Linda Teague.)

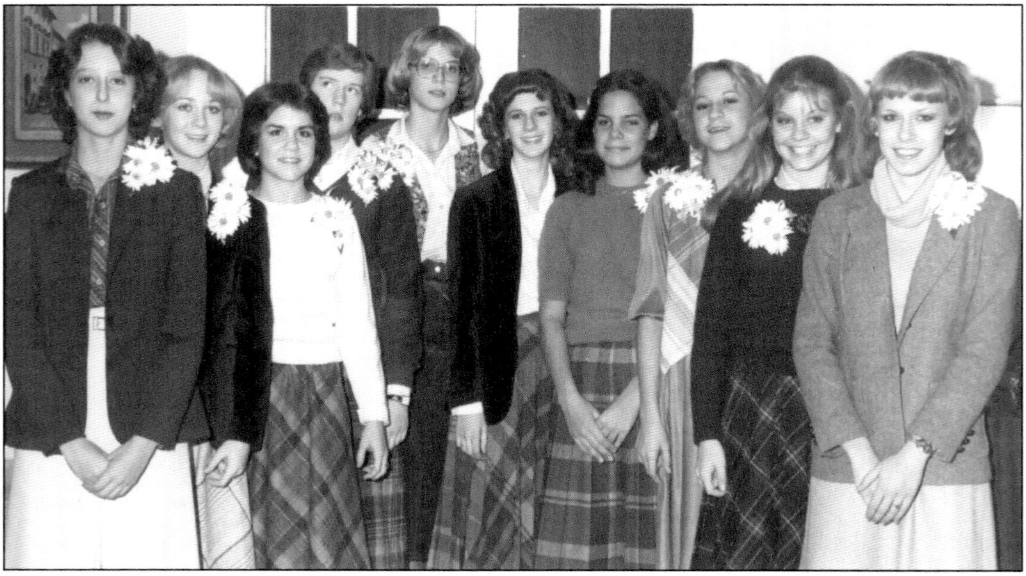

The Junior Sesame Club was organized in 1924. Seen here from left to right are new members initiated in 1980: Jana Loveless, Leslie Fender, Susan Washington, Carol Beard, Leslie Fowler, Marcia Curtis, Stephanie Beaudry, Rose Doskocil, Susanna Showers, and Shelly Shirley.

Nine

HOUSES OF WORSHIP

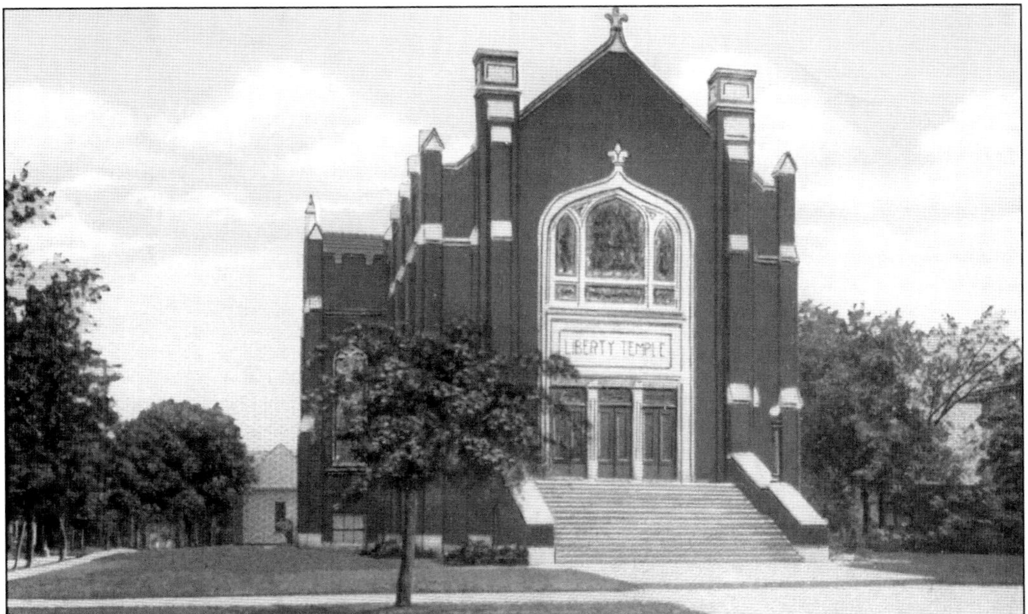

Cumberland Presbyterians first erected a beautiful frame building in 1887 on the southeast corner of Church and Elm Streets, the current location of Citizens National Bank. This lot was deeded to the Cumberland Presbyterian Church in January 1859 by W.R. Nunn. The property was sold to Magnolia Petroleum in 1919 to become a service station, and Central Presbyterian (Liberty Temple) was erected in 1924 on what is now the site of the city administration building on the southwest corner of Elm and New Streets. Liberty Temple closed in 1937 and the building became the Elm Street Church of Christ.

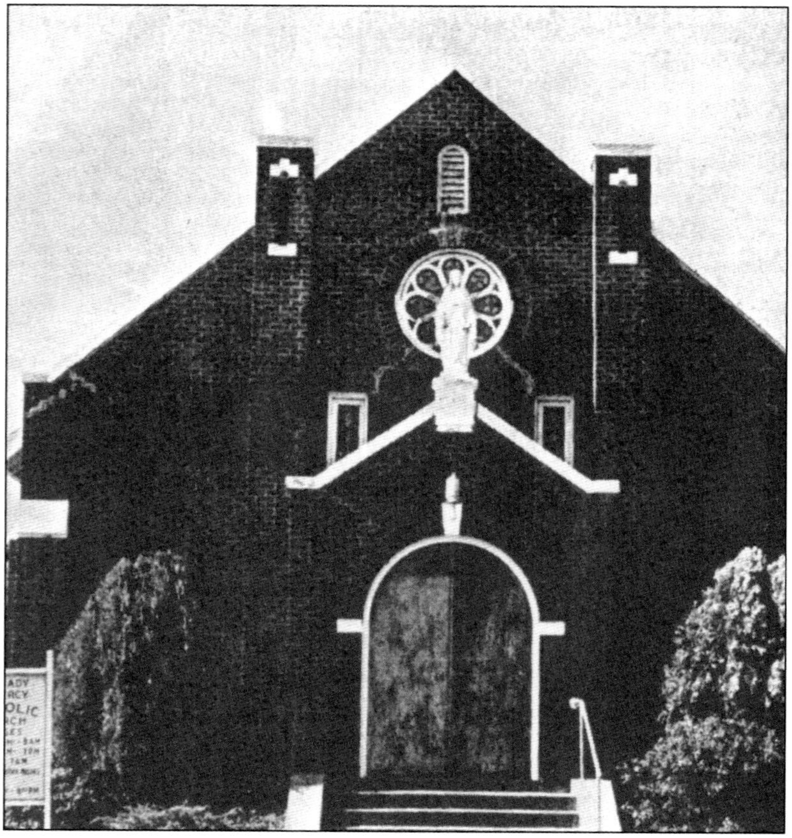

In 1887, Father Alexander Badelon celebrated the first Catholic mass in Hillsboro at the residence of H.P. Harrington. In 1896, the congregation of St. Helen's met at the Culberson School until a frame building was erected at South Pleasant and Walnut Streets. In May 1929, construction began for a church building for Our Lady of Mercy on Corsicana Street. In 1969, it moved to its present location on a hill west of Interstate 35 and north of Old Brandon Road.

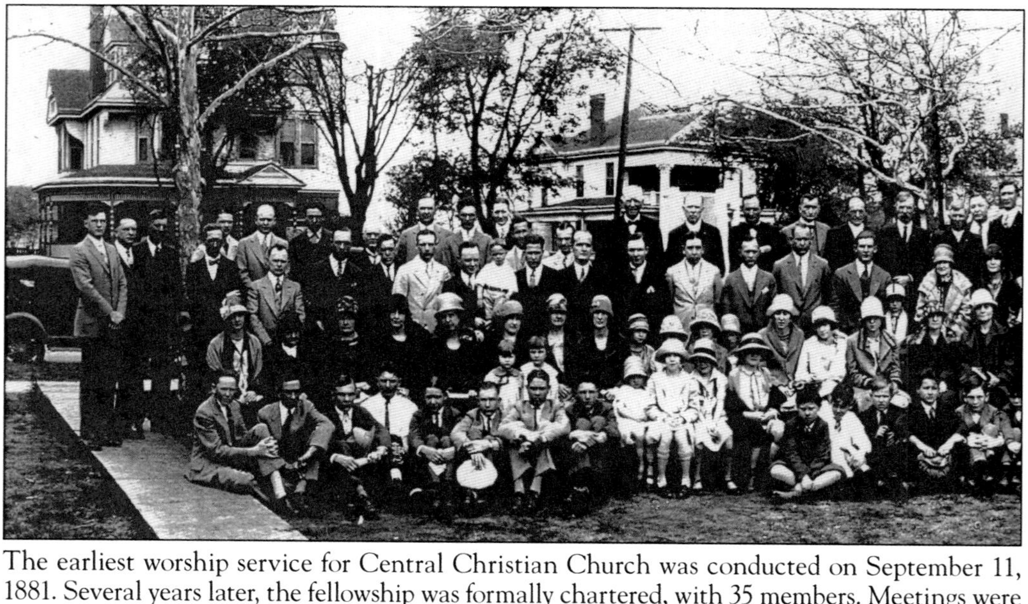

The earliest worship service for Central Christian Church was conducted on September 11, 1881. Several years later, the fellowship was formally chartered, with 35 members. Meetings were held in private homes, at the courthouse, and at the schoolhouse until a sanctuary was built on South Waco Street in 1886. After a fire destroyed the structure in 1892, members built a new church at 200 North Pleasant Street, at Craig Street. In 1928, the frame building was remodeled and bricked.

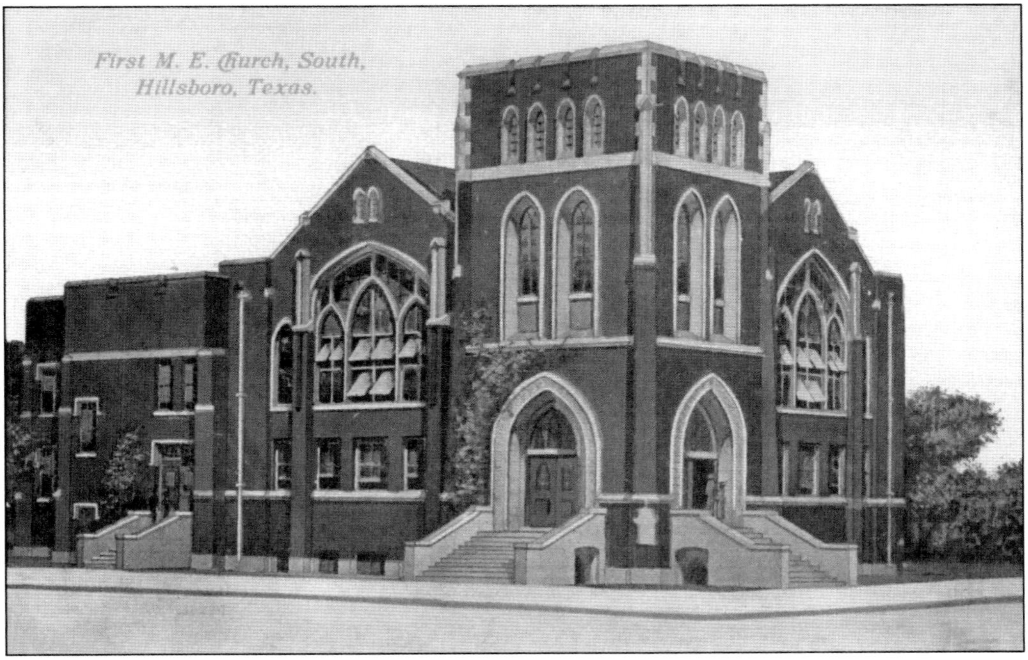

First United Methodist Church is believed to be the oldest organized congregation in the city. Col. T.B. Smith, a charter member, recalled that the church was organized in 1856 by Rev. J.D. Nelms with Thomas B. and Elizabeth Smith, Hannah Booth, and J.M. Moss. The first minister was Jackson L. Crabb. In 1892, a new building was constructed at the corner of South Waco and Walnut Streets (now Brookshires). After 20 years, the growing congregation built on the corner of Elm and Lang Streets under the direction of Rev. John R. Morris. A fire in 1928 destroyed the inner walls of this building, and a rebuilt structure, seen here, opened on the same site in March 1929. Below is an undated photograph of the We Were Young Once (WWYO) class, taught by Lil Eastland. (Both, First United Methodist Church.)

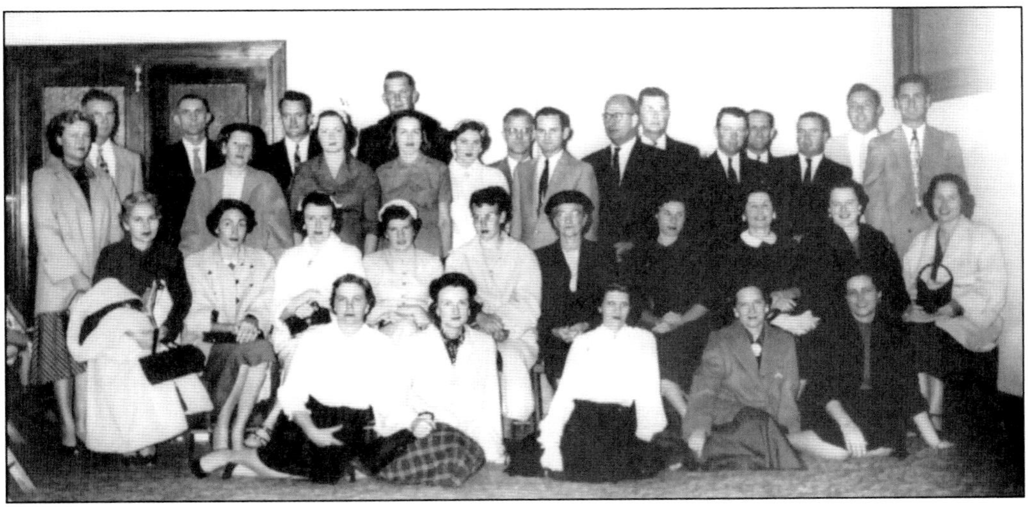

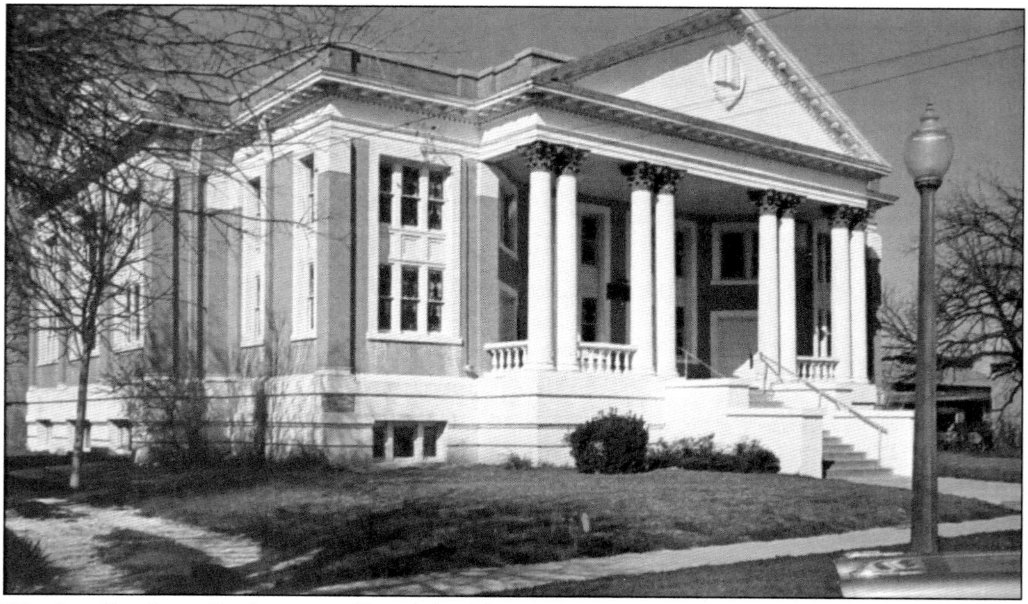

The first Southern Presbyterian Church building was constructed in 1876 at 225 East Elm Street (now Wells Fargo Bank). Judge Jo Abbott chaired the building committee, and the lot was donated by William Sidney Mills in exchange for a farm owned by Capt. S.C. Upshaw. The original frame building was replaced by the Greek Revival structure seen here, erected in 1911–1912 and designed and built by local architect J.O. Galbraith.

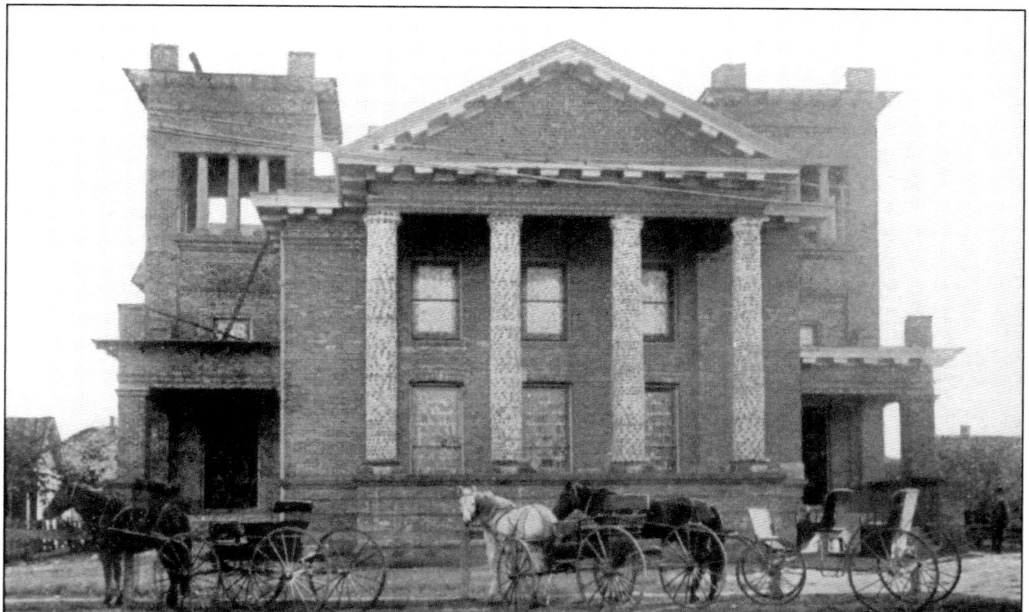

First Baptist Church was organized in 1874 and fully established in 1875 by Rev. P.G. Booth. Charter members were A.M. Isaacs, Nancy and Henry Procise, Fanny Booth, Julia Johnson, Alabama Ponder, and Julia Reavis. The first facility, on South Church Street, was replaced in 1905 by this impressive brick edifice in the Greek Revival style, nearby at 300 East Franklin Street.

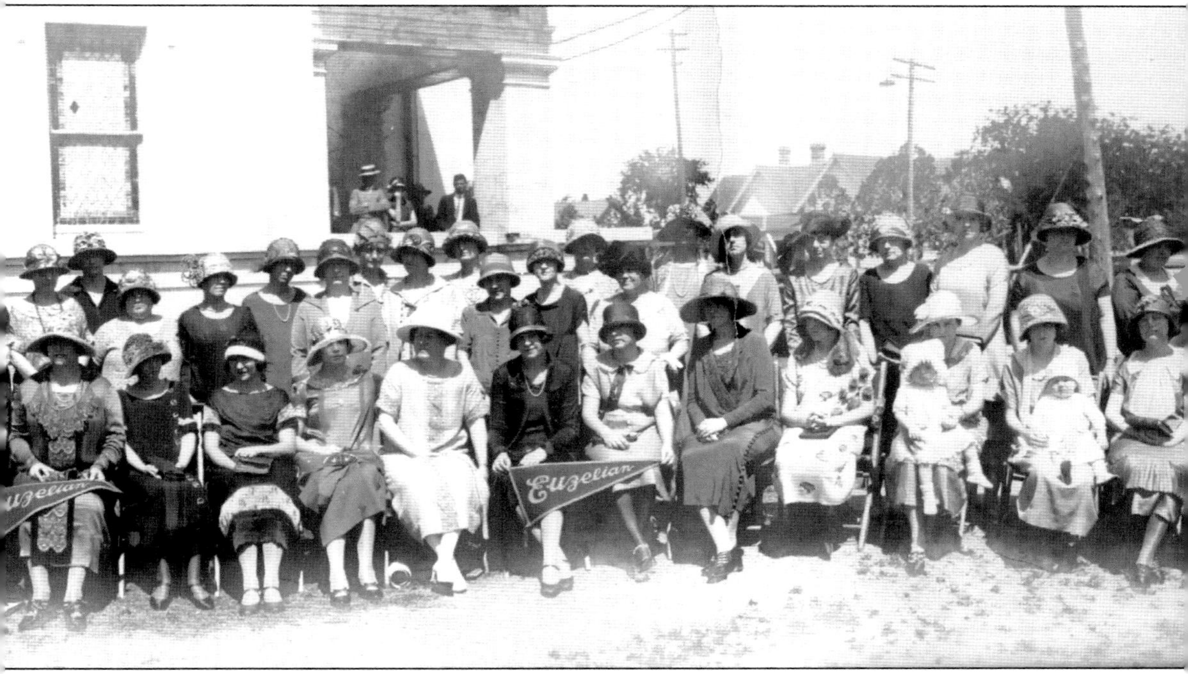

The Euzelian Society was a women's Sunday school class at the First Baptist Church in the 1920s. The society posed for this photograph on the church lawn. One of the stained-glass windows from the 1905 edifice is now on display at the Hill County Cell Block Museum. (Johnson Studios.)

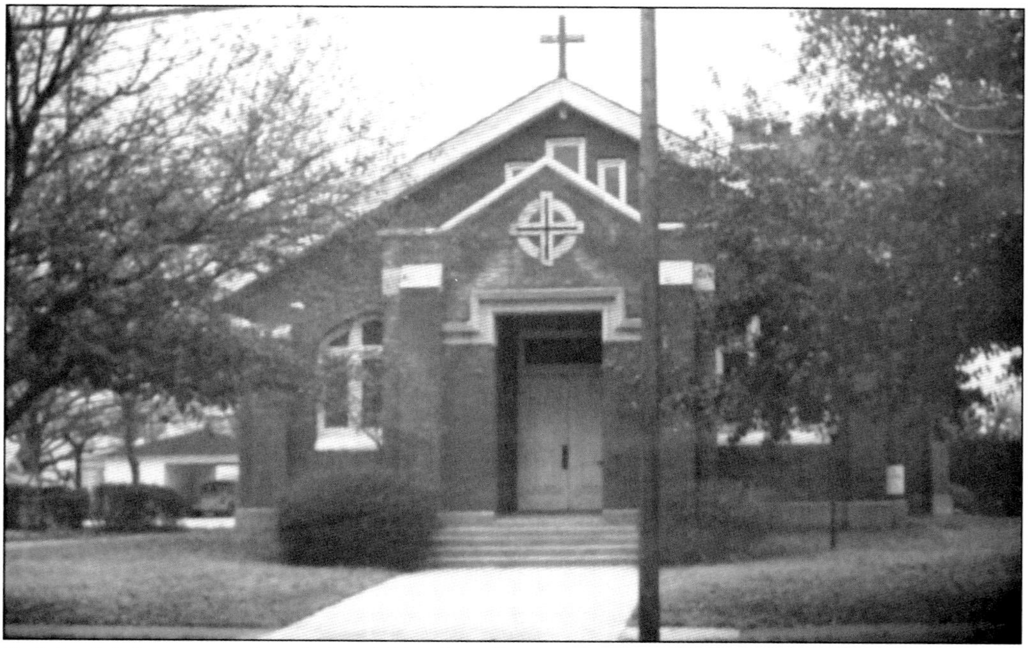

St. Mary's Mission was founded in 1872 when Sarah Sturgis started a Sunday school. On July 30, 1886, Bishop Alexander C. Garrett laid the cornerstone for the first Episcopal church building, which was destroyed by a tornado in 1894 and rebuilt in 1911. St. Mary's became a parish in 1914. Featuring both Gothic Revival and Prairie style influences, it is located at 200 North Abbott Street.

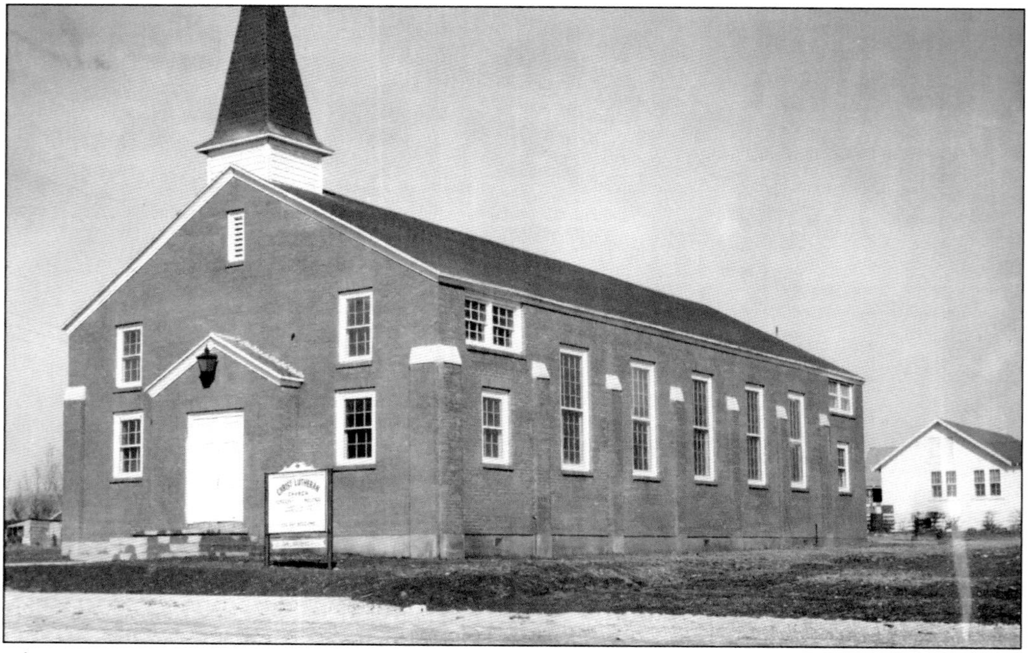

Christ Evangelical Lutheran Church (Missouri Synod) was organized on May 11, 1947, with services held in the Forum Room of the Newman Hotel. Pastor John Herzog was installed on September 14, 1947, and soon after, the congregation purchased a parsonage on Walnut Street. A church building was erected in the 900 block of Corsicana Street using a surplus Army chapel moved from Sheppard Field in Wichita Falls, Texas. (Christ Lutheran Church.)

Ten

From the Courthouse to the Capitol

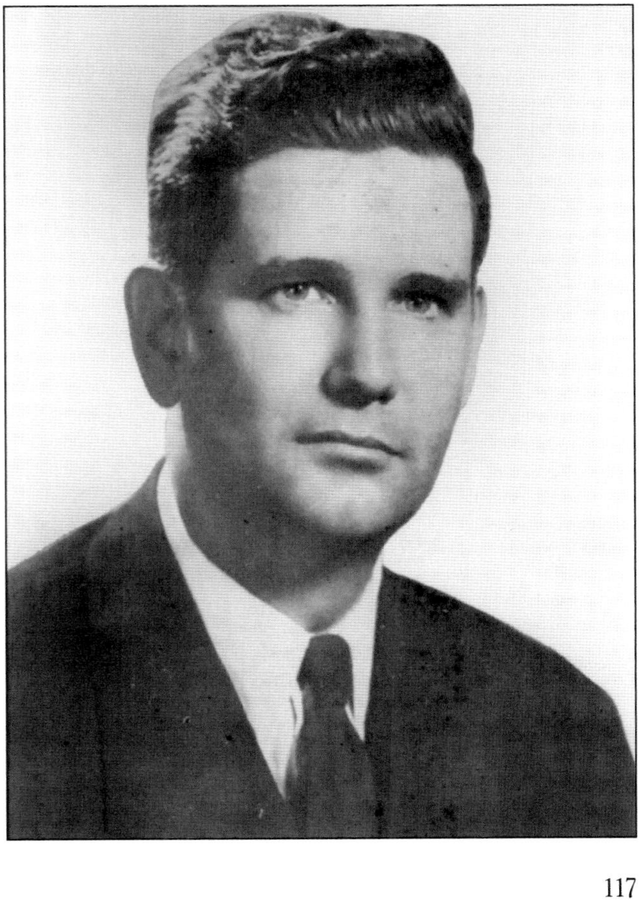

Crawford Collins Martin, a Hillsboro native and a World War II Coast Guard veteran, was elected mayor of Hillsboro in 1948. He went on to hold the Texas Senate seat once held by his father, Will M. Martin, and was elected president pro tem of the senate in 1955. Gov. John Connally appointed Martin secretary of state, and in 1966, he was elected Texas attorney general. Martin practiced law in Hillsboro with his brother William B. Martin.

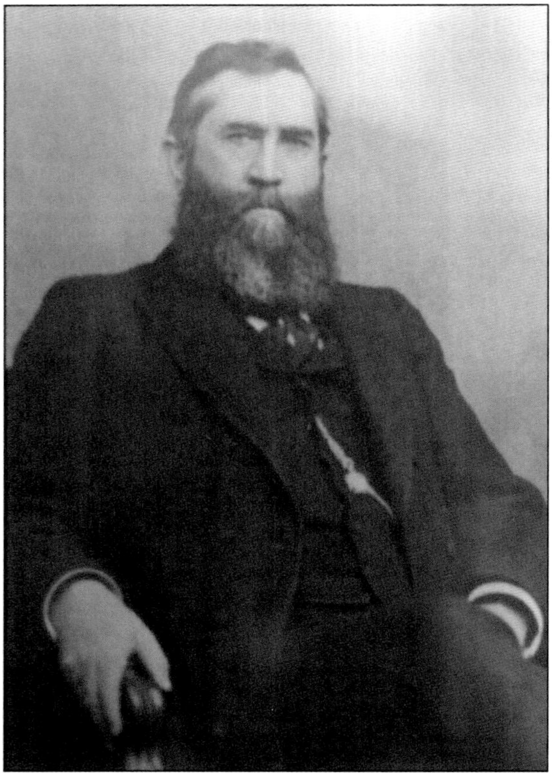

Confederate veteran Joseph "Jo" Abbott came to Hillsboro and began practicing law after the Civil War. He was a member of the Texas House of Representatives in 1870 and 1871. Abbott was appointed district judge of the 28th Judicial District by Gov. Oran M. Roberts, and in 1880, he was elected for a full term. In 1887, he was elected to the US House of Representatives, where he served through 1897.

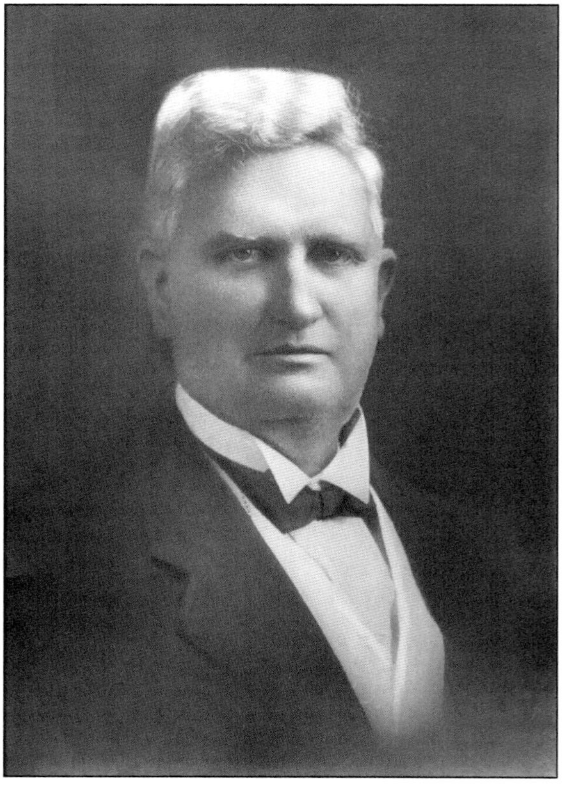

After moving to Texas in 1875, Benjamin Dudley Tarlton practiced law in Hillsboro and was elected to the Texas House of Representatives in 1880 and 1884. Gov. James S. Hogg appointed Tarlton as chief justice of the Court of Appeals for the Second District of Texas in Fort Worth. He was reelected for a second term. The University of Texas Law Library is named in his honor. (Tarlton Law Library.)

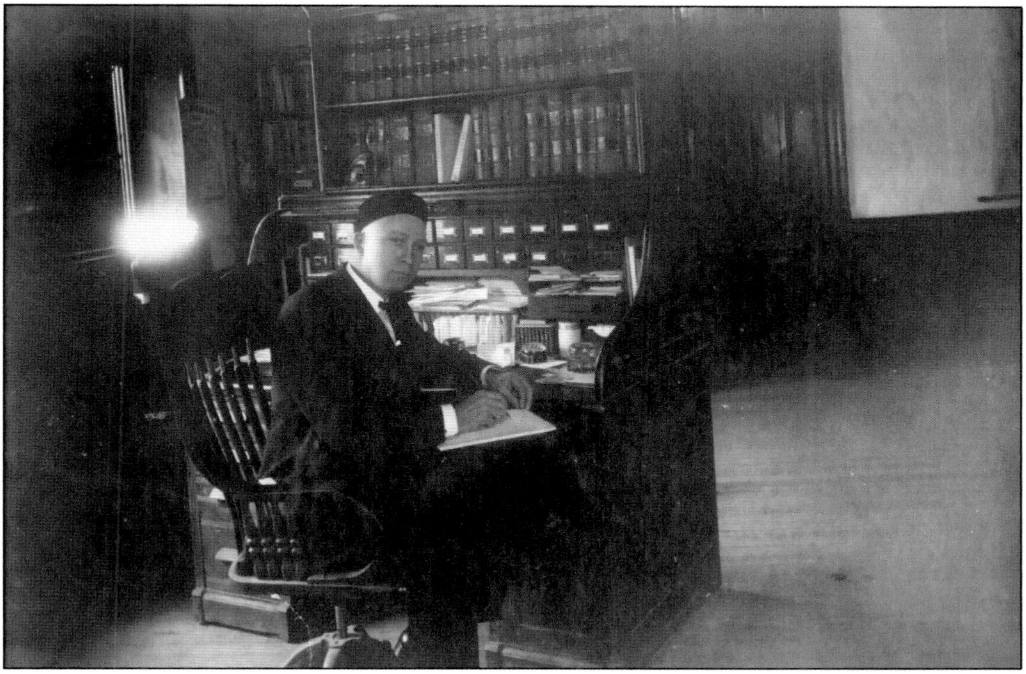

Thomas Slater Smith was elected Hill County attorney shortly after moving to Hillsboro in 1884. He served two terms, and by 1888 had been named to the state Democratic Committee for the 21st Senatorial District. Smith served in the Texas House of Representatives from 1893 to 1895 and was the speaker of the house. In 1896 he was a presidential elector, and he became the Texas attorney general in 1898.

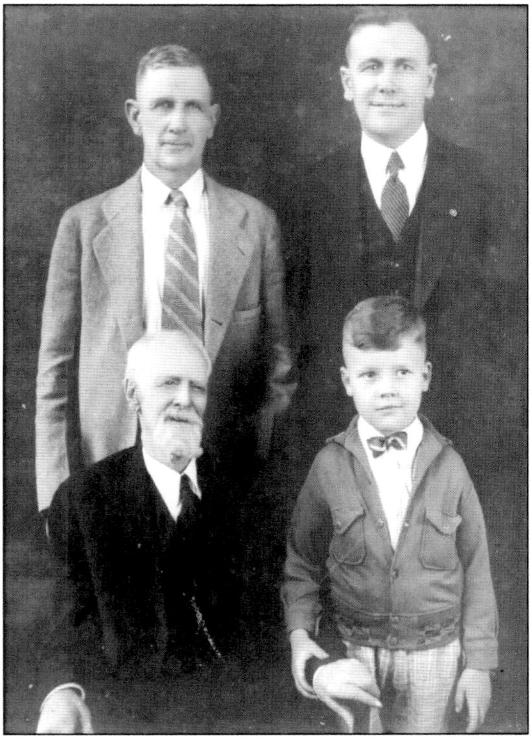

Capt. J.T. Bobbitt (front left) was elected commander of Hill County United Confederates Veterans in 1913. His son, James Alderson Bobbitt (back left) was a progressive farmer and rancher. Grandson Robert Lee Bobbitt (back right) served Texas as speaker of the House of Representatives, attorney general, chairman of the Texas Highway Department, and associate justice of the Fourth Court of Civil Appeals in San Antonio. Robert Lee Bobbitt Jr. (front right) practiced law in San Antonio.

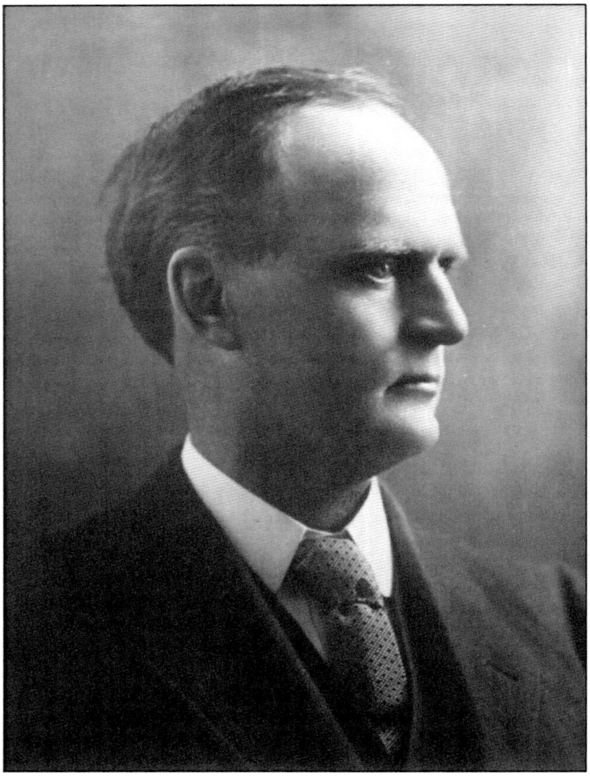

In 1905, district judge William C. Wear (left) was first to preside over the new 66th District Court in Hillsboro. Wear resigned his post in 1910, and Charles Mortimer Smithdeal (below) was appointed to the bench. Wear was an entrepreneur who constructed the Wear Hotel on the northwest corner of Franklin and Covington Streets. He also owned the office building on the northeast corner (now Eastland Title Company). Wear was active in state Democratic politics and chaired the state Democratic Executive Committee. He concluded his career in Austin, serving as a commissioner on the Texas Court of Criminal Appeals. Smithdeal served the 66th court until 1913. Both Judge Wear and Judge Smithdeal are buried in Ridge Park Cemetery in Hillsboro.

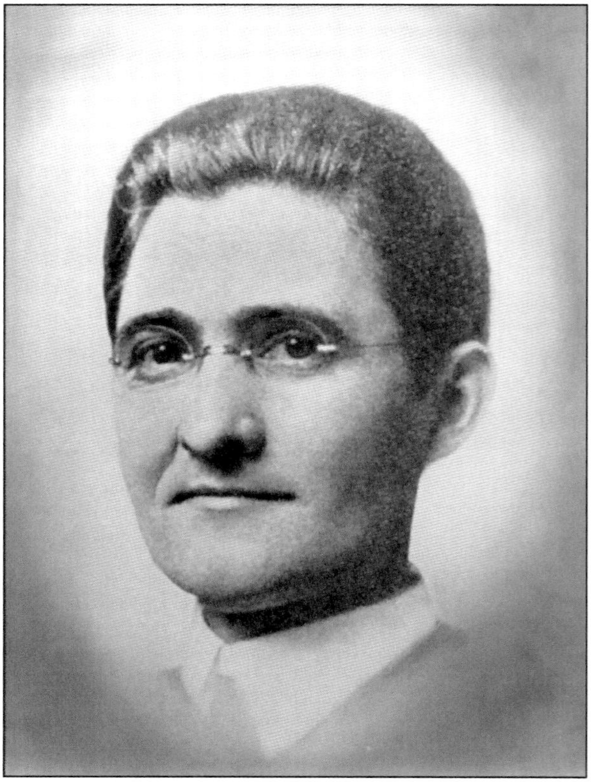

Nelson Phillips was admitted to the bar in 1895 and practiced law with Thomas Slater Smith. In 1904, Gov. S.W.T. Lanham appointed Phillips judge of the 18th Judicial District for two years. In 1912, he was appointed associate justice of the Texas Supreme Court, a position he held until he became chief justice in 1915. He retired to private practice in Dallas in 1921. (Tarlton Law Library.)

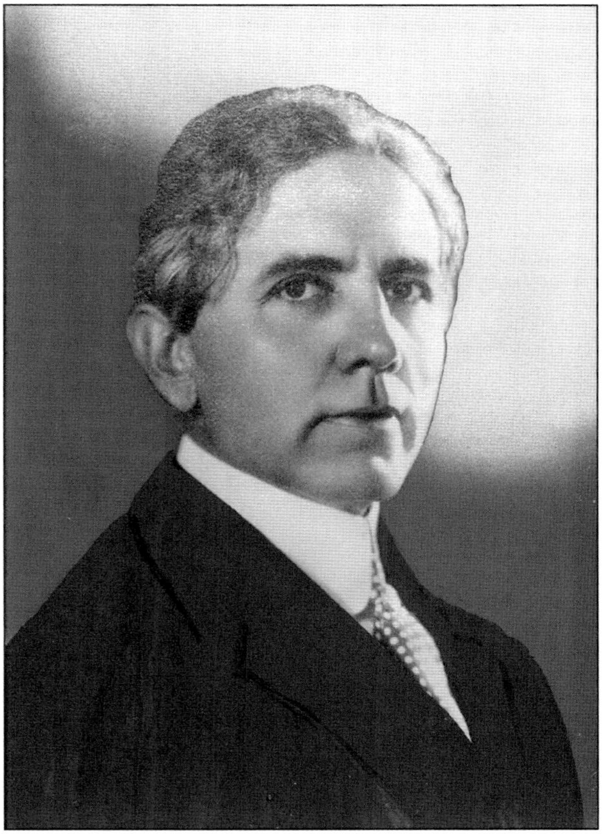

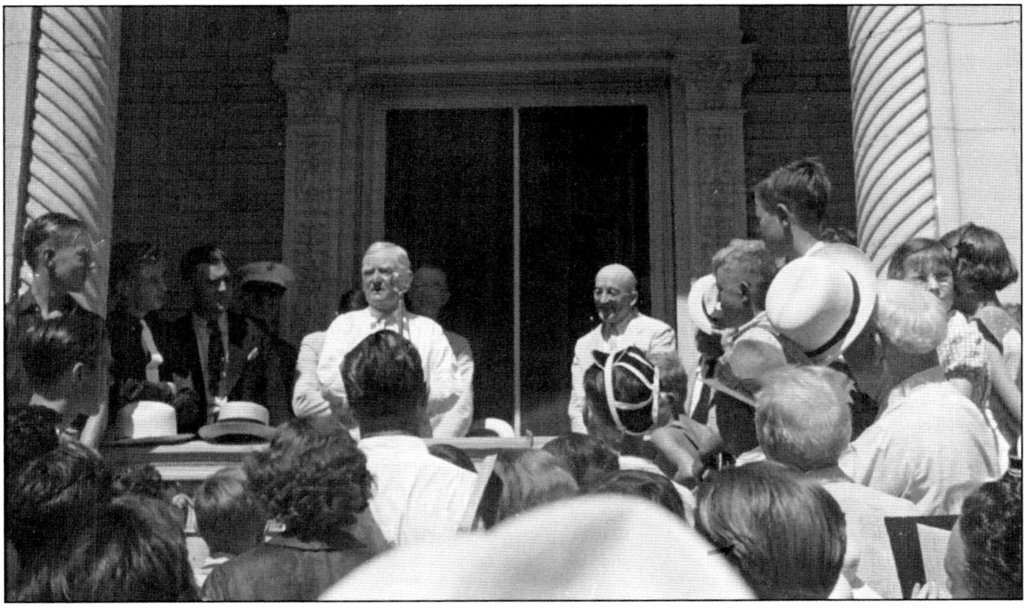

Vice Pres. John Nance Garner visited Hillsboro in 1936 to speak at the chamber of commerce's annual banquet. He was invited by Hillsboro postmaster Burris Jackson, who was an active leader in the state and national Democratic Party. Speaker of the House Sam Rayburn, postmaster general Jim Farley, and Gov. Jimmy Allred also attended chamber events hosted by Burris Jackson.

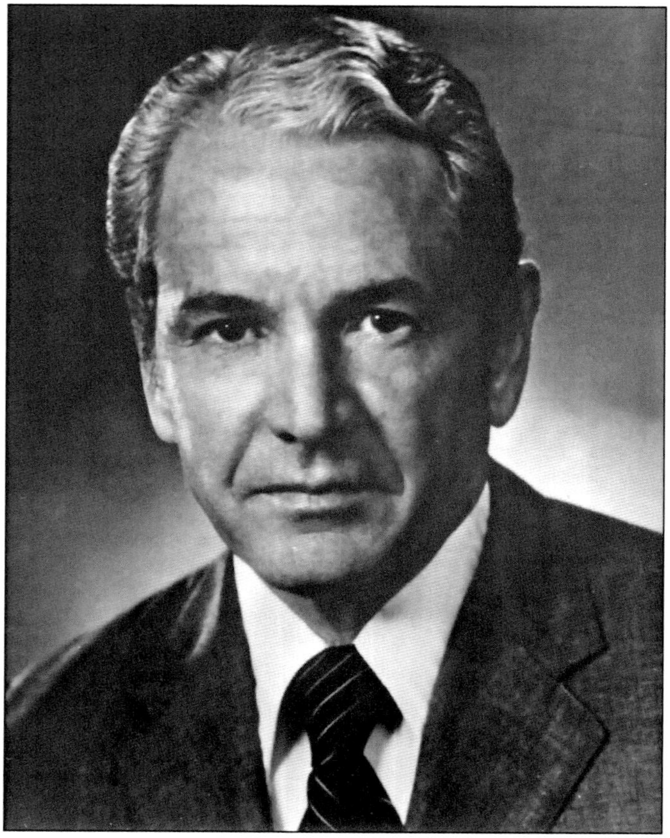

Samuel Dodson Johnson, a Hillsboro attorney, served as Hill County attorney and district attorney. In 1959, he defeated district judge Andrew J. Bryan and took the 66th District Court bench. In 1969, Johnson was elected to the 14th Court of Appeals, where he served until 1973, when he became an associate justice of the Texas Supreme Court. In 1979, Pres. Jimmy Carter appointed Johnson to the US Fifth Circuit Court of Appeals. (Tarlton Law Library.)

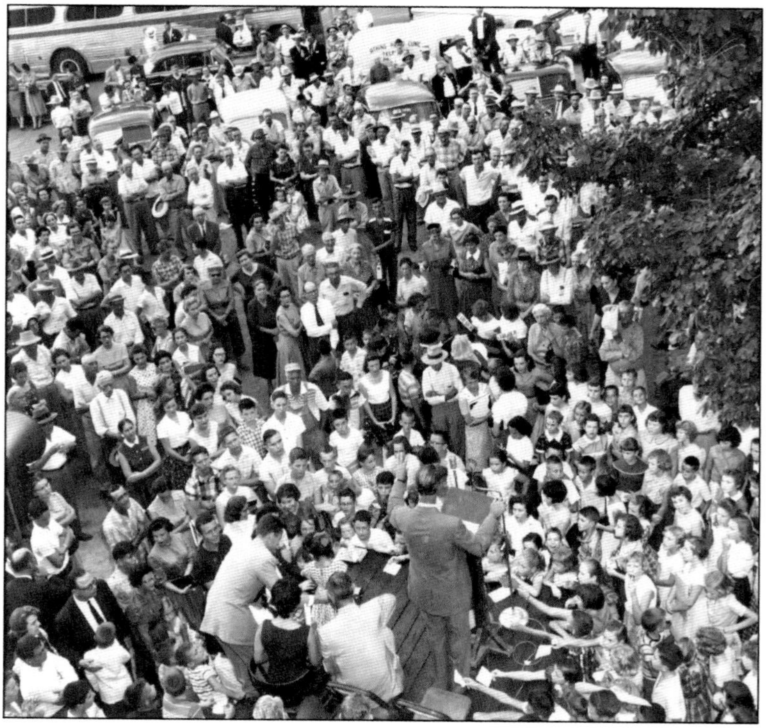

Sen. Estes Kefauver, a Democratic vice presidential candidate with Adlai Stevenson in 1956, speaks to a large crowd on the east side of the courthouse. Since 1853, the courthouse lawn has been the scene of political and patriotic rallies, including sending troops off to fight for the Confederacy in the Civil War, celebrating Armistice Day in 1918, and numerous gubernatorial events, including campaigns by W. Lee O'Daniel and his Hillbilly Boys.

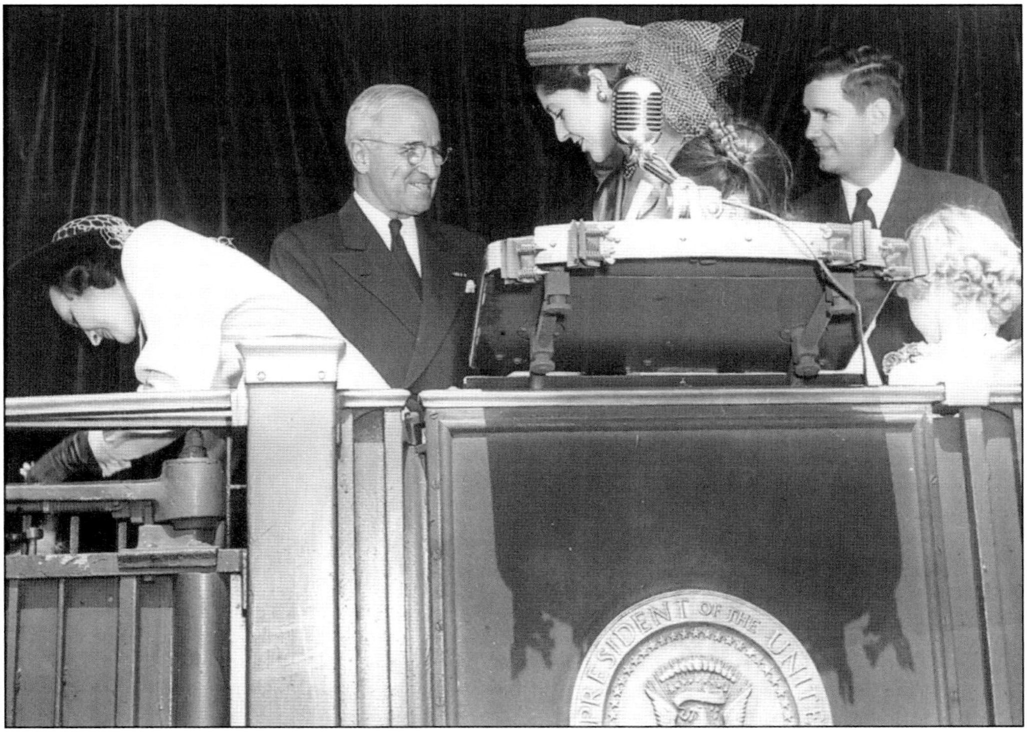
Pres. Harry Truman speaks with (from left to right) Maurine Bacon, Frances Freeland Calvert, and Hillsboro mayor Crawford C. Martin. Hillsboro was a stop on President Truman's 30,000-mile 1948 reelection tour of the United States. A large crowd of well-wishers greeted President Truman at the Katy stop on his way to Fort Worth.

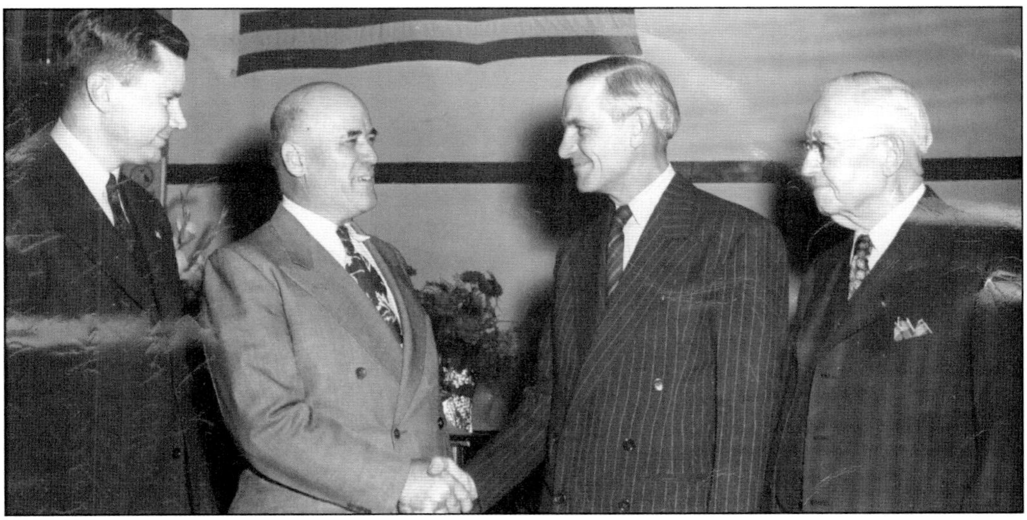
After serving in World War I, Olin Culberson returned to Hillsboro, where he was elected Hill County clerk and county judge. Culberson was appointed examiner for the Texas Railroad Commission and was elected to the Texas Railroad Commission in 1940. Seen here from left to right are district judge Frank McDonald, Culberson, state Democratic chair Robert W. Calvert, and former Hillsboro mayor S.L. Robertson. (Cell Block Museum.)

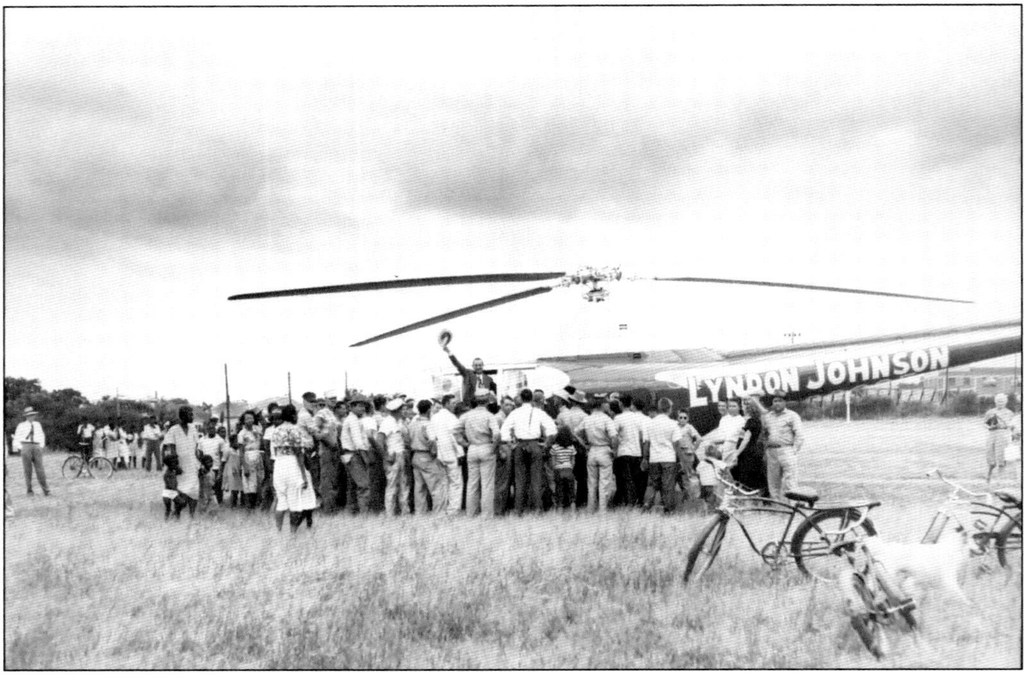

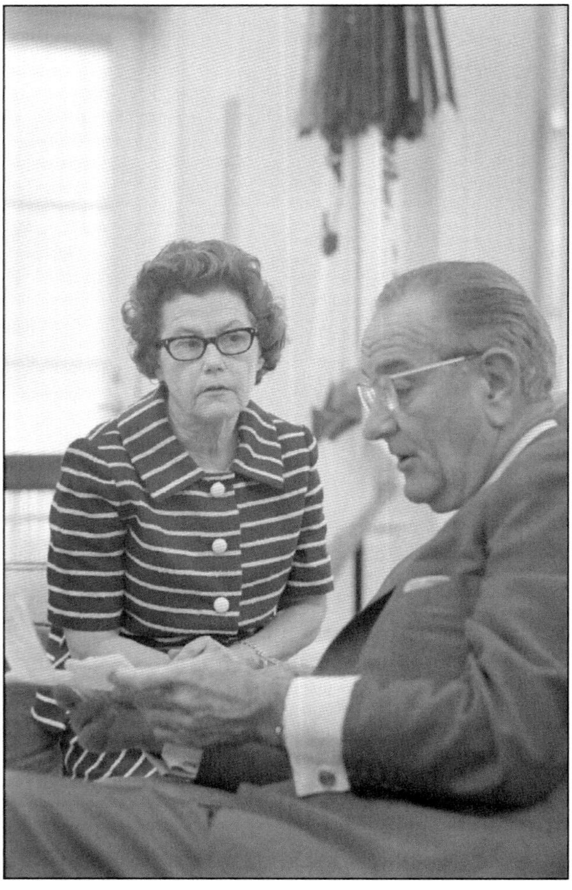

Above, Lyndon Baines Johnson waves goodbye from his helicopter after speaking to a group of Hillsboro residents on June 23, 1948. The speech was part of the future president's US senate campaign; he was a US congressman at the time. A crowd gathered on Bowman Field for the landing and takeoff. (Ben H. Johnson, Lyndon Baines Johnson Presidential Library.)

Beginning in the 1930s, Mary Rather, seen here with President Johnson, served as his personal secretary during his time as congressman, senator, senate majority leader, and for his last year as president, when she lived in the White House with the Johnson family. (Lyndon Baines Johnson Presidential Library.)

Wright Chalfant Morrow practiced law in Hillsboro with his brothers-in-law Greene Duke Tarlton and Benjamin D. Tarlton. Elected district judge in Hill County in 1897, Morrow resigned from the bench and served as a state senator from 1912 to 1916. Morrow was appointed to the Court of Criminal Appeals in 1917, and in 1921 was chosen as the presiding judge of the court, where he served until his retirement in 1939. (Tarlton Law Library.)

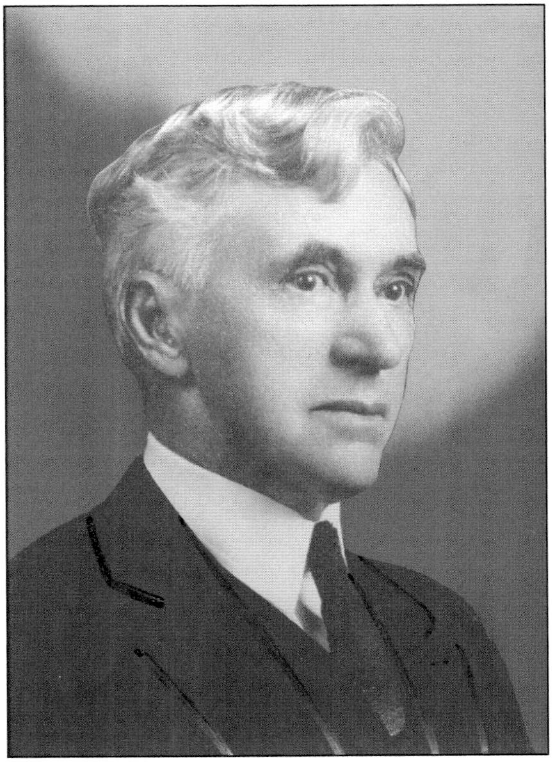

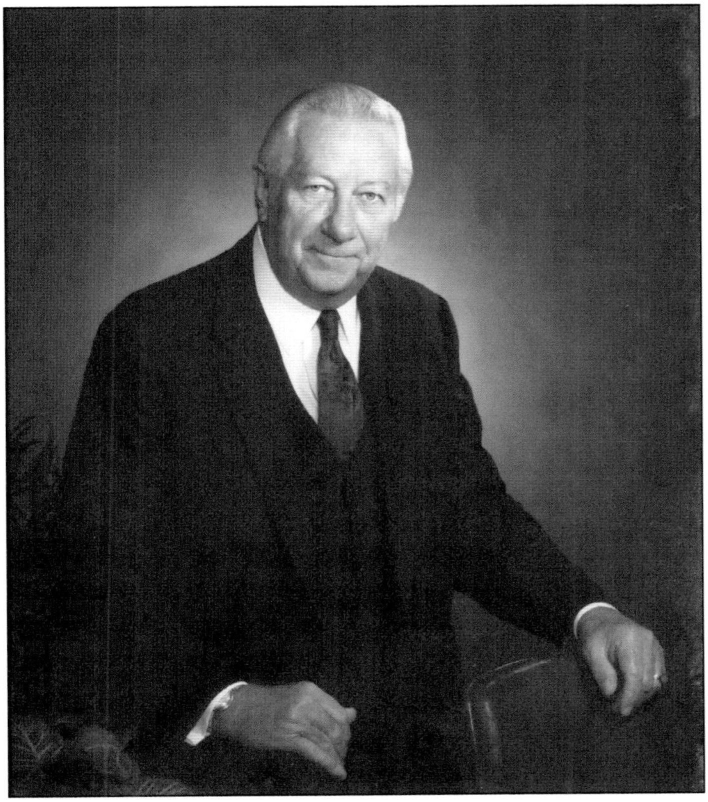

Morris Harrell graduated from Hillsboro High School in 1936 and attended Baylor University, where he earned his law degree. A World War II Navy veteran who served in the South Pacific, he became president of the American Bar Association, the American College of Trial Lawyers, and the State Bar Association of Texas. His father, Oscar "Slim" Harrell, a former professional baseball pitcher, managed Texas Power & Light in Hillsboro.

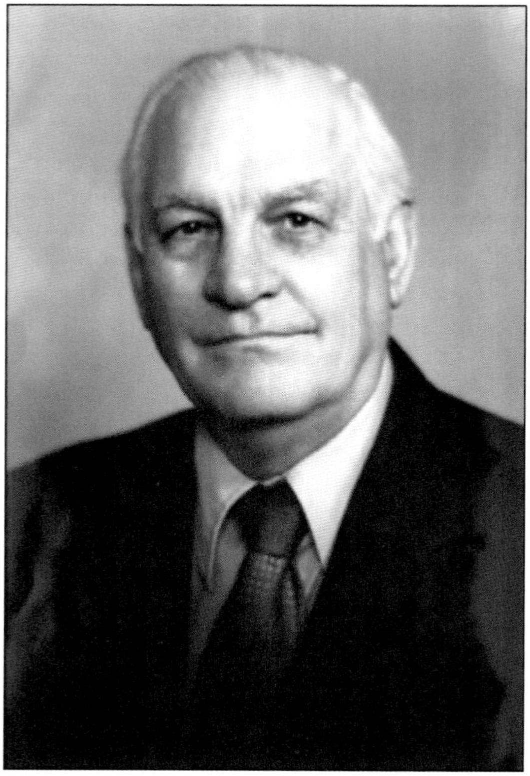

Robert Wilburn Calvert, a Hillsboro attorney, was elected Hill County district attorney prior to his election to the Texas House of Representatives, where he served from 1933 to 1939. Calvert served as the speaker of the house from 1937 to 1939. In the 1940s, he served as Hillsboro city attorney, Hill County attorney, and as president of the Hillsboro school board. In 1950, Calvert was elected to the Texas Supreme Court, where he served as an associate justice before being elected chief justice in 1961.

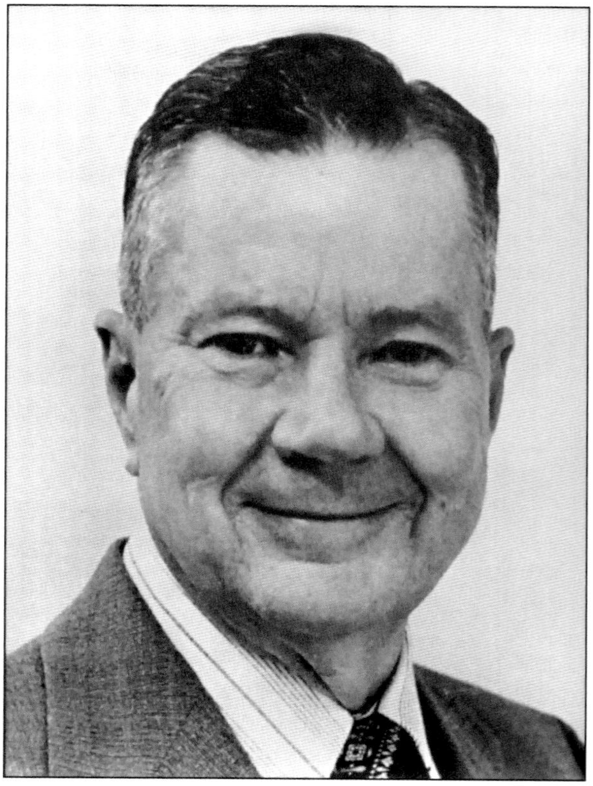

Born in Hillsboro, Frank G. McDonald was the son of Dr. J.F. McDonald and a graduate of Hillsboro High School, Hillsboro Junior College, and the University of Texas Law School. McDonald practiced law in Hillsboro from 1938 to 1940 and served as judge of the 66th District Court from 1948 to 1952. A World War II veteran, he served 36 years as chief justice of the 10th Court of Appeals, as stated in *Heritage of Hill County*.

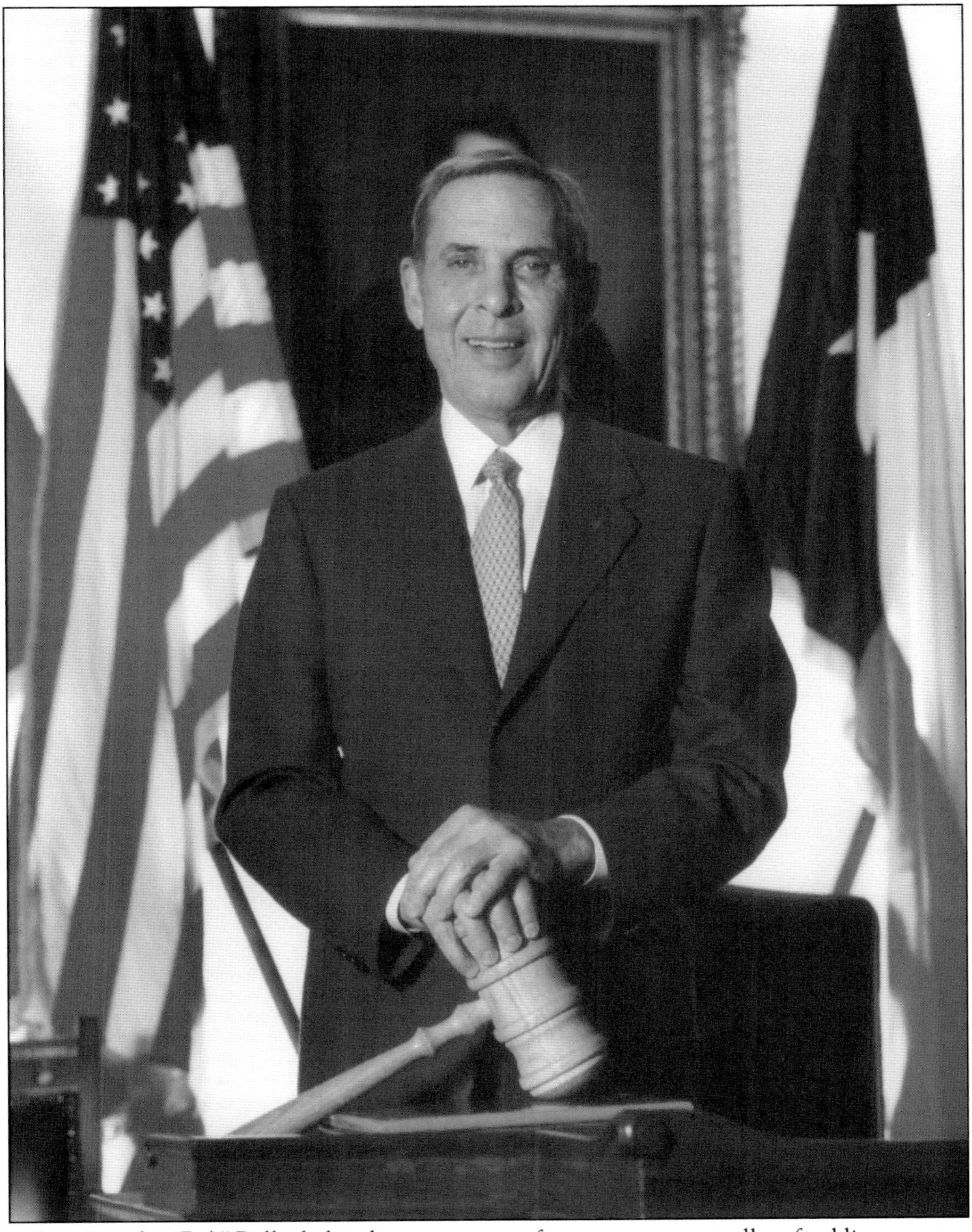

Robert Douglas "Bob" Bullock, legislator, secretary of state, state comptroller of public accounts, and the 38th lieutenant governor of Texas, was born on July 10, 1929, in Hillsboro. He was a third-generation Texan, the son of Thomas Austin and Ruth Mitchell (Abbott) Bullock. His father was a longtime Hillsboro city engineer. Bullock graduated from Hillsboro High School in 1947 and from Hillsboro Junior College in 1949. He is buried in the Texas State Cemetery, and the renovations of the state cemetery are in large part due to his leadership and efforts. (Bob Bullock Collection.)